GILBERT AND SULLIVAN

The Players and the Plays

Works by Kurt Gänzl

1967: *The Women of Troy* (one-act play), volume 3 of New Zealand Play Library

1986: *The British Musical Theatre*, 2 vols. (Macmillan Press)

1988: *Gänzl's Book of the Musical Theatre*, with Andrew Lamb (Bodley Head/Schirmer)

1989: *The Blackwell Guide to the Musical Theatre on Record* (Blackwell)

1990: *The Complete "Aspects of Love"* (Aurum Press)

1994: *The Encyclopedia of the Musical Theatre*, 2 vols., expanded in 2001 to 3 vols. (Blackwell/Schirmer)

1995: *Musicals: The Illustrated Story* (Carlton, UK) / *Song and Dance: The Complete Story of Stage Musicals* (Smithmark, US) / *Die Welt der grossen Musicals* (Bertelsmann, Germany)

1995: *Gänzl's Book of the Broadway Musical* (Schirmer; Macmillan)

1997: *The Musical: A Concise History*, forthcoming 2nd ed. (Northeastern University Press)

2002: *Lydia Thompson: Queen of Burlesque* (Routledge)

2002: *William B. Gill: From the Gold Fields to Broadway* (Routledge)

2007: *Emily Soldene: In Search of a Singer* (Steele Roberts)

2017: *Victorian Vocalists* (Taylor and Francis)

2021: *Petrus Borel: Rapsodies*, with John Gallas (Carcanet)

GILBERT AND SULLIVAN
The Players and the Plays

Kurt Gänzl

Illustrations from the Collections of
DAVID B. LOVELL and DAVID STONE

Published by State University of New York Press, Albany

© 2021 State University of New York

All rights reserved

Printed in the United States of America

No part of this book may be used or reproduced in any manner whatsoever without written permission. No part of this book may be stored in a retrieval system or transmitted in any form or by any means including electronic, electrostatic, magnetic tape, mechanical, photocopying, recording, or otherwise without the prior permission in writing of the publisher.

For information, contact State University of New York Press, Albany, NY
www.sunypress.edu

Library of Congress Cataloging-in-Publication Data

Names: Gänzl, Kurt, author.
Title: Gilbert and Sullivan : the players and the plays / Kurt Gänzl.
Description: Albany : State University of New York Press, 2021. | Includes index.
Identifiers: LCCN 2021030214 (print) | LCCN 2021030215 (ebook) | ISBN 9781438485454 (hardcover : alk. paper) | ISBN 9781438485461 (pbk. : alk. paper) | ISBN 9781438485478 (ebook)
Subjects: LCSH: Sullivan, Arthur, 1842–1900—Performances. | Gilbert, W. S. (William Schwenck), 1836–1911—Performances. | Operetta—Great Britain—19th century. | Operetta—United States—19th century. | Singers—Great Britain. | Singers—United States.
Classification: LCC ML410.S95 G35 2021 (print) | LCC ML410.S95 (ebook) | DDC 782.1/2092—dc23
LC record available at https://lccn.loc.gov/2021030214
LC ebook record available at https://lccn.loc.gov/2021030215

10 9 8 7 6 5 4 3 2 1

Contents

List of Illustrations		vii
Preface		xi
Acknowledgments		xxiii
1	Thespis	1
2	Trial by Jury	11
3	The Sorcerer	37
4	HMS Pinafore	57
5	The Pirates of Penzance	89
6	Patience	119
7	Iolanthe	135
8	Princess Ida	153
9	The Mikado	175
10	Ruddigore	197
11	The Yeomen of the Guard	207
12	The Gondoliers	221
13	Utopia (Limited)	241

14	*The Grand Duke*	255
Appendix: Recommended Reading		265
Index		269

Illustrations

1	Paul Knüpfer and Julius Lieban in *Der Mikado* (Königliche Oper, Berlin).	xii
2	Program for *The Mikado*, directed by "Doc" Gallas.	xiii
3	My rendering of a scene from *The Mikado*, a precocious debut by Kurt Gänzl, aged six.	xiii
4	Lilian La Rue: Who are you?	xv
5	Amdrams: Quintin Twiss, Arthur Blunt, and George du Maurier in *Cox and Box*.	xix
6	Gaiety Theatre star comedian Johnnie Toole in *La Vivandière*.	xx
7	The fate of a too-well-loved volume.	xxi
8	Madeleine Clary: Sparkeion of Croydon.	4
9	An 1858 trial by judge and jury for breach of promise of marriage.	11
10	Nellie Bromley: The blighted bride.	14
11	*The Happy Land*: Messrs. Fisher, Hill, and Righton.	19
12	Fred Sullivan: "I am a Judge, and a good judge, too."	21
13	Cissie Durrant: The bridesmaid who got the bouquet.	23
14	Linda Verner: The cheerleader of the bridesmaids.	25
15	Julia Barber: A Chorine in High Demand.	27
16	Charley Campbell in early *Trial by Jury* days.	30

17	Isabelle Paul: Musical-theater blue blood.	40
18	Fred Clifton as the Notary.	41
19	George Bentham: A tenor of no fixed abode.	44
20	Giulia Warwick: "Happy Young Heart."	52
21	Emma Howson: A prima donna on four continents.	60
22	George Power: A right aristocratic Ralph Rackstraw.	63
23	Harriet Everard: "Sweet Little Buttercup, I."	66
24	Aeneas Dymott (Bob Beckett): "A British Tar."	71
25	George Temple as Samuel.	74
26	Nellie Duglas Gordon as Josephine.	76
27	Henri Laurent as "Ralph Wreckstraw."	80
28	George K. Fortescue as an American travesty dame of a Little Buttercup.	87
29	An Irish King Hildebrand: John Brocolini né Clark.	91
30	Blanche Roosevelt: "The best thing about her singing was her looks."	93
31	George Grossmith: "Yes, yes, he is a Major General."	104
32	Richard Temple: An orphan Pirate King.	107
33	Emily Cross: A piratical maid of unexpected work.	110
34	Rutland Barrington as Pooh-Bah, the Lord High Everything Else.	115
35	Marion Hood: "Yes! 'Tis Mabel."	116
36	Wannabe aesthetes: Messrs. Thornton, Lely, and Temple.	122
37	Leonora Braham as Patience: "I Cannot Tell What This Love May Be."	123
38	Augusta Roche as Lady Jane: "There Will Be Too Much of Me, in the Coming By and By!"	127
39	Jack Ryley as Bunthorne: "Ultrapoetical, superaesthetical."	131

40	Carrie Burton: A less innocent-looking Patience.	133
41	Alice Barnett: "Who taught me to curl myself up inside a buttercup?"	137
42	W. T. Carleton: But half a fairy, and a member of Parliament.	140
43	Jessie Bond: Iolanthe, thou drippest!	145
44	Durward Lely as Lord Tolloller: "Spurn not the nobly born."	147
45	Lithgow James: six feet four inches of sentry or sailor.	150
46	Sybil Grey as Sacharissa: "Cut off real live arms and legs?"	156
47	Team Hildebrand (UK): Messrs. C. Ryley, Bracy, and Lely.	158
48	Florence Bemister and the girls of Castle Adamant: "Man Is Nature's Sole Mistake."	160
49	Mary Beebe: The Boston "Ideal" of a Josephine.	162
50	Team Hildebrand (US): Messrs. Lang, McCreery, and Rising.	164
51	Team Gama (US): Messrs. Earley, Scott, and Cloney.	171
52	Three Little Maids: Misses Grey, Braham, and Bond.	178
53	Bovill the Pickler.	181
54	Bovill as Pish Tush. The same man?	181
55	George Thorne as Ko-Ko.	186
56	Fred Federici as The Mikado.	188
57	Courtice Pounds as Nanki-Poo.	190
58	*The Mikado* at the Standard Theatre, New York.	192
59	Elsie Cameron as Katisha: "A left shoulder-blade that is a miracle of loveliness."	194
60	Richard Temple as Sir Roderic: "When the night wind howls . . ."	198
61	George Grossmith as Robin Oakapple: "A pure and blameless peasant."	200

62	George Grossmith as Jack Point: "I've jibe and joke, and quip and crank."	209
63	W. H. Denny (Shadbolt) and Jessie Bond (Phoebe): "Were I thy bride . . ."	212
64	Kate (Rose Hervey) is the lass who spills the beans.	214
65	W. R. Shirley: The dauntless Leonard Meryll.	217
66	Rosina Brandram as the Duchess of Plaza-Toro: "Baxtaberry, baxtaberry ba!"	223
67	Frank Wyatt as the Duke of Plaza-Toro: "He led his regiment from behind, he found it less exciting."	225
68	Decima Moore (Casilda) and Wallace Brownlow (Luiz): The King and Queen of Barataria.	227
69	Geraldine Ulmar: The first of the fifteen Gianettas.	229
70	Nellie Lawrence (Fiametta): Only the understudy!	231
71	Esther Palliser as a Gianetta looking out for low-flying lagoon birds.	232
72	Leonore Snyder as Gianetta in *The Gondoliers*.	238
73	Kate Talby (Lady Sophy) with her charges: Aileen Burke and Millicent Pyne.	247
74	The Flowers of Progress jam session.	250
75	Ilka Pálmay: International Megastar.	258
76	Rosina Brandram (Lady Sophy) with her Utopian charges: Florence Perry and Emmie Owen.	263

Preface

Gilbert and Sullivan. Magical words. Like ham and eggs, bread and cheese, cakes and ale or fish and chips . . . wonderful separately, but together . . . something sensational.

The "comic operas" that these two men wrote together have a preeminent place in the history of the English-language musical theater . . . and they have, since forever, also had a place in my life. When I was barely emerging from babyhood, the piano (which neither mother nor father could play!) in our green salon featured, on its stand, the German edition of selections from *The Mikado*—you know, the brown one, with Pooh-Bah and Ko-Ko on the front—and when my skinny fingers had mastered *Teaching Little Fingers to Play*, they were tested, next, on the vocal score of *The Pirates of Penzance*. The living room bookshelf held, I remember, alongside *The Search for Bridey Murphy* and *The Black Girl in Search of God*, a book titled *The Savoy Operas*; father's study housed red-bound libretti of several of the shows, marked up with all the "approved" stage moves, by the D'Oyly Carte management; and the first LP recording that replaced our Austrian 78s was *The Gondoliers*. I sang cheerily, along with Ella Halman, my version of "giving him the very best and getting back the very worst," which (diction was never Miss Halman's forte) went something like "baxtaberry baxtaberry baxtaberry ba!"

By the time I graduated to performing "The Ghosts' High Noon" and "A Policeman's Lot" on 2XN radio, I had conducted my College Country Boys' house orchestra of four (after school country boys went to hay out and mow!) in an almost-winning performance of "Poor Wand'ring One" and . . . well, you get the picture. And how jealous was I of the kids at dad's coeducational school, who got to do a G&S opera every year.

1. Paul Knüpfer and Julius Lieban in *Der Mikado* (Königliche Oper, Berlin).

It was "Doc" Gallas, my father, who was behind the productions, which he directed with fine practical flair and the help of Savoy Theatre's little red books, and, at age six, I got to see my first ever stage show: his college production of *The Mikado*. Needless to say, my impressions of the occasion were published by the Wellington *Evening Post*. My graphic skills were never great, but it was G&S who got me into print for the first time. And now, coming full circle, G&S—nearly seventy years later—will be . . . well, maybe not my very last publication, but . . .

In those seventy years, books concerning W. S. Gilbert, Arthur Sullivan, and their producer, Richard D'Oyly Carte, have proliferated like daffodils in the sunshine. There have been splendid scholarly tomes, such as Cyril Rollins and R. John Witts's catalogue of D'Oyly Carte performances (surely due for the promised World Wide Web–age update), annotated editions of Gilbert's libretti, biographies of both Mr. Gilbert

2. Program for *The Mikado*, directed by "Doc" Gallas.

3. My rendering of a scene from *The Mikado*, a precocious debut by Kurt Gänzl, aged six.

and Mr. Sullivan, brief histories, precisely told as adjuncts to exhibition, and now websites and blogs. Which is where I come in.

I have, of course, written at reasonable (and wholly factual) length about the G&S opus, both in my *British Musical Theatre* and *Encyclopaedia of the Musical Theatre*, but I have never been a G&S "specialist." I have always been a man who looks at the wider theatrical view, and G&S were only a part of that panorama. My private affection for them hasn't been allowed to infect my staunchly factual historical writings. I promise. But there are real Savoy scholars out there, who focus wholly on the works of our heroes, and who have helped, by their thoroughness and their devotion, to scour out some of the traditional myths and legends surrounding the pair and their works. The story is getting "cleaner" by the day. And, now, I am getting to be a "Savoy scholar," too. How and why did that happen?

Well, it started thuswise. My last work, which was originally intended only for my own pleasure (keep him off the streets!), in my invalided years, was a collection of brief to not-so-brief biographical notes on singers—opera, light opera, concerts—of the nineteenth century. I completed over nine hundred such articles, and, in 2017, a choice one hundred of them were published, under the title *Victorian Vocalists*. There was the odd Savoyard among the nine hundred, but, truthfully, I wasn't much interested in rootling around researching and writing about folks who had already had a whole book written about them, just to be able to say "that's wrong"; far better to tackle the untackled.

And, so, it came to pass that I was rootling around in the Carl Rosa Opera Company and lit upon one "Lilian La Rue." Now, Lilian not only sang with the Rosa, she was a Cartesian (get used to that word, I use it for anyone who ever worked for Mr. D'Oyly Carte) of some small significance. She was the original Kate in the Opera Comique's *Pirates of Penzance*: "Far away from toil and care, revelling in fresh sea air . . ." Savoy scholars, over the years, had given up trying to find out who she was, and whence she came. Hah! I like a challenge . . . especially when I win.

The result of my investigation was a blog post plaintively titled "Lilian La Rue: Who Are You?" Oh heavens, that name sounds like something out of a New Orleans drag show. Lily Street, maybe? But this airy-fairy Lilian has been a serious mystery to, in particular, Gilbert and Sullivan scholars and students for over a century. Who was she? Would we ever know?

4. Lilian La Rue: Who are you?

Lilian La Rue: Who Are You?

Miss La Rue arrived on the London theater scene in 1879, and was promptly cast by D'Oyly Carte in the role of Hebe, in his second London touring company of HMS *Pinafore*. In January 1880, she was transferred to the West End company. She was "sprightly and agreeable and sang the music with grace and refinement of style." When *The Pirates of Penzance* was produced in London, Lilian was again allotted the mezzo-soprano role of Kate. Thus her fascination for the G&S historians of today.

Julia Gwynne succeeded to the role of Kate, but Lilian was now otherwise engaged. She was to join the Carl Rosa Opera Company. Why? Why would Rosa hire a nineteen-year-old American? Admittedly, he was doing extremely well with American singers, of the ilk of Fred Packard, Julia Gaylord, and Josephine Yorke . . . but a teenager? Why was she not in Italy "perfecting her vocal studies"? Or back in America learning her trade on home ground?

Lilian made her first appearance with Rosa's company, in Manchester, in September 1880, as Mercedes to the Carmen of prima donna Georgina Burns, and progressed to play Frédéric in *Mignon* (the reviewers noted that she "sang carefully and pleasingly," and that "her voice wants power but she sang spiritedly and with intelligence") and Fatima in *The Cadi* ("makes the best of a not particularly strong or brilliant voice . . . looks pretty"). Her next role was Lazarillo in *Maritana*, habitually played by Miss Yorke, the first contralto of the troupe ("sang well and made a good impression"), but there was a yet more dramatic part to come. She was given the star role of *Carmen*, originally the property, like Frédéric, of the sizzling Selina Dolaro and, since, of such stars as Zélie Trebelli. Julia Gaylord and Georgina Burns had played Carmen, and both were still with the company. Why was Lilian being given this plum part, over those experienced leading ladies?

Lilian's first try was equivocal. The critics noted, "Her voice is of peculiar quality . . . [but] no one can doubt her earnestness of intention" and "it is not the Carmen of Selina Dolaro, or of Emily Soldene, or even of Julia Gaylord." She had just weeks in the provinces to work it in, before Rosa opened (14 January 1882) at London's Her Majesty's Theatre. On night four, Lilian was introduced as Lazarillo, and the London critics got to dissect her: "She has a good voice, somewhat alloyed in its purity by a faulty production, as well as by needless use of the tremolo, which renders it doubtful at times to determine the exact note she intends to deliver." But they made allowance for first-night nerves and declared her to be, by far, the best performer in the cast.

Next up was *Mignon*, in which her Frédéric went down much better, before, on 26 January, Miss La Rue brought forth her Carmen. The result was quite surprising. She was hailed for "a very remarkable performance . . . an ideal Carmen." She was declared "fresh . . . new . . . young . . . different." But it was her acting that caught the critics' eyes. "A refined Carmen of the most fascinating kind; a coquettish, wilful, passionate, vain, captivating little witch, utterly irresistible," claimed one paper. Her singing was dismissed, at the end of most reviews, as fair enough, at best "a mezzo-soprano voice of pleasing quality and a considerable degree of dramatic power." After the London season, the company played at the Crystal Palace, and those performances were Lilian's last with Rosa. Strange? Why did she not come back to the company, after all the pains taken to establish her as an attraction?

Lilian returned for a while to America, but, in October 1883, she was back in London, at the Avenue Theatre, featured in a production based loosely on *La Vie parisienne* with a semipasticcio Offenbach score. She played Christine de Gondremarck, now, for "proper" England, the Baron's daughter rather than his wife. Her Christine rather was, naturally, rather less visceral than her Carmen: "A voice of charming quality . . . she acts agreeably and has a ladylike appearance," quoth one critic. "No beauty and less voice," snarled another. She played the role till December, when the show was condensed and Florence St. John, "the queen of comic opera," brought in to replace her. And that was the last that the theater public, on either side of the pond, saw of Miss Lilian La Rue.

Who was this Lilian La Rue? Her identity was never revealed in the press, but I found a way around that. She was said to be an American; everyone was firm about that. Where was the company singing on census night 1881? Birmingham. Yes, there they were—the Gaylords, Josie Yorke, Georgina Burns, and G. H. Snazelle—in theatrical digs. So, I simply went through the whole census for Birmingham, looking for young American ladies who weren't servants or daughters. And, soon, all was explained. There was only one lady who fit the bill. She was twenty-five, and not nineteen, but everything else fit. And she was actually sharing those digs in Bath Street with Josie and Georgina. Lilian was, quite simply, Miss Frances Alice Jones, born in Ohio, the younger sister of Miss Josie Jones aka Yorke. So, that was how she had crossed the ocean, that was how she had swanned into the Carl Rosa, and that was why Miss Yorke had given up, to her, the role of Lazarillo. Lilian was the prima donna contralto's little sister: Fanny Jones, fourth daughter of a soap manufacturer from Cincinnati.

And the rest of the story? Well, the girls returned to America, where Josie had been contracted to Mapleson's opera company. They made the papers when they got robbed in a New York hotel. Josie would return to England and continue her career, but not Fanny. Frances Alice Jones of Cincinnati died in the Grand Pacific Hotel, Chicago, aged thirty, in 1885. So, there's one more Gilbert and Sullivan "mystery" solved. We can now write, encyclopaedically: "LA RUE, Lilian [JONES, Frances Alice] (b. Cincinnati, Ohio, 9 December 1854; d. Grand Pacific Hotel, Chicago, 22 June 1885)."

Chasing Lilian's story didn't immediately turn me from my *Victorian Vocalists* path. But she had planted a seed. Eighteen months later, with my beautiful big red book of nineteenth-century singers, finally, published, I was sitting in my Winter Palace by the sun-sodden Australian seaside, with a glass (bottle?) of wine, and thought: enough. Let the *Vic Vocs* go. Do something else.

I had sent my Lilian discovery to my good friend David Stone, who runs the *Who Was Who* section of the Gilbert and Sullivan Archive, so that he might update his site with the newly found details. And, there, I got waylaid. Okay, Lilian was outed, but what about the many other unidentified folk who created and/or played for Mr. Carte, and who were also listed in this *Who's Who?*: "Emilie Petrelli" (snort), "Ugo Talbo" (howl), "Signor Brocolini," "T. J. Montelli," "Duglas Gordon"—who were, every one, Anglo-Saxon or Hibernian, despite their exotic names. What does anyone know about the original Little Buttercup, the original Ruth, or the original Plaintiff in *Trial by Jury*? The Aussie sun was warm, and it was time to see what I could do to fill some of the gaps in David's splendid collection.

I mean, a piece of theater isn't a real piece of theater until it is lifted off the page and put on the stage: and you can't put a piece on the stage ("unfortunately," as one harassed producer once said) without actors—or, in our case, singers. So, I thought I'd devote my days in the winter sun to trying to find out something more about these people, who have been so long, even to the finest G&S scholars, little more than meaningless names on a program. That was three years ago. And it has been great fun, since, putting lives, stories, and sometimes faces to those names, and delving into the whys and wherefores of the sometimes-curious castings (successful and disastrous) of the Savoy triumvirate. I look at my G&S shows with a different eye now; they have come alive, peopled by real people.

Gilbert and Sullivan before Gilbert and Sullivan

So: Mr. Gilbert and Mr. Sullivan. Or should that be Mr. Sullivan and Mr. Gilbert? I do hate billing problems. I suppose the expression "Gilbert and Sullivan" is now so ingrained in Western culture that it would be pedantic to reverse it. The two gentlemen came together for the first time as theatrical collaborators only when they had accomplished, with other partners or with none, a certain (not to exaggerate!) amount in the musical and theatrical world: neither was a musical-theater novice.

Sullivan, apart from notable fame garnered in the concert world, had had considerable success in the light musical theater, first with the short piece *Cox and Box*, an all-male three-hander adapted from Maddison Morton's greatly popular farce *Box and Cox*, and originally played by society amateurs, and then with the comic opera *The Contrabandista*, played at T. German Reed's St. George's Opera House. Both pieces had had words by Frank Burnand, an extremely well-known and prolific author of burlesque books and comic theater and prose.

Gilbert, like Burnand, was a practiced comic writer of burlesque, pantomime, and variegated theater pieces, not to mention of decidedly successful comic verse. His dramatic work had been frequently praised for both its witty literacy and for its effective theatricality, and had included burlesques of the operas *L'Elisir d'amore* (*Dulcamara*), *La Fille*

5. Amdrams: Quintin Twiss, Arthur Blunt, and George du Maurier in *Cox and Box*.

du régiment (*La Vivandière*), *The Bohemian Girl* (*The Merry Zingara*), and *Norma* (*The Pretty Druidess*), as well as of Giacomo Meyerbeer's *Robert the Devil* for the opening of the new Gaiety Theatre and of Alfred Tennyson's *The Princess* for the Olympic. He had supplied short pieces for the entertainments at the Reed's establishment at the "polite" Gallery of Illustration, and some genuine musical comedies in *The Gentleman in Black* at the Charing Cross and *Creatures of Impulse* (music by Alberto Randegger) at the Court Theatre.

The burlesques had—in the time-honored style—pasticcio scores, made up from well-known tunes set to original songwords. Several of

6. Gaiety Theatre star comedian Johnnie Toole in *La Vivandière*.

the Gallery of Illustration pieces were set to music by manager German Reed, formerly musical director at the Haymarket Theatre. But Gilbert's most fruitful partner, in those years, was amateur musician Freddie Clay, who had supplied the music for both the highly successful little *Ages Ago* and for *The Gentleman in Black*.

After their first collaboration, Sullivan still ventured into the theater with a partner other than Gilbert (e.g., *The Zoo*, with B. C. Stephenson), and Gilbert worked with Reed and Clay on further pieces for the Gallery, and with Alfred Cellier for the Criterion Theatre. With Clay, Gilbert wrote an underloved full-length comic opera, *Princess Toto*, which first saw the light of stage at Nottingham. But from the success of Gilbert and Sullivan's first full-length comic opera as a team, *The Sorcerer*, in 1877, the two men worked exclusively together until circumstances did them part a dozen years later. And in those years, they turned out ten of the fourteen pieces of musical theater that would make them into the stuff of living legends—those pieces that are the subject of our book.

7. The fate of a too-well-loved volume.

So, let's take a wee journey through the fourteen pieces that make up the G&S opus, and peep, on the way, at some of the people responsible for making them popular wherever English is spoken and sung. For the best results, as the cookbooks say, the following pages should be read with the full text of the Savoy Operas at your left hand (alas, my late partner's school-prize copy, from 1932, has, finally, disintegrated under the thumbings of the past few weeks), a CD player and the better recordings, or, better still, a piano and a pile of scores to the right, and the online *Who Was Who in the D'Oyly Carte* (https://gsarchive.net/whowaswho/index.htm) close by, for all those minute details. A bottle of good chilled bubbly and a La-Z-Boy won't go amiss, either.

Kurt Gänzl
Gerolstein, New Zealand
September 2020

Acknowledgments

I don't usually have thank yous in my books, because I'm pretty much of a lone ranger. Not this time! With my former collections now disseminated between Harvard, New York, California, Australia, and elsewhere in preparation for my retirement, I have had to howl for help like never before.

The dual Davids, Stone and Lovell, answered that howl to such an extent, supplying me with photographs from their collections, that they have richly earned under-the-title billing. Thank you, lads.

Andrea Cawelti, Ethan Crenson, Vincent Daniels, Katie Barnes, and J. Donald Smith have come up with the occasional prize pictorial item as well.

Citations and chocolate medals for finding me bits of info and checking my minutiae go to Jamie Findlay, Betsy Miller, Boris Priebe, Moritz Stämmler, Andrew Sandilands, Anne Stanyon, Stephen Turnbull, Will Parry, Leon Berger, Clifton Coles, Michael and Nan Miller, Raymond Walker, Joe Carl White, and the entire membership of Glenn Christodoulou's Facebook forum, the Arthur Sullivan Appreciation Page.

Special thanks, as always, to the impeccable Andrew Lamb.

1

Thespis, or The Gods Grown Old

Grotesque opera
Gaiety Theatre, 26 December 1871

Thespis doesn't, really, have an awful lot to do with the rest of the Gilbert and Sullivan opus. It was written and composed by our two gentlemen, to order, as a Christmas entertainment for the Gaiety Theatre, a new house for which Gilbert had already written a successful pasticcio burlesque. However, following the Gaiety's small triumph with *Aladdin II*, a real, original very comic opera—especially composed for the theater's previous year's festive season, by none less than Hervé, the French "father of the opéra-bouffe"—the theater's manager, John Hollingshead, wanted another original work, to follow in that French "father's" footsteps. O-rig-i-nal.

Gilbert, however, didn't take another traditional pantomime story for his subject matter. Instead he went to the European theater, and to the tale treated in the 1825 Josefstädter-Theater Posse *Die Schauspieler-Gesellschaft in Olymp*. I have no idea whether its topsy-godsy plot—replacing the Olympian Gods, gone on "holiday" with a bunch of ancient Greek actors—originated here or whether this was a version of an earlier piece; I rather suspect it was. And Gilbert, I ween, was not around the Josefstadt (where he might have met my ancestors) in 1825. So, maybe, this quirky idea had been, at some stage, nicked by an English playwright. Anyway, it was a plot that allowed the author to indulge in a version of what has been since christened "the lozenge plot," the reversal or placing in an abnormal context of a piece's character(s). It was a plot element that had been popular as musico-dramatic fodder as far back as Charles Coffey's splendid *The Devil to Pay* (1731), and which had been utilized, more recently, in such joyous French musical theater pieces as *Ba-ta-clan*, *La Chatte metamorphosée en femme*, and many others.

One constraint for Gilbert was that he needed to fit the musico-comical stars of the Gaiety, and most especially those of *Aladdin II*, with prominent roles. Well, the overwhelming stars of *Aladdin II*—the Gaiety's biggest success to date—had been the house's star comedian, Johnnie Toole, as the magician Ko-kil-ko, and breeches-playing Nellie Farren as the titular Aladdin. But they had been superbly supported by J. D. Stoyle as King Ozokerit the lightheaded (a Victorian joke; "Ozokerit" was a brand of safety matches); the incomparable tenor-actor Charles Lyall as a hilarious Remembrancer; Annie Tremaine as a perky maid with a song; rich-voiced Connie Loseby from the music halls as the Princess in the affair; tall, buxom, royal mistress Lardy Wilson in a "thinking" role that enabled her to stroll gape-worthily across the stage; and the delicious Parisian takeover of the part of the genie, "Mdlle. Clary."

Our author filled his brief pretty well. Toole was cast as the titular Thespis, leader of the dramatic troupe, and the other principals—around twenty of them—played the actors and actresses of his troupe, and the gods and goddesses for whom they deputized, during their disastrous stint on the mythological Mountain.

There was only one major problem. By the time everyone had done his or her thing, the two acts of *Thespis* ran for three hours. I suspect—and this is not fact, just a feeling—that author and composer had not worked together. Gilbert had written an entire fairy-tale play, while, separately, Sullivan had written a full score of music. But we don't know for certain, because almost all of Sullivan's music to *Thespis* is lost. It is said that parts of it were reused by the composer in later life, so maybe it was purposely "lost."

We know, from the reviews, about the most popular numbers, particularly the ballad "Little Maid of Arcadee," which, in later times, was interpolated into an American performance of *HMS Pinafore*, to give poor Hebe a number. One chorus was recycled into *The Pirates of Penzance*, and there was "ballet music" that would have no future use, as ballet did not become part of the G&S method. The rest is left to the imagination. Anyhow, the score of *Thespis* has become rather like the Holy Grail to G&S enthusiasts. Something to be eternally, and hopelessly, searched and striven for . . .

So, when we speak of *Thespis*, we speak of something of which we cannot know much, except secondhand, via what was written about it in the contemporary press. And, of course, from what survives as the text.

That text was taken up by the G&S guru of a former generation, Terry Rees. He published a version of it, in the years when it was difficult to get at the censorship copies, for which we were all hugely grateful (*Thespis: A Gilbert & Sullivan Enigma*, Dillon's University Bookshop, London, 1964). But that version was more like one hour than three . . . Well, one hour of *Thespis* is better than no Gilbert at all. And one song (and a few questionable fragments) is better than no Sullivan at all. And an evening with a cast such as the one with which Hollingshead served his writers must have been a treat.

So, whom am I going to feature from the cast of *Thespis*? No, not Johnnie Toole (b. St. Mary Axe, London, 12 March 1830; d. London, 30 January 1906); he wrote his own memoirs: *Reminiscences of J L Toole Related by Himself* (Hurst and Blackett, London, 1889). Nor Nellie Farren (b. Brighton, 16 April 1848; d. London, 28 April 1904), whose famous career has been biographized more recently (G. W. Hilton, *Nellie Farren*, Arthur Sullivan Society, 1997). Fred Sullivan, brother of Arthur? Later. The fine comedians J. G. Taylor and John Maclean? Robert Soutar, who married Nellie Farren for a while? Lardy Wilson, who became the mother of the Duke of Edinburgh's child (whose name was never revealed) and left the stage for . . . what? The really celebrated pantomimists Fred and Harry Payne (nés Schofield), newsworthy features of the original London *La Grande-Duchesse* cancan, and their father's partner, the still undeciphered "Mademoiselle Esta"? The outstanding Annie Tremaine (née Crilman) (b. Woolwich, 27 January 1848; d. Paddington, 12 December 1934), who became Ada Beaumont burlesque star, then Madame Amadi of the grand opera stage and later of the West End musical? Ah! Wonderful woman! She was one of my hundred select *Victorian Vocalists*. Connie Loseby (b. Nottingham, 11 September 1842; d. Red Lion Hotel, Milford, 13 October 1906), originally teamed in a music-hall act with her mother, and here, spotted by Hollingshead, at the beginning of a long stint as a leading singing lady in the British theater.

Yes, it was one heck of a lineup . . . even though a few of these performers had not yet reached the fame that was to be theirs. Mr. Hollingshead was one hell of a casting director, which was and still is not a small part of the reason for any producer's success. So, as a result, many of these folks have been written up (not least by me!) elsewhere. But not all. And that's what I'm here for. I would love to identify "Mdlle. Esta" for you. I have tried for twenty years (and haven't stopped trying!) . . . but let's have "Mdlle. Clary" instead. Unlike Esther, she was a genuine mademoiselle . . . until she became "Sparkeion of Croydon." Hark, ye . . .

"Mdlle. Clary": A Disappearing Act?

For a century and more, one of the puzzles that has troubled folk interested in nineteenth-century musical theater—and Gilbert and Sullivan in particular—is who in tarnation was this "Mdlle. Clary" who was such a success on the London stage in the early 1870s, as star in opéra-bouffe and the creator of leading trouser roles in two interesting musicals? None of us had the faintest idea. She came from Belgium (maybe?), made her hit, and vanished—back to Europe, we supposed.

8. Madeleine Clary: Sparkeion of Croydon.

There was simply nowhere to start, so we didn't really try. When it came to writing a little note on her for my *Encyclopaedia of the Musical Theatre*, I simply grouped her in with some of the other myriad "Mdlle. Clarys" of the nineteenth century—from the Opéra to the Comédie Française—and wrote,

> One Mdlle Clary (née Poirel-Tardieu), equipped with "a remarkably graceful figure, easy movements, a nice soprano voice and a very handsome face" and billed as being "of Saint-Petersburg," went to Britain as a member of Eugène Humbert's Théâtre des Fantaisies-Parisiennes company, which played at the Gaiety Theatre in 1871 (Hélène in *La Belle Hélène*, Roland in *Les Bavards*, etc.). She stayed on, pleading in court, when Humbert tried to force her to return to continue her contract in Belgium, that she suffered too heavily from sea-sickness to make the crossing. Her court performance must have been convincing, for she did remain in Britain, and there she created the rôles of the Grand Duke in Jonas's *Cinderella the Younger* (1871) and Sparkeion in Sullivan and Gilbert's *Thespis*, and played Naphtha in a revival of Hervé's *Aladdin II*, all at the Gaiety, as well appearing as Alexandrivoire in London's *L'Oeil crevé* (1872), Méphisto in *Le Petit Faust* at Holborn, and as La Belle Adrienne in Offenbach's *The Bohemians* (*Le Roman comique*, 1873) at the Opéra-Comique. She then vanished from London and, as far as can be seen, from theatrical annals.

But my friend Sam Silvers more or less challenged me, in response to my articles on Miss Tremaine and Miss Jolly of the *Thespis* cast, to sort out "Mdlle. Clary," so I thought, well, I may as well have a shot. I dived into the musty French records, and—bull's-eye!

Madeleine (yes, she was called Madeleine) was born in about 1846, in France, the daughter of Pierre-Étienne-Émile Poirel and Jeanne-Marguerite-Adelaïde Tardieu. Maybe the parents weren't married, or maybe the hyphenation was just an affectation: anyway, Madeleine was officially plain Jeanne-Marie-Madeleine Poirel. She made what was called her debut on the Paris stage in the hit comedy *Mille francs et ma fille* at the Théâtre Déjazet in April 1868 ("[Elle] joue avec aisance et naturel la piquante Césarine. Elle est jolie et possède une voix agréable, qu'elle sait conduire") and then, I suppose, came the Russian bit, the Belgian bit, the British bit, and the disappearing act. Well, Madeline disappeared for the most common of reasons. No, not death; marriage. On 24 January 1875, she became the wife of Pierre-Marie-Augustin (aka Auguste) Filon. The marriage took place at Rosière-les-Salines in the Meurthe-et-Moselle area of France, so I imagine that either his family or hers hailed from there.

Their son, Louis-Napoléon-George Filon, was born in France, but they later moved, in comfortable circumstances, back to Britain and settled in Croydon. In the 1901 census they can be found at Godwin House, 68 St. Augustine's Avenue. The elders are living on their own means, and Louis is a math teacher. They have a cook and a housemaid. By 1911, Louis has married a Swiss lady, has two children, Madeleine and Sydney (and two servants), of his own and is professor of mathematics at London University. The Croydon dynasty continued, because the grandchildren wed . . . and, well, Sophia Florsted Filon, if you are still in Croydon, in 2021, you are twenty years younger than my Croydon colleague Andrew Lamb, and you could have bumped into him on the railway station or in the supermarket . . . if only we had known!

So, there we are. All these decades we've been thinking "Mdlle. Clary" had disappeared into the darkest Moselle, or a mausoleum, and she was, until her death on 30 December 1930, just down the road, at Godwin House; a short career, but a delicious and memorable one. And now, at last, we know!

Miss Elizabeth Jolly: A Regular "Venus"

Let's go further down the cast list: "Miss Jolly" as Venus. Well, usually when you had "Venus" in a show, you cast the role with the most stunning lady in the company, such as the *pulpeuse* Amy Sheridan. Why, with the "5ft 10 all in proportion" Lardy Wilson in the troupe would you cast Lardy as a boy (in, of course, leg-revealing rompers), and give the part of Venus to "Miss Jolly," mezzo-soprano? Was she another stunner? No one ever indicated it; the critics described her as "graceful and womanly," not quite the Lardy level of beauty, perhaps a plump burlesque. Ah! just so! Venus is described as "an aged deity"! A contralto's fate.

The fashion for duet singing in the 1850s produced some outstanding pairs of singing sisters, topped by the Misses Williams and the Misses Wells, followed by the Broughams, the McAlpines, the Mascalls. Each of these families had the genealogical and musical talent to produce one soprano and one contralto. Mr. and Mrs. Jolly gave birth (among a volley of other babes) to two contraltos.

John Marks Jolly (b. London, 5 December 1790; d. West Square, Southwark, 1 July 1864) was a well-known musician in the London theaters and concert rooms. In his time, he played at most of the principal London theaters, and was conductor at and composed music for several, notably the Sans Pareil as early as 1815, and for a long stint at the Surrey "in its palmiest days." His music was even played before Their Majesties at Buckingham Palace. Mr. Jolly married Sarah Ann Macklan, and fathered a brood, of whom, seemingly, the last two were Elizabeth (b. Somerstown, baptized 1827) and Cecilia (b. York Road, Lambeth, baptized 7 October 1832, d. Peckham Workhouse, 1904), who became "singing sisters."

I first see them out as a pair in June 1849, at Mr. J. Wild's concert, but they got under way and gained wider notice the following year. In November, they were purveying duets of their father's manufacture at the National Hall, Holborn. The *Era* commented that "two sister voices, similar also in timbre, is a circumstance somewhat rare. The enunciation of both ladies is extraordinarily good, their notes have a full clear bell-like resonance." In January 1851, they were at the London Mechanics Institute (singing "The Lost Heart"), after which they went on the road for music publisher Charles Jefferys, as a support act to the boy pianist Heinrich Werner. "They possess voices with remarkably deep tone and very clear intonation which combined [well] with their simple and expressive style of singing," applauded Liverpool, while Manchester opined, "The elder one has a fine organ and they sing well together." Thereafter I spot them at the Strand Music Hall and at various city concerts, and in January 1852 in Glasgow singing at Julian Adams's concerts. In June, they started a season at the Vauxhall Gardens.

In 1853, they were hired by the writer and entertainer Joseph Edwards Carpenter (b. St. George's With East, London, 2 November 1813; d. 20 Norland Square, Bayswater, 6 May 1885), "the distinguished author of up to a thousand songs," to vocally illustrate his scenes and songs from *Uncle Tom's Cabin*, the most enduring of the mass of Uncle Tom shows that followed the fashion for Mrs. Stowe's book. Carpenter lectured about the authoress and her work, and the girls sang songs, with lyrics by Carpenter and music by Henry Bishop, Edward Land, Ernest Perring, Henry Farmer, Bianchi Taylor, Edward Loder, E. L. Hime, and, of course, J. M. Jolly. The pianist was W. S. Rooke, once of *Amilie* fame. The entertainment opened with three straight weeks at the Cabinet Theatre, King's Cross, and progressed to the Manor House, Hackney, and to Crosby Hall, and on 7 February set out from Hastings for a lengthy tour.

When Carpenter's season finished, the Jolly sisters returned to concert singing. I note them at "Signor Borini's concerts à la Jullien" in Dublin on 3 October 1853, duetting Jolly's "The Gipsey Sisters" and performing a duet arrangement of "The Minstrel Boy." Elizabeth sang "The Old Chimney Corner" and "The Last Rose of Summer," while Cecilia offered Lover's "The Land of the West" and Farmer's "The Little Evangelist." The following month they were given their chance, in the footsteps of the Misses Wells, at the prestigious London Wednesday Concerts (9 November, "The Twin Sisters") at Exeter Hall, but this appears to have been a single engagement.

In 1854, they returned to Carpenter for his new entertainment, *The Road, the River and the Rail*, which had been playing since November at the Polytechnic with a Miss Blanche Younge as its musical part. The piece toured till the end of 1855, after which the Misses Jolly took to the music halls—Holder's in Birmingham, the Philharmonic in Glasgow, the Surrey in Sheffield—and to a season at the Surrey Gardens. However, their career as a duo had its last flourish in the halls, and they became a fixture, in the early 1860s, in the choir at the Oxford and Cambridge Music Halls, led by their father. In 1863–64, they are at the Regent Music Hall, but quite what happened next, I am not sure. What careers the girls had thereafter, they, in any case, pursued separately. I see "Miss Cecilia Jolly" on the bill at the Imperial Music Hall at Easter 1864. "Miss Jolly," who, I presume, is Elizabeth, appears at the Regent, at Cremorne Gardens ("a fine contralto") and as principal resident contralto at the Alhambra till 1867.

Next thing, Miss Jolly pops up on the cast lists at the new Gaiety Theatre, playing supporting parts in everything from plays to operas (*Robert the Devil*, *Columbus*, Mrs. Mingle in *Dearer than Life*, Trusty in *The Clandestine Marriage*, Venus in *Thespis*, Sheelagh in *The Lily of Killarney*, Dolores in *Les Cent Vierges*, *Ganymede and Galatea*, etc.), between 1871 and 1874, and as Cogia in *Ali Baba* at the Crystal Palace at Christmas 1871 with W. H. Payne, Annie Tremaine, and J. T. Dalton. It is this Miss Jolly, undoubtedly, who is on the road in 1876 and 1877, as a member of the Cornélie d'Anka and Alice May *La Grande-Duchesse* companies, and this Miss Jolly who is at the Prince of Wales Theatre, Liverpool, later in 1877 playing Clémentine in *Barbe-bleue* with R. W. South. And, just maybe, in 1878 appearing at the Steam Clock Music Hall, Birmingham. She'd be over fifty, now. An aged deity, indeed.

I can't be totally sure, for I now lose Elizabeth, but not Cecilia. Cecilia had a mishap in 1868, and gave birth to an illegitimate daughter, Cecilia Amy King Jolly (1868–1925)—presumably fathered by a Mr. King. Mishaps were to be her lot, it seems, for—still calling herself a "vocalist"—she can be seen in the 1881 and 1891 censi living in the Peckham workhouse. She is still there in 1901, now a "retired vocalist," and she died there three years later.

The family historians say that Elizabeth died in 1916, at the age of eighty-nine. They also say she married one George Green Fenn in 1863. Don't believe a word of it. The Eliza Jolly who married farmer Fenn of Streatham in 1861 was thirty-two, and the daughter of John William Jolly, merchant. So there's yet more searching to do. Venus is still missing.

Thespis: A G&S Mystery

While *Thespis* was playing on the Gaiety bill, a good few of the show's cast were also doing matinées in another seasonal show, produced by Hollingshead, down at Sydenham's Crystal Palace. This one, *Ali Baba*, was a more traditional burlesque-pantomime than Gilbert's "entirely original grotesque opera" (entirely?). Annie Tremaine was leading lady this time, and she and the Paynes, Dalton, Maclean, Miss Jolly, Lizzie Wright, Marie Smithers, Lardy's legs, and Nellie Farren's sister Florence of the *Thespis* cast had to scamper from Sydenham back to the Strand to play in Gilbert and Sullivan's piece in the evening. They played it sixty-three times. And, apart from a performance the following April at Madeleine Clary's Benefit, that was it.

Thespis hadn't equaled *Aladdin II* in popularity. It hadn't followed its predecessor out to the British provinces and into a second Gaiety season; it wasn't to follow the Gaiety's other original musical of 1871, *Cinderella the Younger* (music by Émile Jonas), to productions on the Continent. *Thespis* had simply done the job for which it was created, and then it was put away to make place for the next bit of extravaganza on the Gaiety programs. And it would have stayed away, along with the myriad others of its kind, in spite of the odd murmur of a revival, had it not been the work of Messrs. Gilbert and Sullivan. As such, it has remained an object of interest and curiosity to those who love and study the G&S opus, although, thanks to Dr. Rees and his splendidly scholarly reconstruction of Gilbert's text, we can read, if not hear, what *Thespis* was like.

2

Trial by Jury

Dramatic cantata in one act
Royalty Theatre, London, 25 March 1875

It was three and a half years after the production of *Thespis* before another work from the combined pens of Messrs. Gilbert and Sullivan saw the light of stage. And it was a work considerably different from their first. Gone the three-hour-long visit to world of gods and fairies with its whimsicalities and festivities; *Trial by Jury* was a tight, taut, and thoroughly up-to-date little piece of musical comedy, with a delicious

> **REMOVAL OF THE LORD CHIEF BARON NICHOLSON.**
> The LORD CHIEF BARON NICHOLSON has removed his Judge and Jury Court, and Poses Plastiques and Tableaux Vivans Company, from the Coal Hole to the celebrated
> **CIDER CELLARS, MAIDEN-LANE.**
> The hall is one of the most commodious rooms in London, lofty and well ventilated. It will enable the patrons of the Baron to gaze with the grace and beauty of the Poses Plastiques, and to listen to the wit and humour of the trials without being inconvenienced by the intense heat and stifling vapours they suffered from at the Coal Hole during the representation of the great case of Nogo v. Hero.
> POSES PLASTIQUES and TABLEAUX VIVANS at Half-past Seven and after the Theatres. JUDGE AND JURY at Half-past Nine o'clock every Evening.
> Mr. NICHOLSON begs to offer his most heartfelt thanks for the unprecedented patronage he has received in his new establishment, and to apprise his best friends, the Public, that to-morrow (Monday evening), the JUDGE AND JURY SOCIETY will hear an entirely new case of "BREACH OF PROMISE OF MARRIAGE."
> Tuesday, the Crown on the prosecution of the Parish of "St. Prudence-in-the-Fields against Certain Disorderly Houses." Wednesday, the popular case of "Nogo v. Hero." Thursday, "Breach of Promise." Friday, "St. Prudence." Saturday, "Nogo v. Hero."
> The *Tableaux Vivans* and *Poses Plastiques* are now performed on a scale of splendour unmatched in the history of ancient or modern exhibitions.
> The beautiful model, Miss ETTY GREY, will take her BENEFIT on MONDAY WEEK, FEBRUARY 15, on which occasion will be presented a grand new *Tableau*, illustrative of a "LOVER'S VALENTINE."

9. An 1858 trial by judge and jury for Breach of Promise of Marriage.

flair of modulated bouffonnerie. Once again, the story was a simple one . . . but modern, not mythological . . . and it dealt with a place in which Victorians had found much mirth since the days of the old Cider Cellars and its mock trial of *A Breach of Promise of Marriage*.

Edwin has proposed to Angelina—burlesque already, the names are those of the lovey-dovey hero and heroine of Oliver Goldsmith's *The Hermit*—and, then, has found another lady he likes better. So Angelina sues him for breach of promise of marriage, and they come to court, before a chorus of jurymen and a burlesque judge ("and a good judge too!"). Angelina arrives, weeping, in her wedding gown, with a chorus of bridesmaids trailing behind, in an attempt to bolster the amount of damages to be awarded by a court full of susceptible gentlemen. Edwin pretends that he would be a brute of a husband, and the case is settled only when the judge declares, damme! "I'll marry her myself."

The genesis of the little cantata has been oft described: Gilbert had transformed a comical piece that he had written for the magazine *Fun* into a libretto, allegedly for Carl Rosa and his nascent English opera company. But Rosa didn't do it. His wife, Euphrosyne Parepa-Rosa, who was to be the company's main attraction, died; arrangements for the new company were temporarily shelved, and when they did get under way it was with *Maritana, The Rose of Castille, Lucrezia Borgia, Il Trovatore, The Bohemian Girl, Satanella,* and *The Marriage of Figaro*, with not much place for a comic cantata. So Gilbert put his text aside, without a musical setting.

But chance wasn't long in coming. Miss Selina ("Dolly") Dolaro (née Simmonds)—the "dudes' darling" Jewish soprano who had scored so well in Emily Soldene's opéras-bouffes at the Philharmonic, Islington, and had, most recently, starred in *La Fille de Madame Angot*, at the head of what was described as her own company—decided to play a starring season at the little Royalty Theatre. She was, again, the nominal producer—well, she was indeed the main attraction—but she hired a manager for the season, Mr. R. D'Oyly Carte.

Dolly and her first novelty, *La Périchole*, were well received, even though the star gave the main numbers of the score in French, and the more clenched-buttocked critics objected to the portrayal of a tipsy woman on stage. However, a suitable supporting piece was needed to fill the program. The story has been told that, circa January, Gilbert turned up at Sullivan's house with the script of *Trial by Jury*, and what happened next is anyone's guess, but Sullivan ended up composing the score to the "cantata."

In Victorian times, the little pieces that acted as makeweights, alongside the main show of the evening, in theaters round Britain, were pretty much trifles. These little farces, one-act comedies, or "operettas" with a handful of songs were largely intended to get the audience "in" to the night's entertainment and "out" again, in a merry state of mind—even if they had watched, in between, a gruesome melodrama. Sometimes, these pieces featured a popular actor in a well-worn, show-off role, but mostly they were just little, or reasonably little, pieces of fun, nonsense, or burlesque, either with or without songs. And they were cast accordingly: the stars were in the big piece and, unless you brought in a Julia St. George to star in a bit of burlesque, the afterpiece gave opportunities to the second-string players, including the understudies (if the theater had them) to perform. When *Trial by Jury* was produced, the cast was largely taken from the company already hired, with Miss Nellie Bromley, Fred Sullivan, and Walter Fisher at their head. But the piece, with its choruses, also requires a fairly large supporting cast.

I wonder why Dolly didn't, herself, take the part of the blighted bride in what was to turn out to be the most successful one-act musical in British musical theater. Did she not want to play a rejected woman? It would have been understandable. Her husband—a frightful yob-about-town, involved in gambling, prostitution, and/or worse—can't have endeared her to the institution of marriage. Anyway, whyever, she handed the role of the pretty, forsaken Plaintiff to good friend Nellie Bromley, with whom she had played in the unfortunate *The Black Prince* at the St. James's the year before.

Nellie Bromley (Angelina, The Plaintiff)

Nellie has made her way into all sorts of books and articles and even climbed the exalted heights of Wikipedia, and she was, indeed, a splendid performer. But she is not remembered because of her fine career as an actress—under managers from Pattie Oliver to John Hollingshead, from Alexander Henderson to Edgar Bruce—or for her years of sophisticated comedy successes at the Criterion Theatre. She is remembered for one reason only: she was the first actress to play, for something over three months, the Plaintiff, in Messrs. Gilbert and Sullivan's *Trial by Jury*.

So, what does anyone, really, know about the beauteous Nellie?

Nellie's grandmother, Miss Hannah Shailer, married John Charles Bromley on 5 July 1814. They produced a William, Hannah Charlotte,

10. Nellie Bromley: The blighted bride of *Trial by Jury*.

Jesse, Emily Bertha, Hubert Algernon, Eleanor, and, good heavens, Thaddeus . . . before papa gave up the ghost in 1839. Hannah, however, was tough. She carried on, and in 1841 she can be found living in South Kennington, with her children, Eleanor (fifteen) and Thaddeus (fourteen). It's Eleanor in whom we're interested.

Eleanor went on the stage. When, in 1843, she appeared at the Queen's Theatre as Fanchette in *The Soldier's Secret* and, thereafter, at the Adelphi playing Giannina in *Ondine*, the critics wrote, "Miss Bromley will be a favourite indeed if she continues to carol as sweetly . . . enough to seduce any but a spellbound one from all other allurement." In 1850, Eleanor gave birth to an accidental Eleanor Elizabeth Emily Bromley: our Nellie. Her birth record shows that she was born on 30 September, with her father given as "Arthur Bromley." This looks like a pretty obvious case of virgin birth. I wonder who "Arthur" was. A myth? My last sighting of Eleanor Bromley Sr. is at Christmas 1859. And for good reason: on 15 December 1857, she had married Charles Henry Cook; in 1860, she gave birth to a daughter, and she died in the attempt. After her death, grandmother Hannah took over the care of her two children.

Like her mother, Nellie was young and very attractive when she began her career. In 1866, she hosted a stall at a Crystal Palace bazaar—where actresses would appear to woman the booths as a girlie attraction—alongside the likes of well-known actress Lydia Thompson. Already? How? Why? And by December of that year she was engaged at the Royalty Theatre, playing Dolly Mayflower in Frank Burnand's burlesque on *Black-Eyed Susan*. She stayed at the Royalty for a couple of years, performing in burlesque and comedy, and then went on tour for L. J. Sefton. Back in London, she played at the Globe, the Court, and the Royalty (with the odd matinee at the Gaiety), at the Olympic (under Ada Cavendish), and then moved to the Strand Theatre. There she scored a personal hit in 1873 as Praline in Henry Brougham Farnie's new-style musical comedy *Nemesis* ("What Are a Lady's Wants Today?") and again in its successor, *El Dorado* (Verdurette, "Forget Not to Remember"). Farnie's next effort, the pasticcio *The Black Prince*, found her playing Flossie to the Sybil of Dolly Dolaro; that one was altogether less successful.

Dolly went from *The Black Prince* to the Royalty Theatre to play *La Périchole*, and her "sister" and friend Nellie came too and ended up playing in the afterpieces . . . including *Trial by Jury*. She may have covered Dolly in the main piece—although the vocal power of the one was not equaled by the other—but, anyhow, she got a plum part. There is a myth perpetuated in G&S circles that Nellie was ousted from the role of Angelina, after three months, in favor of Dolly's "friend," Linda Verner, because of jealousy. Bunkum. Don't believe a word of it; Dolly and Nellie remained good friends, toured together thereafter, and in September 1876 holidayed together in Scarborough.

By that time, Nellie had moved on to the heart of her career, at the Criterion Theatre, starting with the hit adaptation of *Le Procès Veradieux* as *The Great Divorce Case*. She became a fixture at the Criterion, featuring in the long-running French farces adapted as *Hot Water*, *On Bail*, and *Pink Dominos* before moving back to the musical theater to play René in the Folly Theatre's *La Créole*. In 1879, she created the role of Amy Jones in another grand success, the comedy *Crutch and Toothpick*, and followed up in the title-role in the Teddy Solomon burlesque *Venus*, and, later, in Lottie Venne's great role of *Betsy* at the Criterion. However, by 1881, lovely Nellie had moved in with the artist Archie Wortley, of aristocratic descent and circles. She would marry him in 1884, more or less retire, and give her four children a father.

Yes, four children; Nellie evidently had a good time around 1870, when she produced two daughters in double-quick time. Their fathers' names are unrecorded but are supposed to have been the Duke of Beaufort and Lord Carrington, respectively. By the time Nellie began living with Wortley, the two girls had been joined by two more children, Valentine Robert (aged two, b. 30 November 1879; d. Canada, 5 July 1950) and John (died in World War I). Again, their fathers are unknown, but the Duke of Alba is whispered as a candidate.

One of Nellie's affairs, however, wasn't a secret. In 1878, some little gossip journalist posited her marriage with a Mr. Baltazzi. The Baltazzis were big. They were the sons of a Smyrnese banker, educated at Rugby, and, I think, both married. Alexander raced horses, Hector rode horses ("en gentleman"), and there were other brothers, too. I think it is Hector who Nellie was reported to have "married." But it's just a guess. Anyway, their marriage was "fake news."

Nellie lived to a nice age, as Mrs. Wortley, and died on 27 October 1939, at Lymington, more than half a century after the role that had made her famous. She is buried at Beaulieu Abbey with the Montagu family.

Walter Fisher (Edwin, The Defendant)

Now, since you have a Plaintiff, you must have a Defendant, and here is the tale of another Victorian player unjustly neglected by fame. He was, in his time, dubbed "the English Dupuis," with reference to the famed José Dupuis, who had so memorably created the tenor roles in the most famous of the Théâtre des Variétés opéras-bouffes. It was a totally fair parallel: Walter Fisher was that rare jewel, an actor/singer who sang as well as he acted, and vice versa—and that was *very* well.

Walter Fisher was born at 9 Bath Buildings, Saint Andrew, Clifton (near Bristol), on 6 April 1848, the second son of James Fisher and his wife Mary Anne (née Powell). James Fisher was an interesting chap, a portrait painter of some repute. And Miss Powell appears, at their marriage in 1839, to have been thirteen years old. They produced an Albert James, Walter, and Amy Florence (b 1850), before Mary Anne seems to have departed—not life but the house, because James is still listed as "married" in 1891.

It has become common to speak of Walter as an actor who happened to have a nice voice. I thought that, too, until recently. But the fact is exactly the opposite: he was a concert tenor vocalist from the age of fifteen. In an advertisement for the Athenaeum Theatre in Bristol, "Mr. Walter Fisher, the eminent tenor" is listed as appearing in a "miscellaneous concert" along with "The Bristol Ethiopian Serenaders," a minstrel troupe, and several others. Another early appearance by the now sixteen-year-old Walter was at the Victoria Rooms in Clifton, where he appeared "in his imitation of SIMS REEVES, as recently performed by him . . . with such distinguished success." Reeves was, of course, the most famous British tenor of the century. On the same bill were Walter's brother, Alfred, who played harmonium solos; a "Mr. Morris," who played flute bravuras; and Miss Farler of Rosemount, Nailsea, who warbled.

Walter made several more appearances, singing at local events, particularly with the Bristol Volunteer Artillery Corps Dramatique, with whom he played ladies' parts in their all-male entertainments. When star actresses Carlotta and Fanny Addison took a Benefit at the Theatre Royal in April 1866, he played Henry Bertram in their performance of *Guy Mannering*, and the critics dubbed him "a local tenor of undoubted ability." A week later, he was heard at the Broadmead Rooms performing "Give Me but My Arab Steed" and "Then You'll Remember Me." In August 1866, the still teenaged Walter was engaged for his first professional theater job, as a "singing man" with J. D. Newcombe's fine company at the Theatre Royal in Plymouth. When Newcombe staged *Der Freischütz*, Fisher was cast as Rodolphe (Max) alongside Marian Taylor. The hometown press reproduced with pride a notice that appeared in the Plymouth papers, describing Walter as "gifted with a magnificent voice, which he can expand or control at will with consummate ease. . . . With a cultured imagination, an elegant taste, and a vigorous poetical element in his composition he ought surely to make his splendid voice heard at no distant day . . . [in] London." From Plymouth, he moved to Nye Chart's Theatre Royal, Brighton, taking time out from acting for concerts, Benefits, and even a performance of Haydn's Fifth Mass back in Bristol.

In 1869, Fisher moved on to his next engagement, one for which the repertoire work with Newcombe and Nye Chart had well prepared him. He joined Captain Disney Roebuck's United Services Dramatic Company. "Captain Roebuck" specialized in multiple productions of well-known plays, and, over the next seasons, the budding actor was to play many, many roles, of all kinds. Occasionally, too, Roebuck featured a burlesque, a pantomime, or an operetta, and Fisher was, naturally, prominently cast in such productions, even appearing as Humpty Dumpty in *Little Goody Two-Shoes*, along with the company's young singing lady, Lottie Venne. A little chap named Billy Elton also took part in this production; a quarter of a century on, wee Billy would be a leading funnyman at the Savoy Theatre.

During this time, actor David Fisher—the sometime fiddle-playing Orpheus of Planché's opéra-bouffe adaptation of *Orphée aux enfers*—tried to capitalize on Walter's increasing popularity to promote his son, a striving comedy actor and buffo singer named Walter David Fisher. In a foolish effort to publicize the boy, he took an advertisement saying, effectively, "managers take care you get the *real* thing"—pretending to warn folks not to confuse his son with (the better-established) Walter Fisher. Walter's lawyer responded tartly in the trade press. Fisher Sr. didn't give up, but to no avail. And our Walter added the middle name "Henry" to distinguish himself from Walter "David" Fisher—who died, anyhow.

Walter and Lottie Venne returned to Brighton, where they played Steerforth and Emily in a *David Copperfield* adaptation, and Kit and Little Nell in another of *The Old Curiosity Shop*, before Walter set out for Glasgow for a brief run as Jack in *The Two Roses*. The following month, he was at Frank Musgrave's Nottingham Theatre, where he and Lottie joined Francis Fairlie's burlesque company. They played in a five-scene "burlesque" of *Chilpéric* with Walter as the King and Lottie as Frédégonde; "If his light tenor voice had more compass his singing would add considerably to his acting, which is very good indeed," wrote the critic. On 20 March 1872, Walter and Lottie were married and, a week later, Walter began his first London engagement, at the Court Theatre.

The Court Theatre was to make Walter into something of a "name." He opened in the drama *Broken Spells* (Ambroise Valamour), where the critics praised him as "a good importation from the provinces." He went on to play in the October 1882 revival, in a shorn-down version, of W. S. Gilbert's *Creatures of Impulse*, taking the role of Sergeant Klooge (originated by operatic tenor William Terrott), while Lottie played the principal boy, Peter. Later that season, he was cast in yet another Gilbert piece, the burlesque *The Happy Land*, in which he played the fairy-story part of Ethais, which role involved his appearing as a burlesque Mr. Gladstone. His imitation of Gladstone, along with the parallel political impersonations of his colleagues, W. J. Hill and Edward Righton, caused a riotous storm. In spite of his other grand work at the Court, Ethais-Gladstone was the role for which Walter would be remembered.

11. *The Happy Land*: Messrs. Fisher, Hill, and Righton.

But, all in all, by the end of their time at the Court, the young couple had wholly established themselves as West End leading players.

Walter played with Henry Neville's company at the Olympic Theatre, and then, on October 3 1874, he opened at the Philharmonic Theatre, cast, now, as an opéra-bouffe leading tenor. *Giroflé-Girofla* had been a huge success as played in London in its original French version, and Charles Head, owner of the "Phil," had forked out for the sole English rights. And he had cast it pretty richly: Julia Mathews, London's original Grande-Duchesse, had the star role; Harriet Everard, the plum comic role of Aurore; the splendid contralto Jenny Pratt (sometimes "Prati") was Paquita; and the rival husbands were played by Teddy Rosenthal of touring opera renown, and Fisher, as Marasquin. The newspapers marveled that the "actor" Fisher could sing so well.

By January 1875, Fisher was in a new job: he joined old colleague, Dolly Dolaro, from the Court Theatre, in her season at the little Royalty

Theatre, to play opéra-bouffe. Walter Fisher was becoming, veritably, as *Punch* labeled him, the "British José Dupuis." At the Royalty, Fisher took on a role actually created by Dupuis, the "hero" Piquillo in *La Périchole*; Dolly, of course, was the heroine. But the success of the season was not *La Périchole*, it was Mr. Gilbert and Mr. Sullivan's one-act musical comedy *Trial by Jury*. That tried-and-true interpreter of Gilbert's works, Walter H. Fisher, tenor, was cast in the role of the Defendant, and the rest is history.

Fisher didn't remain in the cast throughout the run, however. He returned to Henry Neville's Olympic Theatre, to play in the drama *The Gascon*, with the beauty-star Clara Rousby. *The Gascon* had a long run, after which Mrs. Rousby and Walter played *The Wife* until his contract ended. He then joined an ambitious opéra-bouffe company in Manchester managed by, again, Mr. D'Oyly Carte, and featuring, again, Madame Selina Dolaro. Fisher played his Piquillo with Dolly, and Ange Pitou in *La Fille de Madame Angot* with Pattie Laverne and Bessie Sudlow. But the company suffered from a surfeit of prima donnas, Dolly walked out, things got messy, and, by October, Walter was back in London playing *David Copperfield* and *Dombey and Son* for Charles Wyndham at Crystal Palace.

Fisher went on to appear with singer Kate Santley's company, he worked again with Dolly, and he appeared opposite Florence St. John as the juvenile Hector in London's *Madame Favart*, before accompanying Camille Dubois on the road in the same role. As in the case of Dupuis, opéra-comique was not as much his strength as opéra-bouffe had been; Hector was a straight Don Ottavio–style juvenile.

Then Walter disappears from my periscope; he who has gone so visibly, for years, straight from one great job to another. It has been said that he succumbed to the allure of the demon drink, and, possibly, thus lost his wife. In the 1881 census, Walter is living at home with his father; his wife and family are in Lewisham. He made a few more appearances in the early 1880s, but nothing after 1884, until Carte hired him again in 1887. Alas, he got "ill" again and had to have a long break. Was it an illness or was it the drink? He returned again to Carte in 1888–89, playing all kinds of roles, until the time came when he was heard of no more. On 28 November 1892, Walter was admitted to the Cleveland Street Infirmary at the Strand Union workhouse, where he died on 1 January 1893.

12. Fred Sullivan: "I am a Judge, and a good judge, too."

Fred Sullivan (The Learned Judge)

The third important personage in *Trial by Jury* was, of course, the Learned Judge, which part was played by Fred—brother to Arthur—Sullivan.

Frederic Thomas Sullivan (b. London, 25 December 1837; d. London, 18 January 1877) worked, for many years, as an architect and surveyor, but he turned to the stage late in his short life for a brief but high-profile career, ending with his death, at the age of thirty-nine.

He first appeared on the stage as Bouncer (1869) and later as Cox (1871) in *Cox and Box*, and went on to play in burlesque with Henrietta Hodson at the Royalty Theatre, and as Punch in W. C. Levey's operetta

Punchinello (July 1871). He then formed Mr. Sullivan's Operetta Company, which appeared in several provincial venues, giving performances of *Cox and Box*, *The Rose of Auvergne*, and *Breaking the Spell* (August 1871). He repeated *Cox and Box* at the Alhambra Theatre in October 1871, and then took a supporting role in brother Arthur's next work, at the much more demanding Gaiety Theatre, as Apollo in *Thespis* (1871). He enjoyed sufficient success in that part to be cast with the theater's stars, Nellie Farren and Connie Loseby, as Midas in the four-handed *Ganymede and Galatea* (*Die schöne Galathée*).

Fred played *Cox and Box* and *A Mere Blind* (*Les Deux aveugles*) at the Gaiety, was seen in repertoire with the Gaiety touring company, returned for the operetta *Fleurette* at the Gaiety (1873, Marquis Beaurivage), and repeated both *Cox and Box* and *Die schöne Galathée* at the Crystal Palace (1874). Then, he once again tried his hand at management, presenting *Cox and Box* and *The Contrabandista* for fortnights at the Prince's, Manchester (11 May) and Birmingham (25 May), with Alfred Cellier as conductor, and himself playing Grigg and Cox. When things went poorly, he added Fred Evans's comic ballet *Fra Diavolo* and Offenbach's *Lischen and Fritzchen*. The agent for the season was Mr. D'Oyly Carte.

Fred returned to performing in *Ixion* at the Opera Comique (1874) and as the Duke of Rodomont in *Melusine the Enchantress* (1874) at Holborn, and then landed the principal comic role of the Viceroy in London's first production of *La Périchole* (1875). That led, of course, to the part of the Judge in *Trial by Jury* (1875). Fred would play the Learned Judge at the Royalty, on the road, and at the Opera Comique (1876) with no less than three different main pieces. During this run, he was taken ill, and such was his importance to the piece that *Trial by Jury* was suspended until his return. He subsequently toured as the Judge, Pomponnet (*La Fille de Madame Angot*), and Cocorico (*Geneviève de Brabant*) with Emily Soldene.

It was announced that he would further his producing activities by staging the first full-length work to be written by his brother and W. S. Gilbert the following season at the Globe Theatre. However, fate willed otherwise, as Fred took sick and shortly thereafter died. *The Sorcerer* was ultimately produced by Richard D'Oyly Carte at the Opera Comique, some months after Fred's untimely death. Fred Sullivan is perhaps best remembered today through the song "The Lost Chord," which Sullivan composed "in mourning for my brother."

The Bridesmaids

The bridesmaids—the Royalty's "big nine": in other words, the front line of the Dolly chorus—were originally portrayed by Linda Verner, Amy Clifford, Julia Beverley, Cissie Durrant, Annie Palmer, and Misses Lassalle, Villiers, Graham[e], and Lee "and others." Julia Barber and Laura Carthew were not originals, but, when the piece became a hit, soon became appreciated additions.

Cissie Durrant turned out to be more than your average chorine—and she ended up a wealthy wife and mother. Cissie was born in London, as Caroline Cicely McDavitt, in early 1852, one of the seven children

13. Cissie Durrant: The bridesmaid who got the bouquet.

of a Glaswegian engraver, James McDavitt, and his wife Rosa Caroline (née Nash). Her father pops up occasionally in the musical world: I see him in 1856 in concert at the London Mechanics' Institute, conducting and singing at Evans's Supper Rooms (the press described him as having a "fine tenor voice") and as conductor at the Islington Philharmonic.

In 1873, Cissie joined the chorus of Emily Soldene's famous company, playing in *Geneviève de Brabant*, *La Fille de Madame Angot*, and later *La Grande-Duchesse*. She played Bacchus in Amy Sheridan's "unclothed" *Ixion Re-Wheeled* at the Opera Comique, and then rejoined Soldene for more opéra-bouffe. But, instead of going with Soldene on her American tour, Cissie joined Dolly Dolaro at the Royalty and, thus, became a bridesmaid in *Trial by Jury*. She went on to tour with Dolaro—now promoted to First Bridesmaid and a Cousin in *Périchole*—but then turned back to Soldene, playing good supporting roles, for Soldene's famous 1876–77 tour to America and Australia. She left midtour: cause, marriage.

Cissie wed wealthy Sydney landowner Harry McQuade. They had three children, and lived happily and comfortably until Harry's death in 1898, at which point Cissie inherited the lot. "The lot" included the ground ownership of Sydney's Her Majesty's Theatre, which she teamed with J. C. Williamson to rebuild after its destruction by fire in 1902. Cissie died on 14 August 1938, at the age of eighty-six, of cancer, in Chelsea, London. Her daughter, Amelia Rose, was the wife of the 'cellist Jean Géraldy.

The featured chorine among the original *Trial* girls was Linda Verner, who played the First Bridesmaid and, later, took over as the Plaintiff. She would have a proper theatrical career, of nearly twenty years, as a supporting singing actress. Of course, Linda Verner was not her real name.

Hannah Sarah Palmer was born in 1855 (baptized on 2 September), in Lambeth, the daughter of Thomas William Palmer and his wife Hannah (née Newton). I imagine that it is she, appearing as "Miss Verner," who played in Dublin, in 1874, with the Julia Mathews/Catherine Lewis *La Fille de Madame Angot* company, but it may not be. There were a number of "Miss Verners" around—in jobs ranging from music hall to the drama—so I can't be wholly sure that all these early sightings are our Linda.

Anyway, our Linda succeeded Nellie Bromley in *Trial by Jury*, played the Plaintiff at the Royalty and on the road, and then took part in Carte's production of the bowdlerized *The Duke's Daughter*. She joined

14. Linda Verner: The cheerleader of the bridesmaids.

Emily Soldene to appear in *Geneviève de Brabant*, played Princess Sabra in the pantomime at the Alexandra Palace, and Princess Badroulbadour at Liverpool. If she took some time off, it was understandable: because "Linda" had become the wife of George Potier, a "wheel-band manufacturer." Between 1876 and 1885, she would bear him five daughters and a son.

When Dolly brought her *Périchole* back to town in 1879, Linda was there, and when Dolly produced *Another Drink* to follow, Linda was still there. Next up, she (and fellow ex-bridesmaids Misses Barber, Clifford, and Carthew) traveled to Dublin with burlesque's brilliant Lydia Thompson, after which she played more pantomime, and then returned to London's Opera Comique Theatre, featured in Lila Clay's all-woman troupe (*An Adamless Eden*). In 1884, she took a tour with Carte's *Princess Ida* company, playing Lady Psyche. In 1886, she appeared in *Herne the Hunted* and as Arabella in *Billee Taylor* at Toole's Theatre, before taking on the leading role of Madeleine in *Le Postillon de Lonjumeau* at the Empire. She supported Florence St. John in *La Béarnaise* and, now a little less young, found herself a job at the Gaiety Theatre, playing Madame Gondelaurier in the second edition of the burlesque *Miss Esmeralda*. She would become a fixture in the Gaiety's new burlesque productions, going on to play not only in London but also in the provinces, America, and South Africa with George Edwardes's companies. She died of the weather in Johannesburg, while on tour, on 24 August 1892. Fred Leslie's biographer relates that Leslie raised one hundred pounds to aid her five children and her "long incapacitated" husband. Incapacitated? Not entirely. He promptly remarried and had four more children before his death in 1908.

Death intervened rather earlier in the case of Julia Cecilia Beverley (b. Leeds, 26 February 1854; d. The Barracks, Clonmel, Tipperary, 20 December 1885). Julia was one of the brood of illegitimate children of commercial traveler George Beverley and Liverpool grocer's daughter Ellen Emma Bankes, of whom three—Louise (the most successful), Julia, and Blanche—appeared on the London musical stage. Julia started as a teenager, at the Alhambra, in *Le Roi Carotte*. She later toured with Joseph Eldred's comedy and burlesque company, and played, after her bridesmaid stint, at the Olympic. On 28 March 1883, she married Assistant Commissary-General Major Alfred Ely of the Commissariat and Transport Staff and died two years later in what appears to have been childbirth.

Julia seems to have been the only one of the original bridesmaids to have worked under her veritable name. "Miss Lassalle" and "Miss Villiers" are as instantly recognizable as stage names as would be Miss Cholmondely or Miss Paunceforth-Brown. Finding out who such ladies were and what became of them is almost impossible. Miss Grahame? Perhaps the Clara Graham[e] who was, for fifteen years, a very pretty feature of so many London shows?

So, that leaves "Miss Amy Clifford" and "Miss Annie Palmer," who had, at least, the kindness to have a first name; some of the time. Both, also, were definitely not—as Misses Villiers and Lassalle were—ephemeral.

Was Amy Clifford her real name or not? She worked under that name for something like a decade. Again, there were numerous "Miss Cliffords," but the first time I see "Amy Clifford" mentioned as such is as a member of the Thespian Literary Club's amateur company in 1872. In 1873, Amy turns up in the cast of *Black Crook* at the Alhambra, getting a pretty mention in the little role of Florican. And there she is singing seriocomic numbers at Crowder's Music Hall (dubbed by the critic "a young lady with a clear, placid countenance and a gentle, graceful carriage . . . sang, and danced beautifully"). Then, she returned to the amateur companies, playing, good heavens, Pauline in *The Lady of Lyons*! She appeared, next, at the Charing Cross Theatre in

W. H. C. Nation's company (*The Last of the Legends*), before being hired for the Royalty Theatre.

She was one of a number of the cast members of *Trial by Jury* who followed Dolly and Carte into their production of *The Duke's Daughter*, after which she joined Kate Santley in her touring company, playing Cupid in *Orphée*. In 1878, she shows up (with Julia Beverley) in *The Two Orphans* at the Olympic, and in 1879 both in *Alcantara* at the Connaught and in pantomime at Exeter, where she remained for a season. And in 1880 she was back at the Royalty, appearing in Kate Lawler's *Don Juan Jr*. And then . . . is she the Amy (seriocomic) playing the halls in 1890? And/or the "Amy Clifford" (real name: Amy Jenkins) touring in *The Shop Girl* in 1897?

Was Annie Palmer her real name or not? It seems strange that, while Miss Hannah Palmer changed her name to Linda Verner, another member of the same cast decided to be Annie Palmer. Odd, too, that "Linda" actually had an elder sister, Annie. (Linda's sister Annie was born in Rotherhithe on 22 March 1846.) Odd too, that a "Miss Verner" appears briefly in *Périchole* before vanishing to be replaced by a "Miss Palmer." But I'm just guessing. This Annie went on to play with the Soldene troupe et alia, all as part of a solid front-row-of-chorus career through the 1870s.

Two of the most memorable "bridesmaids" however, were two of the not-quite-originals: Julia Barber and Laura Carthew. Like Cissie Durrant, Julia was to be part of that comic opera company that became celebrated as the greatest in antipodean musical theater history: the Soldene troupe. Julia Grace Smith or Barber was born in Lambeth on 24 July 1855, daughter of Samuel Taylor Thompson Barber and Emma Isabella (otherwise Smith), and went to work as a dancer. She joined the Soldene outfit and can be seen, as "Miss Julian Grace," at the Opera Comique, playing one of the four Maids of Honor in *La Grande-Duchesse* (Misses Durrant and Carthew were two others) at the Lyceum. She visited America with the Soldene company, toured Britain, and made the famed voyage to Australia, where she was often featured in the Soldene shows as solo dancer. This fidelity to the corps was the result of her relationship (which lasted ten years and produced four children) with Johnnie Wallace (né John Henry Clark), the stage director of the troupe and Miss Soldene's "left hand." The "Wallaces" returned to

15. Julia Barber: A Chorine in High Demand.

Australia after the main trip, but in 1884 they split, and Julia married a much younger man by the name of Edwin William Stidolph, of the acrobatic Faust family, and quit the antipodes for America. She died there on 14 October 1914, under her married name of Mrs. Ted Faust, and was eulogized as an actress who was "loved by the profession the world over."

Laura Carthew was one of those chorines everybody wanted to hire. She worked solidly through the 1870s, in the best companies with the biggest stars, often in tiny featured parts, but never as anything more demanding. Yet, it was she whom Soldene chose to replace the beauty queen of her company, Clara Vesey, in her pants role, when the latter was too ill to appear on its New York opening night. So she clearly had some ability and attraction. When she came to the Royalty, Laura had been four years at the head of the Soldene chorus: at the Philharmonic, on the road, at the Opera Comique, at the Lyceum, and on tour in America, often in little "step-out" roles. And when she had finished her interlude playing a bridesmaid in *Trial by Jury*, Laura went right back to the management of Soldene and Charles Morton, for more of the same. Next, she joined up with the other most visible company of the day: Lydia Thompson's "Blondes," playing with Lydia (plus Misses Verner, Beverley, and Clifford) in her *Carmen* burlesque. She also appeared at the Strand in *Champagne*, and at the Folly Theatre, in a wee step-out (with billing), in the record-breaking *Les Cloches de Corneville*. But after that I'm not quite sure. A "Miss Carthew" turns up on odd occasions—but she'd been billed as "Laura Carthew" for years. So, alas, I lose her.

The Gentlemen of the Jury

The gentlemen involved in *Trial by Jury* were a mixture of the to-be-famous, of eternal choristers and bit-part players, and of veritable amateurs—with, it seems, a dash of nepotism thrown in. There was even one remarkable character who started out in the Jury, moved up to be Foreman, then to the part of the baritonic Counsel for the Plaintiff . . . and ended up playing the star tenor role all around the world!

C. J. Campbell (né Charles James Cleaver, b. Newington, 13 March 1849; d. 181st Street, New York, 27 February 1918) was the son of a carpenter from Saint Helier. His career took off in 1873, when he joined the company at the Liverpool Prince of Wales Theatre, where he appeared with Dolly Dolaro in *La Fille de Madame Angot*. After touring in that piece, he joined Dolly, in a small part, in *The Black Prince*, and then followed her to the Royalty for *La Périchole* and *Trial by Jury*. Charley then turned his loyalty to Emily Soldene, and it was with Soldene that he was to make his name, fame, and begin a grand career. On November 18, 1876, Emily began her "world tour." Her lead tenor was the boyish Knight Aston (né Thomas White); Charley played "other baritone parts." But Aston got into troubles (he had married a convicted confidence trickster) and left the company. Emily, stranded

16. Charley Campbell in early *Trial by Jury* days.

without a leading man, simply promoted her handsome light baritone. Charley was a total success. Post-Soldene, he remained in America, where he played for many seasons with the best comic-opera companies. He worked once more with Carte when he headed the management's Continental Company to Europe. In later life, he penned a number of musical comedy libretti with some success.

Charley was not, however, to be the biggest star to come off the Royalty Theatre jury bench. William Sydney Penley (b. Margate, 18 November 1851; d. London, 11 November 1912), an ex–Chapel Royal chorister, after an apprenticeship in the musical theater, went on to enduring fame as the star of *The Private Secretary* and, above all, as the original Fancourt Babberley in *Charley's Aunt*.

So that leaves Mr. Hollingsworth (Counsel), B. R. Pepper (Usher), Charles Kelleher (Foreman), J. B. Husk (Foreman), and Messrs. T. Healey and Cairns (Associate), plus choristers Messrs. T. Cheen[e]y, Bradshaw, West, Grundy, Fraser, Marshall, Walsh, Nolan, Plating, Blackworth, and G. Paris. And I will tell you right away that, although the first four present no problems, few of the others mean anything to me.

Let's start with Hollingsworth. He was not a Hollingsworth. He was born in Wokingham in June 1841, son of a shoemaker, and christened plain Charles Hewett; Hollingsworth was his father's middle name. This was almost the only time that Charles worked in a named part in the musical theater. He began in life as a miller in Marcham, Berkshire, where, on 28 October 1861, he married Miss Sarah Reading. The registration certificate for that marriage holds a curious item. Most of the witnesses are members of the spreading Chesham families of Reading or Hewett—but one is the teenaged Richard D'Oyly Carte. There is a suggestion that the two men were cousins. However, feedback to my blog posts on this subject revealed that there is illegitimacy in the Carte and Hewett families, and that we have to go back to one grandmotherly Sarah Bartlett (later Shepherd) to find the link between them. Anyhow, he was obviously Carte's "relation" in some degree.

Charles, as a young man, sang and played the flute in the semi-professional Reading "Penny Readings," and he underlined his affection for music and the stage by naming his first child Adelina Patti Hewett. And then suddenly he turns up at the Royalty Theatre, playing professionally—and perfectly soundly, it seems—in a "dramatic cantata." How? Undoubtedly through his Carte connection, especially given that Carte later employed two of Charles's sister's children.

Anyway, by the 1881 census Charles was back in Berks, working as a "bleacher and dyer employing nine men." But he must have caught the theaterlust because, by 1891, while his wife and children were plaiting straw in Luton, he was in Amwell, insisting he was a "vocalist." He began calling himself "Hollingsworth" instead of Hewett, went into the millinery manufacturing trade, married a second wife, Fanny Meller, after Sarah's death, and continued making hats at Islington's Gibson Square up until his death on 2 August 1911.

In contrast, Belville Robert Pepper (b. Marylebone, October 1850; d. Manchester, September 1888) was a thorough professional. He was born into a family of wood-carvers, the son of Montague Pepper and his wife Sarah (née Carden), and orphaned in his teens. He seems to have made his first theatrical appearances at Great Yarmouth, in a two-month summer season of potboilers stage mounted by one George Ashton. In 1872, he advertised "the 44th week of Messrs B. Booth and R. B. Pepper's London Comedy and Burlesque Company." Oddly, I can't spot mention of any of the other forty-three weeks. Mr. Pepper then changed tack, and changed his name, as well. As "Mr. Robert Belville" he joined up with the Soldene company. Originally a chorister, he rose to playing the Burgomaster in *Geneviève de Brabant* and Cadet in *La Fille de Madame Angot*, after which, he decided to become Pepper again. He played at the Royalty, then on tour with Kate Santley, and rejoined Soldene in the little part of Bonaventura in *Madame l'Archiduc*. After that I lose him for a bit, until "Mr. R. Bell Pepper" turns up as Sandy Sixanate in the Glasgow *Puss in Boots* in 1878–79. In 1879, he was seen in Glasgow in concert, in *Paul Pry*, and in *Trial by Jury* with J. A. Shaw and Lucy Franklein—until the theater burned down. The next Christmas, Pepper was King Rat in *Dick Whittington* with Alice May and the Lupinos; played the Usher in yet another *Trial by Jury*, this time with George Mudie and Alice Burville; and took part in a tour of Cellier's *The Sultan of Mocha*. That company also included "Miss Pepper": Robert's dancer wife, née Elizabeth Mary Wilkinson. He toured with Wyndham and D'Oyly Carte's *Olivette* company, with a little piece called *Innocents Abroad*, then joined up with a *Fille de Madame Angot/Geneviève de Brabant* company led by Duglas Gordon. He was now thirty-one years old. What happened? I see him again only at Christmas 1883, in pantomime in Todmorden—and five years later, he was dead.

Charles Joseph Kelleher (b. St. James's, London, 1851; d. 76 Regent Street, September 1878) survived *Trial by Jury* only a short time. Three of the sons of Irish tailor Francis Kellard—or Keller or Kelleher (b. Macroom, Cork, 1815) and his wife Jane (1816–1899)—became vocalists. While the eldest, tenor Alfred, disappeared off to a good life in music in America, both Charles and Louis made promising careers in the British musical theater before early deaths.

By the 1871 census, Charles was already claiming the surname Kelleher, rather than Kellard, and describing himself as a singer. My first sighting of him on the stage is in 1874, as a minor member of Fred Sullivan's operetta company touring in the midlands. He followed up in the good role of Fernando in Kate Santley's *Cattarina* company, then rejoined Sullivan at the Royalty in *La Périchole* (Pedro) and *Trial by Jury*. He played Nicolo when Miss Santley brought *Cattarina* to town, toured again with her, and ended up, first, at the Criterion Theatre with Walter Fisher and, then, at the Royalty, for Carte in *The Duke's Daughter*. Between 1874 and 1877 he was seen widely in the most popular pieces of the time, playing classic roles from General Boum to Larivaudière to John Styx in *Orphée aux enfers*. He appeared at the Aquarium, giving once more his Usher in *Trial by Jury*, but my next sighting of his name is in a letter written by D'Oyly Carte to the *Era* newspaper. Kelleher had "for some time" gone insane and, around the end of September 1878, he died, at the age of twenty-seven.

Opéra-bouffe was, it seemed, bad for the brain. Already, the original Royalty company had lost the flamboyant twenty-five-year-old Charles Wilton Norton (d. 60 Osney Crescent, Kentish Town, 17 February 1875) to insanity and delirium tremens. But some of the chorus were a little more stable and durable. And the most stable of all was Mr. Husk.

James [Baker] Husk (b. Somerset, 7 March 1811; d. London, 18 May 1879) was a basso profundo vocalist who plied his trade from the Isle of Wight to Edinburgh, and from the concert platform to the music halls to the theater. And he did it (when not teaching music, bricklaying like his father, and/or producing eight children) for more than three decades. When he joined the Royalty company in *Trial by Jury*, he was sixty-four.

While he was still officially a bricklayer, in the 1840s and 1850s, Husk sang in minor, suburban, and provincial concerts. On 3 April 1855 he sang second bass to Tom Lawler in the London Sacred Harmonic Society's *Elijah*. The soprano, on that occasion, was the great Charlott Anne Birch and, when the oratorio was repeated the next year, she was replaced by the "Queen of Northern Song," Susan Sunderland. However, that was not Mr. Husk's usual type of engagement. Much of the time, he was a bass chorister and sometimes soloist in London's music halls. At some of them—including the loftiest of them all, the Oxford and the Holborn (1869)—he even acted as the chairman of the entertainment. It seems to have been only later in life that Husk took to the stage. His wife, Mary Ann Charlotte (née Taplay), and one of his five sons, William, were in the chorus of *Little Faust* in 1870, but often the chorus members were not listed, so this probably wasn't the first or only time that they appeared on the stage. Husk joined Augusta Thomson's *Chilpéric* tour, doubtless playing the Druid, and, after *Trial by Jury*, moved to the Alhambra, where he was included in the cast for *Lord Bateman* and for Soldene's *La Fille de Madame Angot*. He seems to have been "in the saddle" right up to his death at the age of sixty-eight.

Of the other jurors there is little to say. Mr. T. Healey's Royalty job seems to have been his only engagement of interest in a "career" of small parts in stock companies from Newcastle to Southampton, but mostly in the smaller venues of Liverpool. I see an occasion in 1878 when, cast to play a bit in *Hamlet* with Charles Dillon, he didn't appear and wasn't to be found. It seems that Grundy is "Australian" Tom Grundy, unless it's his father, who was also called Tom Grundy when he wasn't billed as "Mr. Badzey." "West," I think, must be Joseph Sebastian West (1852–1898), because "Miss [Annie] St. George" (née Annie Elizabeth Augusta Mansfield) joined the *Trial by Jury* cast, too; she was West's wife. Later, they toured for years with Soldene.

The only Mr. Parris to be found in the records is a printer. Another stage name? No, it is he. George [John] Parris (1830–1910), the son of shoemaker John Parris and his wife Elizabeth, ran a stationery and printing firm with his younger sister Emma (1842–1919), from number 57 Greek Street, Soho, for at least forty years. We know this is he, because his death notice stated that he was a "long-time Savoy chorister." So, I presume that Mr. Parris was stage-named Mr. Paris, and that he appeared also in *The Sultan of Mocha*, and at the Philharmonic, with Emily Soldene; in my *Emily Soldene* book I have him noted as chorusing as early as 1870, when he was already forty. Before that? I see several advertisements in the press for publications from his house, as well as in the "Situations Vacant" notices, an "employment agency" sideline of many bookshops. George and Emma even find their way into a 1903 book, *Men and Women of Soho*. He was obviously a man with three hands.

If I've gone rather extravagantly into the cast of *Trial by Jury*, it's because I consider it the real beginning, the hen's nest, of Gilbert and Sullivan's comic opera opus, and I don't feel that any player who participated in that momentous production should be utterly forgotten. So, this is my best shot. No one else has bothered with the "workers" behind the stars, and probably no one ever will again. So, the bridesmaids and jury . . . this is your moment.

Trial by Jury's Legacy

Trial by Jury was, of course, a huge success. It ran right through Dolly's Royalty season, and was taken by her on her provincial tour—where it proved the best-loved item on her programs—for four months. It then returned to the Royalty, where—when *La Périchole* was replaced by the Dollyfied *La Fille de Madame Angot* (a perversion that slanted that perfectly proportioned double-headed star vehicle ludicrously toward its Dollystar and omitted almost all of one act), *Trial by Jury* remained, truthfully, the main attraction. It was pirated in America by Alice Oates and by an English team at New York's Eagle Theatre. More notably, it was taken up by Madame Soldene to play at the Opera Comique, where, like Dolly, she delegated the role of the Plaintiff to another, in this case her little sister, the stunning but only slightly soprano Clara Vesey. Fred Sullivan was again the Judge, Charley Campbell was now the Defendant, Amy Clifford rose to first bridesmaid, and Mr. Healey to the Associate. Then, in 1877, it was featured for the first time as a gala piece, with a huge all-star cast, on the occasion of the Compton Benefit at Drury Lane. The grand George Honey was the Judge; "Pauline Rita" (Mrs. Maggie Phillips), late of the Italian Opera, was the Plaintiff; W. H. Cummings, the future head of the Guildhall School of Music, was the Defendant; and the top milk of London's musical players (including Walter Fisher!) played Jury, Bridesmaids, and the Crowd in Court. These Benefit galas became the fashion, and the performances staged for Nellie Farren (1898) and Ellen Terry (1906) included crowds of theatrical royalty in their lineup. At both these last two matinées, Gilbert himself took to the stage as the Associate.

Trial by Jury has an unchallenged place in the history of the musical theater, and even if it has finally slipped somewhat from the produced repertoire in the twenty-first-century days of sound systems, click tracks, and chesty howling, it remains—speaking "from bias free of every kind"—a little gem in the idol's forehead of English-language comic opera. And, of course, historically, the first real stone in what was to become the edifice known, perhaps a little inaccurately, as "the Savoy opera." But I like the term, and we all know what it means, so let's stick with it, even if it is a wee bit semantically inaccurate.

3

The Sorcerer

Comic opera in two acts
Opera Comique Theatre, 17 November 1877

Following upon the great success of *Trial by Jury*, it was natural that Gilbert and Sullivan should collaborate further, and it was equally natural that Carte should want to be, again, at the helm when they did. Rumors, of course, flew, as to their plans, and the papers printed some of those showbiz squibs of the kind, still current, which bear more relation to guesswork and fancy than truth. Among the rumors were the assertion that Fred Sullivan was to take a London theater and produce the duo's next work; and that that new work would be a musicalized version of the famous farce *Le Chapeau de paille d'Italie*, of which Gilbert had already created an English-language version for the Court Theatre. It wasn't, of course, either of these.

The same method was followed for the new piece as for the last: a humorous magazine piece of Gilbert's was elaborated into a two-act comic opera, peopled not with gods and fairies but with recognizable, contemporary characters and, well, just the odd creepy immortal to engineer the tale's fateful twist. For, yes, the humor of this piece, just like that of Gilbert's metempsychosis musical play *The Gentleman in Black*, just like that of his subsequent *Creatures of Impulse* (both scores, alas, gone the way of that of *Thespis*), just like the classic *Devil to Pay*, rested on the piece's peripeteia, magical, of course, the alteration of someone—or in this case, nearly all, the characters—by magical means, into something they are not. One can't help thinking of Donizetti's *L'Elisir d'amore*, earlier burlesqued by Gilbert as *Dulcamara*, or of Scribe's *Le Philtre*, when one reads the plot of *The Sorcerer*, but the differences are greater than the similarities. In the older pieces there is no supernatural element and l'elisir in question is nothing but a flask of good old vino rosso.

On the day of his village wedding to the sopranic Aline, tenorious Alexis hires a London magician, Mr. J. W. Wells, of "Seventy, Simmery Axe," to come to spread joy, equivalent to that experienced by the bridal couple, among the villagers. This involves an "elisir d'amore," which is slightly more satanic than vin rouge. In what was already becoming recognized as "Gilbertian" style, the magic potion dropped into the bridal-festal teapot leads the bewitched characters into all sorts of follies before the spell is lifted, by sacrificing the Sorcerer to whatever demon lives under the stage. It wasn't a perfect book: the later Gilbert would have found a cleverer twist for his finale—this one was a bit too *Don Giovanni*—but it gave plenty of rein to the author for ludicrous situations and he colored them up delightfully.

The Sorcerer, with its homely setting and (give or take a magician) characters, owed nothing to the current rage for French opéra-bouffe, with its hysterically humorous historical-burlesque style. Nor even to the burlesque/extravaganza/pantomime genre that Gilbert had practiced successfully since his beginnings. It was a pure descendant of the English musical comedy as purveyed, most recently and relevantly, at the Gallery of Illustration and St. George's Hall, by German and Priscilla Reed. The work of both Gilbert (*No Cards, Ages Ago, Our Island Home, A Sensation Novel, Happy Arcadia,* and *Eyes and No Eyes*) and Sullivan (*Cox and Box*) had been featured at the Reeds' establishments over the last decade, and the proper, polite image of their product encouraged many of the surprisingly large number of folk who still considered the theater a plant pot of all the vices through their doors. At the Reeds' place, wit, cleverness, charming music, and excellent acting could be enjoyed without the risk of a glimpse of ankle or thigh, or a whisper of baby-blue dialogue.

Well in advance, Carte had looked after the practical side of getting *The Sorcerer* to the stage. In 1876, he had formed a "Comedy Opera Company" with the avowed aim of producing full-scale theatre works in the Reedian vein (he'd written a few little ones himself!) by English authors and musicians. Mostly, those of his social circle. But, particularly, the new work of Messrs Gilbert and Sullivan. He went into print with his credo on 4 November 1876; it could have come straight from the pen of German Reed. In Carte's productions, there would be no "meretricious displays of costume—or, rather, absence of costume," no "objectionable suggestiveness of motive or dialogue."

The directors of Carte's company, who I imagine were also the principal moneymen, included Metzler and Chappell, music publishers; Collard, piano manufacturer; and Mr. E. H. Bayley, cleaning contractor. Among the others who took additional smaller shares in the company was a musician named George Benjamin Allen who apparently borrowed the cash to buy his way in, and never repaid it. Allen had recently returned from a long period in Australia where his de facto wife, known as "Alice May," had made a splendid career as an opéra-bouffe star. It was, therefore, hardly a surprise when Miss May was cast as *The Sorcerer*'s lead soprano and Mr. Allen appointed conductor.

Carte had promised that the "actors and actresses" in the production would "all [be] English," and, technically, he kept his word. But there had also been agreement between Gilbert and Sullivan (who had reserved for themselves the casting rights) that they would not engage any established opéra-bouffe stars with "established mannerisms." Well, Miss May was a special case. She, like Britain's first star in the genre, Julia Mathews, had done her bouffe-ing in Australia, where they ain't got no time for mannerisms. As a result, their casting was slightly "out of left court": of the other eight principals, three came from the realm of opera, four from the world of the parlor "Entertainment," and only one from the regular London and provincial theaters. I wish there were room here to give you extended biographies of them all, but George Grossmith—the Entertainer at the Piano who was plucked from a society amateur performance of *Trial by Jury* to fill the role that had probably been intended for the deceased Fred Sullivan—wrote books of his own and has been biographized mightily; Rutland Barrington, too, who at this stage was also a supporting player in an Entertainment, after two autobiographies, left us nothing new (except corrections and verifications) to be said; and the story of Alice May and "Grievous Bodily Allen" would fill a book, and it has: the late Adrienne Simpson's *Alice May* (Routledge) is quite simply one of the best and most factual Cartesian biographies ever written.

There was, however, in the cast, one veritable and established star. Mrs. Isabelle Jane Paul (née Hill, sometime "Miss Featherstone"; b. Newton Street, Holborn, 1 April 1833; d. Bedford Park, 6 June 1879) had had a splendid career, in the greatest theaters of England, and on the country's foremost concert and operatic platforms, before being manipulated by her husband into the lucrative field of the Entertainment. Isabelle, as versatile as she was talented, vanquished all obstacles (the greatest of which was that husband) to become a star on both sides of

17. Isabelle Paul: Musical-theater blue blood.

the Atlantic, appearing not only as a protean solo entertainer but also in pieces such as *La Grande-Duchesse* and *Geneviève de Brabant*: here, at the age of forty-four, she was to play a *komische Alte*—an ageing character lady. Mrs. Paul has not had a book devoted to her, but she has a pretty exhaustive thirty-seven-page biography in my *Victorian Vocalists*. A couple of those pages are spent on the antics of the husband and the merriment created when a newspaper, erroneously, thought him dead and published a stinging obituary!

So, of our cast, that leaves the three opera singers—Richard Temple, Giulia Warwick, and George Bentham—our one remaining entertainer, Fred Clifton, and our one confirmed, but not celebrated, actress, Harriet Everard.

Fred Clifton (Notary)

Yes, the whole world of Gilbert and Sullivan scholarship knows of Fred Clifton: he's the comic actor-singer who almost was; the man who after having played supporting roles in *The Sorcerer* and *HMS Pinafore* (Bobstay), initiated the role of the Sergeant of Police in *The Pirates of Penzance* in America. But Rutland Barrington begged, successfully, so he tells us, for the part in London, and Fred's chance for fame was pretty well lost. He remained a supporting actor and small-part player, a striving writer and composer, for the rest of his life. Well, Mr. Barrington isn't the very most reliable of autobiographists, and I think there was a little more behind Fred's American exile than that—as we shall see.

So, to start with, who actually was Fred? We have for a long time been told that he was born in Birmingham, on 29 May 1844. And guess what, half of that, I now discover, is right. And, amazingly, it is the date that is right! "Fred" was actually born in Dudley, and it was his father's name that was Fred; he was Tom. There they all are, in Castle Street,

18. Fred Clifton as the Notary.

Dudley, in the 1851 census: father Fred, the hairdresser, from Peterborough; mama Eliza; and four children, of whom Tom is the oldest. Oh, and their name is not, of course, "Clifton"; Fred was born Thomas Hu[n]sler Green. How did I discover that? Well . . .

Let's dip into his early career. Someone said that Fred started at Reading in 1861. Perfectly possible, but the first reference I've found to "Fred Clifton comique" (as opposed to the starry Harry Clifton, or Edward Clifton), in tiny provincial concerts, comes a year or two later. But, very soon, the billing was expanded to "Mr. and Mrs. Fred Clifton." Really? I have to admit I never really believed it. Marriages were not always of a registrarial fact in the Victorian theater. But this one was a fact! And the lady? She was Mdlle. Therese Brunelli, from Italy, pupil of San Giovanni (or sometimes Don Giovanni), prima donna soprano of La Scala, Milan. But, wait a minute: in 1859, already, "Miss Brunette" and Mr. Clifton are touring with Fred Younge's Vaudeville and Petite Opera company!

Anyway, the *soi-disante* Mdlle. Brunelli may have never seen La Scala, but she wasn't rubbish. During her career, she sang major roles in London. And she was no Italian. Of course, she didn't know that census records would, one day, be on the Internet, so, in 1871, when Tom was pretending to be "Fred Clifton," she blithely put herself down as Mrs. Ellen M. Clifton, born in Teignmouth, Devon. Well, she was actually born Ellen Matilda Hird, in Shaldon, across the water from Teignmouth, in 1843, and she married Tom Green on 13 November 1862 at Liverpool. And it was from that marriage record that I found out that "Fred Clifton" was really Tom Green.

The couple performed together in music halls and the like for several years, as "Mr. & Mrs. Fred Clifton, burlesque operatic, high and low comic, duettists and solo comic and sentimental singers," often performing around the Hull, or Sculcoates, area where Ellen's folk (her father was a customs tide-watcher) lived. They appeared in dioramas, operettas, and music-hall sketches—I have a long list of minor dates—until Mr. D'Oyly Carte (agent) "discovered," in particular, Therese. And, next thing, she was up on stage, at London's vast Alhambra, starring in the title-role of *Black Crook* (1872), and appearing in *Lord Bateman*, *Le Voyage dans la lune*, and *La Fille de Madame Angot*.

At the same time, Fred was fulfilling little stand-up engagements, playing in the odd operetta, and traipsing round with the Eldred opéra-bouffe company, and as a support to Jolly John Nash, doing his "musical, mimetic, Protean" act. And then, somehow (maybe through Therese?), he, like Messrs. Grossmith and Barrington, moved out of the Entertainment business and into Mr. Carte's company. Also, like so many middle-aged men, he dropped his more-successful wife and waltzed off with a younger lady who appears to have been a chorine named Mary or Marie Glover.

On Fred's return to England, after the American *The Pirates of Penzance*, he was seen in a wee part, as the Registrar General, in a botched version of Léon Vasseur's *La Famille Trouillat* (*La Belle Normande*), for Charles Wyndham. Therese was, around the same time, starring on tour in *Pygmalion and Galatea, Joan of Arc*, and *Jane Shore* for the saner of the Maitland brothers.

The new "Mrs. Clifton" promptly had a daughter (while Therese, righteously, still billed herself as "Mrs. Clifton"), and then Fred and Marie, as bigamists, real or effective, had a habit of doing in those days, fled back across the Atlantic. There, Fred would find a moderate career, stretching over twenty years, and an obviously fulfilling family life that produced six more (illegitimate) children, before his death in Boston on 7 September 1903. Therese put an end to her singing career in the early 1880s, and can be seen in the 1891 and 1901 census working as an attendant at the Lunatic Asylum at Banstead in Surrey. So there you are: the details and facts that the various articles that concentrate on Fred's professional career don't tell you.

I wonder, most unhistorianally, what would have become of Fred if he had played "A Policeman's Lot Is Not an 'Appy One" in London instead of Barrington. And, indeed, what might have been the story of Alice May had Carte not transferred her to another of his projects, the production of an English version of the glorious French *Le Petit Duc* at Islington. For, yes, the Comedy Opera Company at the shabby old Opera Comique was not yet a sufficiently stable thing (as, indeed, would be proven), and Mr. Carte needed to keep his finger in other pies. *Le Petit Duc*, amazingly, failed—twice.

But, back to *The Sorcerer* and its players. The piece was an indubitable success. The Vicar's Song ("Time Was When Love and I Were Well Acquainted") became the takeaway tune from the show, being sung frequently in concert by baritones from the loftiest professional to the most out-of-tune amateur. Even Aline's "Happy Young Heart," probably the favorite solo in the show with the first-night critics, could not compete!

George Bentham (Alexis)

Now it's time to look at the tenor. Because we shan't see him again. The part of Alexis is, as was quickly noted, one of an up-himself prig: an idea fully and deliciously, developed (by others) in *Billee Taylor* a very few years later. So, maybe it wasn't a silly idea to cast the part with a society amateur turned professional opera tenor: "Signor Bentami" (otherwise George Bentham). A better idea, undoubtedly, than would have been the originally mooted candidate, American ex-child singer Johnnie Chatterson, later to be known as "Signor Perugini" and, briefly, "Mr. Lillian Russell."

George Buchan Bentham was born at Clifton, York, on 9 December 1843, the son of Captain (later Lieutenant-Colonel) John Bentham, son of an army general and variously of the 6th Dragoon Guards, 52nd Light Infantry, and the 3rd East Lancashire Militia, and his Leeds-born wife, Emma Sophia (née Ikin), the "youngest surviving daughter of Thomas

19. George Bentham: A tenor of no fixed abode.

Ikin, Esq of Leventhorpe House." In the 1851 census, John and Emma and children were living with Emma's widowed brother, Thomas Bright Crosse, "magistrate and deputy lieutenant" and sometime MP for Wigan, at Shaw Hill, Whittle-le-Woods, Lancashire, in a household that also included a governess and nine servants, including two nurses, a nurserymaid, and a governess. The Crosse family "of Crosse Hall, Chorley," as well as being of ancient lineage, was decidedly well off.

The young George took employment in the war office and, since he had an attractive tenor voice, he also got involved in the amateur music making that was a feature of high society life in London. By 1866, the date of the first concert programs in which his name seems to feature, he had won his way to the top of that particular tree. The earliest I have found is a concert in January 1866, given by the Margate Volunteers at the local Assembly Rooms. George performed that veritable chestnut "The Message"; Mrs. Talfourd, the widow of the well-connected playwright Francis Talfourd, gave the florid "Carnival of Venice" variations; and the two joined together in the duet from *Rigoletto*. Mrs. Talfourd's singing teacher, Emmanuel Aguilar, also took part. Maybe he was young Bentham's teacher too, but it is never said. Anyway, the press raved: "Rarely do concert-goers hear such a tenor as Mr. Bentham . . . his singing . . . was something superb." A couple of months later, he is at Torquay, singing at a concert given by "some members of the Wandering Minstrels." The Wandering Minstrels was the foremost gentlemen's amateur singing club in Britain, and it appears that George Bentham had, already, at twenty-two years of age, been nominated their tenor. Later in the season, he and Mr. Whitworth Jones (the former and very appreciable professional opera basso known as "Henry Whitworth") were the soloists in a very high-society concert given by the group at the West London School of Art.

At the end of March, George was featured in the concert of the Civil Service Musical Society at the Hanover Square Rooms, and the London critics added their praise of his vocalizing: "He has a beautiful tenor voice which was heard to much more advantage in Mr. Frederick Clay's very graceful song 'The Shades of Evening,' accompanied by the composer. . . . Besides possessing a voice to excite envy, Mr. Bentham has real musical feeling and sings with expression as true as it is unaffected." Along with his ballads, George also tackled opera, joining a Mr. Swain in a duet from Saverio Mercadante's *Eliza e Claudio*. In April he visited Canterbury for a concert given by the professional vocalist Eleanor

Armstrong. He gave his "Shades of Evening," won a double encore for his rendition of "Spirto gentil," and the critic nodded "[he has] a very good tenor voice and sings somewhat after the sweet manner of Mr. Hohler."

The magic name: the comparison to Hohler had to come. For indeed, the two men were drawn from one and the same well. Both came from a wealthy and high-social background, and both had fine, true English tenor voices with, it seems, true English enunciation and pronunciation; both had been stars of the Wandering Minstrels; both had been civil servants. But Thomas Hohler was a particular case. Rare it was—and, indeed, I can think of no previous example—that a society amateur should quit the amateur ranks and take on a full-size career as a professional vocalist. Most didn't want or need to. Singing was a pleasurable and social activity, not a job. But, just a few years earlier, Hohler had done it, and done it with more than a little success. George Bentham, metamorphosed for the nonce into "Giorgio Bentami," would follow where Hohler had led.

Quite where and how George started his transformation, I do not know. He is still there in May of 1866, singing at a Civil Service Society concert ("he created quite an effect with the audience"), but he then disappears from my view for the whole of 1867. Was he studying singing in Italy? Some sources credit him with his having "made his operatic debut at Brussels' Théâtre Italien du Cirque under the name of Bentami in 1869"—which is certainly not right. My first sighting of the Italianized Bentham is in 1868, when a correspondent of the *Musical World* reported from Copenhagen on "a new English tenor" who was appearing there in *Il Trovatore*, describing him as having "a great surprise . . . a soft, sonorous, sympathetic voice . . . intonation as pure as the sound of a silver bell." When he sang *Rigoletto*, alongside Pantaleone and America's Mlle. Calisto, the international music press credited him with "eine hübsche Stimme, aber kein Spiel." Well, you can't expect a tenor to have "Spiel." By October, the reports were coming from Amsterdam, where he was "primo tenore in the opera of the city. He has just signed an engagement as primo tenore for the Royal Theatre at Stockholm, for ten weeks."

After that, it seems, George proceeded to Italy, because—when he finally made it back home—he was billed as being "of the principal theatres of Italy." It is always a suspicious bit of terminology, that is, and the truth of the matter is that the unnamed principal theaters are usually nothing of the kind, if, indeed, they exist at all. But, anyway, Bentham was on his way in his new career, and good tenors being as hard to find in the nineteenth century as they are in the twenty-first, it is likely that he found gainful employment wherever he may have been.

The career of Tom Hohler had been launched by impresario Mapleson of the London Italian opera, and the experiment had been a success. Now, Mapleson put the newest civil service tenore under contract, and Giorgio Bentami was able to return to Britain with a three-year contract for the Italian opera in his pocket. He began the British part of his professional career in Scotland (March 1871), where Mapleson's company was playing a pre-London season: Glasgow voted his Almaviva "manly and musicianlike"; Edinburgh reported that as Elvino, to the Sonnambule of Ilma di Murska and of Clarice Sinico, "his tasteful vocalisation elicited hearty applause"; and, as the company headed south, Birmingham approved his "voice of agreeable quality" though finding "his acting and singing somewhat amateurish."

Bentami made his London debut playing the role of Carlo, opposite di Murska, in *Linda di Chamonix* (20 April 1871), and the critical response was fairly satisfying—but only fairly. The *Times* opined that "he must abide his time and acquire experience. That he possesses a voice to be envied none can dispute; moreover, he has talent into the bargain," and added that he was much less nervous on the second night. Another writer referred to him as "a cultivated English amateur" and compounded the slight by stating that Bentham had "a nice tenor voice of the tender rather than the robust order and of these there is always an ample supply. His manner is quiet and modest, and his style careful, neat and small, more suited for musica di camera than the area of the Grand Opera."

Nonetheless, the "new tenor" was much in demand. On the 20 May Bentami appeared at the New Philharmonic concerts in a concert version of *Idomeneo*, alongside Therese Titiens; two days later he shared the vocal duties with Clarice Sinico at the real Philharmonic Society, singing "Un aura amoroso" and provoking, again, a review noting that he had "a delightful tenor voice, but much to learn." It was a refrain that the gentleman in question would hear often in the years to come. On 24 May *Idomeneo* was repeated, and on 25 May Bentami joined di Murska, Edith Wynne, J. G. and Janet Patey, Sims Reeves, and Signor Foli as soloists with Henry Leslie's choir. In the early days of June, Signor Bentami appeared with some of his opera confrères at the Crystal Palace; he took part in Mr. Aptommas's concert singing Donizetti and joining in "Un di se ben" ("he improves"); he sang at Wilhelm Kuhe's concert;

at Wilhelm Ganz's concert at St. James's Hall, sharing the vocals with Titiens, Natalie Carola, Vernon Rigby, and Jules Lefort; and at Henry Leslie's concert with a large portion of the opera company. And in the midst of all this activity, il tenore Bentami launched into a new role at Her Majesty's, featured as Idreno to the *Semiramide* of Titiens, alongside Zélie Trebelli, baritone Luigi Agnesi, and Foli. The press opined that the role was "a tenor part only to be completely filled by an intelligent singer . . . [he] added to the general efficiency."

On the occasion of Mapleson's Benefit in July 1871, Giorgio was put forward as Lionel in *Martha*. The press commented, "Years back petty jealousy and prejudice would have given a young English tenor no such chance as that which has favoured Mr. Bentham." The concert engagements continued on till the end of the season, and, in the interregnum between the London opera season and Mapleson's provincial tour, George snared another top job: an engagement at the Gloucester Festival, sharing the tenor music with Vernon Rigby and Edward Lloyd (*Elijah*, selection *Azor et Zémire*). Presumably he didn't sing on the last day of the Festival, 8 September, for that day he was in London, at All Saint's Church, Kensington, tying the knot with his twenty-year-old mezzo-soprano colleague, Cecile Fernandez.

The newlyweds crossed with the Mapleson company to Dublin, where George stepped in to deputize for Vizzani in *Il Flauto magico*, and Cecile scored a success with her Smeaton in *Anna Bolena*. But Mr. Bentham took umbrage when Zélie Trebelli was then given the role of Smeaton, and he refused to allow Cecile to go on in *Il Flauto magico*. He flounced off with his wife to sing in Hallé's concerts in Manchester and booked them for Brighton, in defiance of their Maplesonian contracts. As Mapleson's troupe proceeded on to Liverpool and dates beyond, Bentham was still with them, but he doesn't seem to have done much. It seems he may have been suspended. Anyway, his manager sued him, claiming he had "violated his contract by singing at the Gloucester Festival and at Dover last Sept. without consent." And so, it was back to the concert halls—the Crystal Palace with "Il Mio tesoro" or "Ah si ben mio," Ganz's Saturday evenings with "O Caro imagine"—and to reviews ranging from "there is little doubt that he will ultimately become one of our most popular tenors" to the too-familiar "he ought to do more than he does with so much voice as he possesses."

And then they were up and gone: Mr. and Mrs. Bentham quit England and headed for Italy. News seeped back to Britain of their performing—one, the other, or both—in Udine, at the Pergola in Florence, and at the Teatro Bellini in Palermo. In January 1873, he sang Faust, and she—for heaven's sake—played a mezzo Marguerite in Malta to enthusiastic reviews; in June, he was reported as singing *Don Pasquale* in Faenza, while she was doing Rosina in Ferrara. Later, Bentham appeared at the Teatro della Valle in Rome (*L'Ombra*).

And in Florence, on 24 March 1873, Cecile gave birth to a little Jack A. Bentham. I don't know what happened to little Jack, but something seems to have happened around about this time to George and Cecile. He returned to England, but she stayed in Italy, playing at the Teatro Malibran in Venice. When she did return, they were no longer working together, as they so often had before. And, according to the censi of 1881, 1891, and 1901, neither were they living together. She still billed herself much of the time as Madame Bentham-Fernandez, or Fernandez-Bentami, or some other suitable variation. But sometimes she is just Cecile Fernandez. It does seem as if their marriage may have had a very short effective life.

Back in London, George began to work busily. He took part in the Monday pops, replaced Vernon Rigby in the London Ballad Concerts, gave "Salut, demeure chaste et pure" at the British Orchestral Society (to a dubious notice: "Mr. Bentham proved his advance as a vocalist but to be frank he has yet much to learn in point of style"), sang again with Henry Leslie's Choir, and appeared in concert at the Albert Hall ("When Other Lips"). And then, on 27 April, he reappeared with Mapleson at Her Majesty's Theatre. *Faust* was the vehicle chosen, with Marie Roze as Marguerite, Signor Rota as a splendid Mephistopheles, "Signor de Reschi" (otherwise de Reszke) as Valentine, and Trebelli as Siebel. But the result was the same:

> Mr. Bentham, having been absent three years, has improved the time by study so that many of the faults that were but too patent before have vanished. To be frank, there is yet something to acquire and something to discard ere Mr. Bentham will take that position which his excellent voice should enable him to do ultimately. But every sign of advance should be welcomed and the young tenor had no reason to complain of the coldness of his audience, for kindly applause followed every effort . . . perhaps most successful in the third act. The "Salve dimora" was a little beyond his powers, but his

rendering of the music was creditable and the duet especially showed him at his best.

A Faust for whom "Salve dimora" is beyond his powers? When *Faust* was put up again, Italo Campanini and Christine Nilsson took the starring roles. I suspect George Bentham may have been hired as a spare tenor or a general tenor understudy. However, later in the season he was put up as Tamino (*Il Flauto magico*). This time, the press found that "his chief fault was his lack of animation." There was always a fault of some kind, it seems. When he again played Tamino on tour, the Liverpool critic grumbled that he was "scarcely equal to the demands of [the part]."

But engagements were not lacking. In September, Bentham returned to the Gloucester Festival, singing in the Rossini *Stabat Mater* with Titiens, Trebelli, and Agnesi; Weber's *The Praise of Jehovah*; Rossini's *Messe Solennelle*; and the tenor music in *Elijah* ("beautiful voice and faulty intonation"). When that was done, he continued on to the Liverpool Festival (29 September), where the other tenors engaged were Sims Reeves and Edward Lloyd. On 14 October he joined Campanini and Lloyd as the tenor soloists at the Leeds Music Festival ("an agreeable tenor voice . . . not always free from errors . . . painfully flat"), and in November he traveled to Edinburgh for a performance of Julius Benedict's *St. Peter*. In the early part of 1875, Bentham sang another *Elijah*, at the Albert Hall, and, yet again, there was complaint about his intonation—not something that had been a problem before.

In 1876, George Bentham returned to the operatic stage. But this time it was not the Maplesonian opera; those days were gone. He joined up with something called the Imperial Italian Opera Company, a touring outfit of dubious stability run by the ambitious Scottish baritone who called himself Enrico Campobello. It had a limited life, during which George sang Alfredo to the La Traviata of Emma Howson. In the early part of 1877, however, he did return to Mapleson. Not for opera, this time, but as part of a very superior concert party tour that featured Titiens, Alwina Valleria, Agnes Bonn, Giuseppe del Puente, and a future Cartesian John Brocolini. In Manchester the press was able to report "he has seldom been heard to such advantage . . . he has an exceptionally fine voice under perfect control and his singing was thoroughly artistic." No faulty intonation? No lack of energy? No "voice on legs"? All those faults that George Bentham had seemingly had since day one, and of which he had apparently never succeeded in getting rid, had they all disappeared at last? Would, and could, his career, at 33 years of age, finally take off as Hohler's had done.

The job that George Bentham got in the last part of the year 1877 was precisely the one that could and should have suited him to perfection; it could and should have allowed him to achieve that takeoff. He was cast in the leading tenor role of Alexis in Gilbert and Sullivan's new English comic opera *The Sorcerer*. It should have been a doddle. It was ideal casting; the music was exactly right for his not-too-robust English tenor voice. And act? He didn't have to act. He simply had to play himself, with a certain amount of burlesque humor, of course, or at the least of understanding of burlesque humor. Well, apparently it wasn't a doddle. George Bentham wasn't bad as Alexis; he just wasn't good. It seems that the humor of the thing quite escaped him, that even acting himself didn't make him act convincingly. And that the languidness that had, apparently, always affected him as a performer was still there.

George Bentham played the role of Alexis for the opening months of the run of *The Sorcerer*, and then, when the show's initial touring company was sent on the road, he was redeployed to play his original role in the provinces, while another upper-class—nay, aristocratic—English tenor, George Power, took over at the Opera Comique. George Power would go on to create the tenor roles of HMS *Pinafore* and *The Pirates of Penzance* during his handful of years in the professional theater. And George Bentham? Once the tour of *The Sorcerer* ended, he simply and quietly removed himself from a musical profession in which he, seemingly, could find no suitable niche—at the age of thirty-four.

George Bentham, "of independent means and no fixed abode," was sixty-seven when he died, at the Strand Palace Hotel, on 25 March 1911, of fatty degeneration of the heart for unnumbered years culminating in a sudden heart failure. He had been ill, reported his death certificate, "for a few minutes." Madame Bentham didn't come to register his death; "A. T. Crosse, cousin" did the honors. "No fixed abode" seems to have described this lost, vaguely talented man rather well.

Giulia Warwick (Constance)

There was one other principal member of the *Sorcerer* company who didn't stay to become a member of the Savoy troupe. Sullivan had obviously put faith in her, and she had a career, but . . . well, Miss Julia

20. Giulia Warwick: "Happy Young Heart."

Ehrenberg, daughter of an expatriate Polish-Jewish tailor, has suffered from some foolish biographical notes in the past: it's time for her history to have a wash- and brush-up.

The three musical Ehrenberg sisters were born in London, the daughters of Jacob Ehrenberg and his wife Evelina (née Elias). They were set to the piano at a young age, and Julia (b. 46 Warwick Street, St. James, 15 January 1857; d. 12 Rathbone Place, London, 13 July 1904) studied under the well-known musician Sigismond Lehmeyer. She appeared, at the age of twelve, at the Beethoven Rooms (16 June 1869) as a pianist, before mutating into "Miss Warwick" (allegedly named for her birthplace), and becoming a vocalist, under the tutelage of Madame

Sainton-Dolby and the patronage of the Countess d'Avigdor and Baroness Lionel de Rothschild.

Julia and her sister Annie sang regularly at the Berkeley Street Synagogue, but my first sighting of the young soprano on a public platform is on 24 February 1873, all of sixteen years old, singing in a performance of William Jackson's *Isaiah* with the Kilburn Musical Society. Later the same year, she sang in the Covent Garden Promenade Concerts, alongside such vocalists as Rose Hersee, the Siedle sisters, Clarice Sinico, and Helene Arnim. In 1873 and 1874, she appeared at the Albert Hall, with William Carter's choir, singing the minor music in *Elijah*, and later at Cambridge, singing the Mermaid in a concert version of *Oberon*.

In later 1876, she became "Miss Giulia Warwick," to give a handful of performances with the Carl Rosa Opera Company. She was tried first (7 October 1876) as Zerlina to the Don Giovanni of Frank Celli and the Anna of Cora Stuart at the Alexandra Palace, and on 4 November she appeared as Arline in *The Bohemian Girl*, alongside J. W. Turner and Celli, in the regular Rosa season at the Lyceum Theatre. Julia repeated that role for the last night of the season (2 December) and, apparently, also played one performance as Marcellina in *Fidelio*, vice Julia Gaylord. When the company moved on to Liverpool, she paid a flying visit to that city for one more Arline.

Shortly afterward, Julia was cast in a curious five-act opera titled *Biorn* through a forced run at the Queen's Theatre, but that engagement doesn't seem to have stopped her taking part in a concert party tour with the violinist August Wilhelmj, singing *Israel in Egypt* in Belfast and at Kuhe's Brighton Festival, visiting Leeds with Wilhelmj ("an excellent soprano"), or repeating her Carter *Elijah*. When *Biorn* had been buried, Julia returned full-time to the concert stage—the Crystal Palace, and the Covent Garden and Agricultural Hall proms ("attempted Elsa's Dream" from *Tannhäuser*)—until she was, again, hired for the theater and secured her place in the reference books.

Julia was cast, "of the Carl Rosa Opera Company," to play "seconda dama" in a new opéra-bouffe at the Opera Comique: *The Sorcerer*. As Constance Partlett, the pew opener's juvenile daughter, she was seen to have "something to learn as an actress." However, she did well enough that, when producer Richard D'Oyly Carte redeployed leading lady Alice May to his newest show, and Gertrude Ashton and Mrs. Ware had assured the interim, she was given the part of Aline for the remainder of the run. She also appeared in the forepieces *Dora's Dream* and *The Spectre Knight*.

However, Julia did not continue with what would become the Savoy company; her first engagement with Carte was her last. When the run at the Opera Comique ended, she rejoined the Carl Rosa troupe, as a supporting soprano. Over some three years, she appeared as Anne Chute in *The Lily of Killarney*, the Gipsy Queen in *The Bohemian Girl*, Clara in *The Siege of Rochelle*, Elena in *Piccolino*, Bianca in *The Taming of the Shrew*, Ritta in *Zampa*, Paquita in *Carmen*, the mother(!) in *I Promessi sposi*, Donna Inez in *Moro*, and Martha in *Faust*, inter alia, to fair and usually brief notices, before ending her time with the company in mid-1882.

Julia returned to concert singing for a while but then moved definitively into the field of comic opera and musical comedy. In 1884 (7 May), she was hired by Alexander Henderson for the second role of Jessamine ("The Song of the Clock") in *Nell Gwynne* at the Avenue Theatre, and she subsequently went on the road for the same producer, playing Edwige behind the Falka of Tillie Wadman. She took up the role of the titular Falka in the number two tour, run by Auguste van Biene and Horace Lingard, and on 8 April 1886, at the Comedy Theatre, played the role in the show's one-thousandth performance.

She went on to play Daphne in the short-lived *Glamour*, and was then reengaged by van Biene to tour in *Pepita* and in *The Old Guard*, an engagement culminating in a return to the Avenue Theatre as Fraisette in *The Old Guard* and Princess Etelka, behind Marie Vanoni, in *Nadgy*.

In 1889, Julia toured as Frédérique in *La Girouette*, and in 1890 she took part in the Globe Theatre production of *The Black Rover*, replacing the composer's insufficient wife in the large leading role of Isidora. In 1891, she went out at the head of the "Giulia Warwick Opera Company" playing the complex title-role in the French musical comedy *Madame Cartouche*, after which she ended her time on the touring circuits. On 29 March 1892, she mounted a concert of her own at the Prince's Hall, with a fine bill including Valleria, Hilda Wilson, Ben Davies, Michael Maybrick, and her sister Alexandra, who had also switched to singing from the piano. In the later part of the year, she took a turn in the music halls (still billed as being late "of the Carl Rosa Opera Company") singing alongside Cora Stuart—who was now playing comedy—and some performing dogs and cockatoos, from the Empire Palace, Edinburgh, to the Star Theatre of Varieties, Dublin.

In 1894, Miss Warwick was appointed to the staff of the Guildhall School of Music in the department of "gesture, elocution and deportment," but she had not yet finished with the stage. In 1896, the "very tiny woman, with a big voice and vivid personality" was cast as Aunt Barbara, alongside star May Yohé, in *The Belle of Cairo*. Miss Yohé and the show turned out to be failures, and Julia returned to the Guildhall. In 1896, following her sister's death, she succeeded to her post on the vocal staff of the school, where she remained until a couple of years before her death, at the age of forty-seven.

The Sorcerer Makes a Hit

The Sorcerer was a decided success. In a London town devoted to the frisky and fashionable French opéra-bouffe, where most of the few home-made musicals of consequence had been spectaculars made for the vast auditorium of the Alhambra, it even had something of a flavor of the "new" about it. How did one manage it, especially with three-fourths of a board of directors who'd had from the show what they wanted—lucrative sheet music for the country's million pianos—and were more concerned with not losing money than with taking a gamble on making more. It was an attitude that would lead, soon, to a split. For Mr. Carte had the bit between his teeth, and he kept "his" show on the boards of the Opera Comique—which, like the old Philharmonic in Islington in Soldene/Morton days, had gone from being a despised venue to a fashionable one, thanks to one production—for six months.

During that six months, the cast stayed fairly stable. Alice May and Bentham were deployed elsewhere by Carte; a little pupil of Gustave Garcia, known as Lisa Walton (née Elizabeth Isabella Watkin; b. New-castle upon Tyne, 5 December 1857; d. 11 Prior's Terrace, Tynemouth, 26 August 1879) was brought in to replace the promoted Giulia Warwick, and the American concert soprano Irene Ware (née Adams; b. Lewiston, Maine, c. January 1850; d. New Malden, Surrey, 8 March 1909), "an excellent soprano, somewhat weak in her top notes" and the talented, foolish Gertrude Cave Ashton (née Gertrude Eva Andrews; sometime Gertrude Ashton b. 27 West Square, Southwark, 17 April 1855; d. 34 Devonshire Street, Cavendish Square, 30 March 1886) filled the inter-regnum. None stayed. Mrs. Ware had a modest career and retired to teach music. I suppose she has the distinction of being the first of the American sopranos hired, over the years, by the Carte organization—alas, generally unsatisfactorily. Lizzie Watkin died at the age of twenty-one, and Miss Ashton's strange, strange tale also ended in an early death.

But the bulk of the initial casting proved highly successful. Messrs. Temple, Grossmith, and Barrington would become long-term Cartesians, and famed as such, through many a show, as would the young lady who deputized for the failing Mrs. Paul as Lady Sangazure: thirty-two-year-old London cab proprietor's daughter Miss Rosina Brandram (née Rosina Moult, Mrs. Champney Charles Butcher). Unkind fate would deprive the company too soon of Mrs. Paul and Miss Everard, as well as Miss Walton, and marital misbehavior would exile Clifton to America, but almost all of the rest of the cast would continue on into the next show at the Opera Comique. And that next show would be a history maker . . .

4

HMS *Pinafore*, or The Lass That Loved a Sailor

Comic opera in two acts
Opera Comique, 25 May 1878

Who knew? Who knew, on that day in May, that theater history was being made?

HMS *Pinafore* was, basically, the mixture as before. Gilbert put together a simple tale—captain's daughter prefers tenorious able seaman to lofty knight, and of course, as in all good fairy stories, gets him—from his published comic writings, and detailed it in a delicious welter of burlesque humor; Sullivan decorated said tale with a delightful score of laughing and almost sentimental music, with just a sufficient burlesque flavor . . . Ah! Did ever an operatic soprano bewail her lowly love in such tuneful but tongue-in-cheek tones?

Well, it is easy, in the twenty-first century, to say . . . oh, it's obvious. But it wasn't that easy. And the piece and its makers had to master a few steeplechase fences both on the show's way to the stage and even more thereafter as HMS *Pinafore* established itself as the most appreciable comic opera in the English-language theater of the 1870s.

Rutland Barrington was Corcoran, the well-bred captain of the HMS *Pinafore*, who assures his crew that "though related to a peer, I can hand, reef and steer" and that he is "never, never sick at sea." Gilbert would never tire of sticking pins into the aristocratic bearers of titles and employments won by birth rather than by ability, and Corcoran—even though endowed with a beautiful ballad by Sullivan—is reduced to the ranks by the final twist in the tale.

Corcoran is looking to rise in the social scale by marrying his daughter, Josephine (prima donna), to the First Lord of the Admiralty,

Sir Joseph Porter, a patter-singing knight molded around the now proven capabilities of George Grossmith. Alas, the prima donna is already devoted to the primo tenore, A. B. Ralph Rackstraw, as represented by Bentham's *Sorcerer* replacement, George Power. They plot an elopement (aided, of course, by the entire, and very vocal, chorus) but are betrayed by a misanthropic tar by the name of Deadeye (Richard Temple). However, nemesis is at hand: The bumboat woman, Buttercup (Miss Everard) is a retired nanny, and she reveals that not all is "as it seems." She was a wayward wet nurse and she muddled up two of her little charges: it is Ralph who is the relation of a peer, and Corcoran who is of lowly birth. And since love does not level rank "as much as that," a happy ending is reached.

Although this tale and text seem perfect to us today, they are not wholly what was intended originally. One major character had to be excised from the libretto and score: Hebe, the dragonistic head girl of Sir Joseph's gaggle of accompanying sisters, cousins, and aunts. Hebe was intended to be the Lady Sangazure of the piece, and to be played by Mrs. Howard Paul. But Mrs. Paul was ill; before *HMS Pinafore* sailed out of the Opera Comique, she would, alas, be dead. She had to be replaced in her "especially written for" role. I don't know why they didn't call on Miss Brandram, who had played Sangazure in poor Isabelle's place, or some other *komische Alte*: instead, they largely erased Hebe's role and hired an obscure concert contralto to play what was left of it. Miss Jessie Charlotte Bond (who tells us in her unreliable memoirs that she wasn't "hired to" but was already in the cast as . . . a member of the chorus?) would become a well-loved fixture with the Carte companies for the best part of her career. But the relationship between Sir Joseph and his hawkeyed cousin Hebe disappeared from *HMS Pinafore*.

Other folk yearn to find the score of *Thespis*; I would love to see the text and score of *HMS Pinafore* with the character of Hebe, and, undoubtedly, her "aria(s)" intact—if they were ever written. Anyhow, with the character of Hebe virtually gone from the piece, the originally secondary contralto role of Little Buttercup, the Mrs. Partlett or Inez (*Gondoliers*) of the piece, became the main contralto part; with Harriet Everard to play it, it turned out to be a delightful creation. This didn't stop Gilbert from hastening back to his gorgonic and booming contralto dames in future works. Little Buttercup, somewhat by accident, stands rather alone of her kind in the G&S opus.

HMS Pinafore, as she was launched, was labeled a comic opera. But, like *The Sorcerer*, it was comic opera of a rather different kind from such classics bearing that description as *The Duenna, The Cabinet,* or *Love in a Village*. It included, as the new wave of French opéras-bouffes did, the elements of burlesque, parody, and comical craziness previously featured, in England, more in pasticcio burlesque productions. Because this was England, however, the burlesque content was in a cultivated rather than in a wholly iconoclastic Hervé-like mode. And, because this was England, the objects of the burlesque were objects relevant to the British theater and to British culture. So, what more obvious playground could present itself than the vastly popular Jolly Jack Tar-style of theater, as crystallized in pieces such as Douglas Jerrold's *Black-Eyed Susan?* But *HMS Pinafore* was not in the same world as the many previous burlesques of things naval: to start with, there was music—new music—from a glorious glee to a mock operatic aria to the ditsiest song-and-dance trio you ever did hear.

Emma Howson (Josephine)

Alongside our stalwart "backbone" Cartesians, the first night cast included one or two performers who were not to become vertebrae in the G&S operas. And the greatest of these was the prima donna. It took the team several shows before they lit on a soprano who would, and could, join Grossmith, Barrington, Temple, et alii as a durable member of what was, by then, the Savoy team. In the meanwhile, they had, however, employed several fine performers. The first of consequence to follow Alice May was another "Australian," and, in this case, a homebred Australian. But although Emma Howson (b. Hobart, 28 March 1844; d. New York, June 1928) was Tasmanian-born, she was from a thoroughly musical English family: a niece to the celebrated operatic mezzo-soprano Emma Albertazzi and . . . well, I've covered the history of the Howson family—parents, brothers, sisters—in my *Encyclopaedia of the Musical Theatre*. They are a wonderful bunch. I wonder why no one has fully biographized them. They left volumes and volumes of fascinating diaries.

By the time she created the role of Josephine, Emma had been before the public for nearly twenty years. She was thirty-four years old and had lived the tough life of a touring performer for much of that time. As a young teenager in Australia, she had been seen in good and leading roles in operas such as *The Night Dancers, The Mountain Sylph, The Rose of Castille, Il Trovatore,* and *Guy Mannering,* as well as in concerts, pantomimes, and burlesques, often with her sister or her brothers,

21. Emma Howson: A prima donna on four continents.

and on occasion with the whole lot of them together. In June 1866, the family left Australia for San Francisco. They remained there for three years, giving performances operatic and popular, concerts, oratorios, burlesques, and the West Coast's first performances of *La Grande-Duchesse*, *La Belle Hélène*, and *Barbe-bleue*. Emma was leading lady in whatever they played and was acclaimed by the local press "the best operatic artist now in California."

Then the family set off eastward. They wouldn't all make it to New York. Father Frank succumbed to a cancer of the jaw in Omaha, and that was the end of the family troupe. Months later, Mother Emma died too. Emma joined up with the Caroline Richings company, played at Niblo's Garden, was Cunégonde in the spectacular New York production of *Le Roi Carotte*, and appeared as everything from Reiza in *Oberon* to Susanna in *The Marriage of Figaro* to Agathe, Maritana, Arline, and Martha—until, in June 1873, she headed for Europe. She made her European debut in *La Sonnambula* at Malta but soon headed for England, where she went out on tour with the Campobello company . . . and ended up at the Opera Comique. She was a fine, no-nonsense Josephine. Hardened, like Julia Mathews, by years of repertoire performance and one-night stands in Australia, and on the exhausting, health-breaking touring circuits of America, she played her role efficiently, charmingly, and thoroughly until her contract was up. And then she returned to America, where, fairly soon, she retired to teaching music in Brooklyn.

While Emma was being leading lady at the Opera Comique, her elder brother, John, was also in London. The only production to challenge that of HMS *Pinafore* in current popularity was the English version of Robert Planquette's *Les Cloches de Corneville*. And the leading man of that production was none other than John Howson. John would appear in American productions (pirate and proper) of many of the earlier works of Gilbert and of Sullivan—as the Judge in *Trial by Jury* with Alice Oates; as Cox in *Cox and Box*; in *Creatures of Impulse*; as Wells in *The Sorcerer*; and as Bunthorne in *Patience*—before his death in 1887.

And what about Ralph Rackstraw, the "audacious tar"? Well, George Power, an almost accidental Victorian vocalist, left his name engraved in the history of the British musical theater, thanks to his being around and in the right social and singing circles when Messrs. Gilbert and Sullivan were taking their most important steps toward fame.

George Power (Ralph Rackstraw)

George Power (b. Kilkenny, 24 December 1846; d. 31 Addison Road, Kensington, 17 October 1928) was a younger son of Sir John Power, Bart, of Kilfane, County Kilkenny, and his wife, the former Miss Frances Elizabeth Wade of Clonabreany, County Meath. George was educated at Cheltenham College and at Trinity College, Dublin. Being the possessor of a pretty light tenor voice, he elected, following his education, to draw some enjoyment from the cultivation of his musical gifts. To this end, he set out for Italy, where, we are told, he studied "under Barilli, Graffigna, Lamperti and others." Achille Graffigna of Mantua and Milan was known as "the teacher of Nilsson." Francesco Lamperti was, seemingly, the teacher of a good half of the thousand foreigners who visited Italy in search of a voice and, most importantly, a clever and influential agent. Power, however, took his training seriously, and he became a lifelong devotee of "the Italian method." It was doubtless Lamperti, with some help from the Power family bank balance, who secured the young *tenorino* a first outing at that most purchasable of debut theaters, the Teatru Manoel in Valetta, Malta. We are told that the role chosen was that of Almaviva in *Il Barbiere di Siviglia*, but, sadly, I have not yet succeeded in unearthing a report or review.

On his return to Britain, Power was hired for a short season of English opera being given at Her Majesty's Theatre, in which a number of young native vocalists were being given the chance of a first appearance. Power was chosen to sing on opening night (26 December 1877) but, sensibly, was not thrown into any large or hefty role. He was cast alongside Pauline Rita as Daniel in the little *The Swiss Cottage*. In the event, Mdlle. Rita didn't appear, and her place was taken by Helene Crosmond (Mrs. Hannah Turner). Miss Crosmond—daughter of Madame Rachel of the scandalous trial "beautiful forever" ill fame—made a notable success, and Power and George Fox, in the baritone role of Max, were thoroughly outshone. Power was nodded to as "an agreeable tenor" and the *Era* chronicled "a satisfactory first appearance." It would also be George Power's last appearance in opera.

Mr. W. S. Gilbert and Mr. A. Sullivan, both frequenters of, or, more frankly, devotees of, the aristocratic amateur musical and dramatic circles of London, were at this time running the wholly professional comic opera *The Sorcerer* at the Opera Comique, in the Strand. When the time came near for *The Sorcerer* to head for the provinces, the writers and their manager, Mr. D'Oyly Carte, side-wound their original leading man into the touring troupe and, to replace him at the Opera Comique, they took on George Power. Thus, on Saturday, 23 February 1878, less than two months after his London debut at Her Majesty's, Power was installed as an opéra-bouffe leading man in the Strand. The choice was a good one. Power was a pretty fellow, with nicely gentlemanly, and even aristocratic, ways and manners, the ability to wear clothes well, and a decidedly true and well-cultivated light tenor voice.

When *The Sorcerer* had run its course, Messrs. Sullivan, Gilbert, Carte, and the Comedy Opera Company replaced it with *HMS Pinafore*. In a manner that would become a habit, the production team cast most of the new piece's roles with the cast of their previous show and, thus, it was George Power who was handed the role of the tenorious tar, Ralph Rackstraw. Ralph's role, consisting of good looks, sweet singing, and earnest though burlesque dialogue, it would have scarcely been possible, at the time and in the place, to cast the part more happily. Alongside the showier parts and performances of the piece, Powers's Ralph was often only dignified in the reviews with "a very capable" or "pleasing" tenor, but his performance was not to be underestimated. He sang "A Maiden Fair to See" and went melodically and melodramatically to his dungeon cell in a perfect English light-tenorious fashion.

From Power's comments in later life—when he was regularly called upon to tell tales of the production of Gilbert and Sullivan's great hit—it is clear that he did understand the burlesque nature of the piece and his part, so I think we may give him credit for comprehended "mock sentimentality" rather than, uncomprehendingly, the real thing.

Power played Ralph Rackstraw for most of the show's long run, and he was still the leading-tenor-in-title of the Opera Comique company when it came to the time to produce *HMS Pinafore*'s successor, *The*

22. George Power: A right aristocratic Ralph Rackstraw.

Pirates of Penzance. In *The Pirates of Penzance*, he had a role as like to its predecessor as could be, as a fine, put-upon young fellow who sings longingly in duet with his soprano before their plight is all untwined, and their final curtain clinch can be clinched. The reviewer in the *Era* gave him a tad more space than usual, allowing him "a very agreeable light tenor voice and a pleasing style, qualities which have already gained for him no little favour in the previous opera . . . [he has] good taste vocally and a fair amount of histrionic skill," before returning, at a later date, and finding him "in every way excellent. He acts the character with a mock sentiment which always renders the part amusing . . . his pleasant tenor voice is used with great effect." George Power played the role of Frederic, "the slave of duty," for six months before he relinquished his second consecutive long-running role and returned to a less-professional mode of life.

For the next ten months, he was seen out only in fashionable concerts and in occasional parlor operettas and other amateur or semi-professional theater performances. He played in Henri Logé's *Incognito* (May 1881), Freddie Clay's *Out of Sight* (as Lt. de Blanc-Mange, 1881, opposite Mrs. Godfrey Pearse, daughter of the tenor Mario), and, more surprisingly, in a French production of Émile Augier's play *L'Aventurière*. When François Cellier produced *The Pirates of Penzance* ("by permission"; director: Richard Barker) with amateurs at Kingston, Power popped down to Surrey to repeat his original role. He must have been surprised to find there a stunning Mabel, a certain "Mrs. Loveday," who was either none other than the former Gaiety star Annie Tremaine or her sister-in-law Elinor, a former Opera Comique Josephine.

Power returned to the concert platform, and "charmed everybody by the beauty of his voice," in many an aristocratic drawing room, before, on 20 August 1881, returning to the professional stage. Michael Gunn of Dublin, an important backer of the Carte regime, had begun a series of English comic operas with which he hoped to rival Carte's Gilbert and Sullivan productions. He had made a splendid beginning with Edward Solomon and Henry Pottinger Stephens's *Billee Taylor*, and now he was producing its successor, *Claude Duval*. He was determined to cast the "lovers" of *The Pirates of Penzance* as the lovers of his new piece, so Marion Hood and George Power joined Frank Celli, in the title-role, and the composer's brother, Fred Solomon, as chief comic, at the head of the cast for the new show. Alas, Mr. Stephens, in particular, had sadly failed to come up with the goods a second time, and it was reckoned that "Mr. George Power made as depressing a melancholy lover as could well be found to play a depressing part." Fred Solomon's comic turn held the show together for a couple of months, before it closed, and, with it, George Power's career as a professional comic-opera tenor.

Between 1885 and 1895, George Power performed in concert and occasional operettas, mostly on society occasions. He seems to have played some performances with "Percy North's Operetta Company" alongside the equally equivocally picturesque Hayden Coffin; he turned out at Cannizaro House in Wimbledon, at Mr. and Mrs. Leo Schuster's Benefit for the Colonial Emigration (for other people, doubtless) Society, at the London matinees given by Minnie Bell, Arthur Wellesley, and Templar Saxe, and he was in the cast with David Bispham and Mrs. Pearse (Madame Rachel's noisiest "victim") when the Stock Exchange amateurs produced the burlesque *Joan, or the Brigands of Bluegoria*. In 1890, he appeared in *Frou Frou* for charity, and my last sightings of him as a singer are in March 1894, at the Palazzo Rinuccini in Florence, when he performed Ralph Rackstraw with the local society glamateurs, and in November of the same year at the Green Park Club (for ladies), London. To the end of the century, Power continued to appear in occasional society amateur dramatics, but by this time he had become a singing teacher, known for his severe adherence to the Italian method.

In 1903, George Power succeeded to his father's baronetcy. He had been umpteenth in line to the succession, but following the death of brothers and nephews—several of whom had taken to the military with its inherent risks and final results—he unexpectedly found himself ennobled, if hardly in a position to continue the line. In fact, at the approach of the age of seventy, he did finally marry. His wife was Eva Gertrude Boulton, the daughter of Sir Samuel Boulton, Bart. of Copped Hall, Totteridge, Herts, with whose brother and family he was "old friends." It goes without saying that there were no children, and the baronetcy died out at Power's death at the age of eighty-one.

Harriet Everard (Little Buttercup)

During my forty years wandering in the Victorian musical theater, I developed a devotion for, among others, the lady who called herself "Harriet Everard." Bit by bit, I studiously put together a record of her career, that career which culminated so famously with her creation of the role of Little

23. Harriet Everard: "Sweet Little Buttercup, I."

Buttercup in HMS *Pinafore*. And because, seemingly, no one else had done so, I decided to tell the story of that "plump and pleasing person."

Miss Everard (or, later, Miss H. Everard) was actually born as Harriet(te) Emily Woollams. (I can't remember whether I was the first to reveal that fact, one hundred years ago, but anyway, fact it is.) She was the daughter of John Woollams—variously described as a builder and a decorator—and his wife Harriet (née Graves). That doesn't sound particularly interesting, does it? But it is. "Builder and decorator" may sound like a local handyman, but . . . no way. Mr. Woollams was a shining star in the British wallpaper world. His father was an even bigger star: "William Woollams of 31 Wigmore Street, paper stainer." I won't detail his importance. If you are interested, there is a splendid book on the Web detailing the Woollams' influence on wallpaper. William married a Huguenot-descended lady by the name of Mary Ann Aumonier . . . and, well, it all gets genealogically vast after that . . . but they had a bunch of sons, all but one of whom went into wallpaper. That one, David Woollams, started life as a "carver and gilder" but apparently became a singer "in the Opera." He died a rich man, so I suspect he also had a day job. After grandad's death, the next generation took up the wallpapering: son William at 110 High Street Marylebone, and a John at 69 Marylebone Lane. They won prizes at the Great Exhibition and other trade fairs . . . well, the book tells all, even if it is sometimes difficult to sort out the Williams and the Johns! So, enough of that; let's get on to Harriet.

Harriet was born at 96 High Street, Marylebone, on 12 March 1844, and was, seemingly, brought up by her aunt, Emily, and her husband, goldsmith Frederic Aumonier, at 754 Old Kent Road, while father and mother were producing, in succession, Adela Louisa, Percy Raynor, Walter John, Kate, Alma, and Maude, among whom several also pursued theatrical careers. I'd always supposed that Harriet, like so many, stage-named herself "Everard' because it sounded aristocratic. Never presume; I now find her great grandparents were Jean Aumonier and Marie . . . Everard!

Harriet began her stage career at Exeter with actor-manager Frederick Belton. But it is not quite evident when. Some say 1860; Belton opened his theater on 26 November 1860 with a company including future star Harry Beckett. But the theater seemed open mostly to allow the military amateurs of the local Volunteer Corps to strut their stuff. Belton plugged on through short and shorter seasons until, for his winter season, he scored a small coup: Charles Kean and wife came to his theater for three performances. They brought just three supporting players with them, but they played large plays, so Mr. Belton hired a "winter company." First a Miss Elise de Courcy, then a Miss Plucknett, and—amid the host of musical and burlesque performances—I finally find a notice for the "beautiful singing" of Miss Everard in *Guy Mannering*. Mr. Belton moved on to manage the Swansea Theatre for a season, and Harriet went too. She sang "My Pretty Jane" between the parts ("in a style that commanded an encore"), and played in *Rob Roy*, opposite the company's first singing man, Maurice de Solla ("the singing of Miss Everard is much admired"; she is "really a great favourite here"). From Swansea, she and de Solla continued to Plymouth in October to repeat their *Rob Roy*, and they remained there as part of the strong local company until Easter the following year, she playing such roles as Pekoe in *Aladdin*, Abricotina in *Ruy Blas*, *Fortunio*, and so on).

I don't know exactly what happened next. Harriet was strongly established in a fine provincial company, there was talk of her going to J. A. Cave at the Marylebone Theatre . . . but for the rest of 1863 she is unfindable. Was she ill? Pregnant? Experiencing family problems? She resurfaces in the new year, at the second-rate Surrey Theatre in Sheffield, singing "The Chink of Gold" in *Sinbad* and appearing in *Guy Mannering* and *Rob Roy* with de Solla. I notice among the other names in the company a certain Mr. Parry, from Sheffield, whose name will appear again.

Harriet progressed to Jersey's Queen's Assembly Rooms for a summer season. It wasn't quite as end-of-the-pierish as it might sound: the two principals were tenor Elliot Galer and his wife, Fanny Reeves. They were both well-known English operatic performers, but Galer had had a bad accident, and they were now touring an Entertainment of little operettas, which they had recently been performing in London (*Cousin Kate, The Haunted Mill, Blonde and Brunette*, etc.). For their summer season they hired two supernumeraries: Harriet and "Mr. W. Parry." Why do I insist on Mr. Parry? Because Harriet says that she married him. They advertised together from Jersey . . . and then, unless he's "Mr. W. Parry from Cirencester" playing *Whitebait at Greenwich* at Gloucester . . . I lose him. Well, not totally. In the 1871 census, Harriet is back living with the widowed Mrs. Aumonier; she is listed as Harriet Parry, and accompanied by an Arthur Parry, born Covent Garden, aged thirty-four. And when Harriet later (re?)married, she did it as the widow Parry. Well, I've wasted enough time on the Parry puzzle. Someone can check the Jersey registers . . . Suffice it that, after her holiday (honeymoon?) in the Channel Islands, Harriet returned to town and joined Sefton Parry's (oh no!) company at the New Greenwich Theatre (it was mentioned that she "appeared after a lengthened absence") playing Leicester in *Kenilworth*, Charlotte in *The Stranger*, Sybil in *Jack in the Giant Killer*, and Apollo in *Ixion*, and then, dammit, I lose her again, for all of 1865.

Harriet was still only twenty-one when she joined the company at the Olympic Theatre, alongside such rising gals as Nellie Farren and Amy Sheridan. She appeared as Prince Pecki in *Princess Primrose* ("a skilful songstress with a finely developed figure"; "displays talent as both a vocalist and an actress"; "so melodious a voice and with such brilliancy of expression"; "a decided success"), was the comedy relief as Cordelia Jemima in the drama *Love's Martyrdom*, and created the rather approximate version of Clémentine in the first very approximate English version of the opéra-bouffe *Barbe-bleue*. She was already marked out as the coming "Desclauzas" of England . . . a plumpish, pleasing character lady . . . at the age of twenty-one! And, yes: I think her "finely developed figure" was already heading the same way as that of Marie Desclauzas!

In 1867, Harriet played a season with Miss Marriott at the Victoria Theatre (*Jeannie Deans*, *The Hunchback*, *Hamlet*, *The Broken Sword*, *Raymond and Agnes*, *Tricks of the Turf*) and then visited Liverpool, to play at the local St. James's Hall with Maria Simpson. She was Mopes the maid in *Pygmalion*, Princess Bariatinski in Tom Taylor's *The Serf*, Mrs. Raby in *Miriam's Crime*, and she created the role of the elderly, flirtatious Marchioness in a burlesque of *La Fille du régiment*, titled *La Vivandière*, authored by Mr. W. S. Gilbert.

Then, after a brief return to Greenwich, Harriet was hired for the Queen's Theatre by manager Alfred Wigan. Only, Wigan was but a front. The Queen's Theatre was a lust gift from Henry Labouchère to his married mistress, the actress Henrietta Hodson. Miss Hodson played endless juvenile leads at her theater and, either enormously cannily or blithely unaware that she was being acted off the stage, surrounded herself with a most amazing company: Lionel Brough and Johnny Toole as chief fun makers, the young Henry Irving, John Ryder, even, for a while, the delicious Polly Markham and the rising Kate Santley—and Harriet as chief comic soubrette and old woman. She reprised her role as the Marchioness in Gilbert's burlesque ("cleverly represented without too much exaggeration'), was Mrs. Corney to Brough's Bumble, "an intriguing lady of a certain age" in *The Gnome King*, Mrs. Spriggins in *Ici on parle français*, Polly in *Not Guilty*, Mrs. Fielding in *Dot*, and Mrs. Subtle in *Paul Pry*, and took on many other like roles during a whole eighteen months at the Queen's.

Harriet fulfilled a season at the Royal Alfred Theatre (Hecate in *Macbeth*, Blouzabella in *The Invisible Prince*), before landing another substantial engagement, in Mrs. John Wood's company. Mrs. Wood played a good repertoire (*Milky White*, *Bombastes furioso*, *The Heir at Law*, *Paul Pry*, *To Oblige Benson*, and the burlesque *Vesta*), but her trump card was the burlesque *La Belle Sauvage*. It was Mrs. Wood, of course, who played Po-co-han-tas (as John Brougham's piece had originally been named), but the show had been rewritten since its first productions and was now a burlesque of the hit play *School*. Harriet was the schoolmistress Kros-as-can-be: "One of the most genuinely grotesque parts on the modern stage. A sort of French bonne in German style." She all but stole the show from the star.

Harriet returned to the Hodson house for *The Last Days of Pompeii*, joined an aspiring Edith Bertram at the Royalty Theatre for a month as a garrulous landlady in *Bohemia and Belgravia* and Mme. Deschapelles in *The Lady of Lyons*, and even took part, alongside such stars as Lionel Brough, Mrs. Billington, and Mrs. Howard Paul, in the money-splashed-everywhere spectacular *Babil and Bijou* at Covent Garden.

In 1873, she appeared at the North Woolwich Pleasure Gardens, and then moved to the Princess's Theatre, where she appeared as the Spirit of Memory in *Undine*, in *The Will of Wise King Kino*, *Griselda*, and in *The Sleeping Draught*. She played the Queen of Catland in the panto *Little Puss in Boots* singing "How Nice to Be a Fairy," and was applauded as "a very buxom and substantial fairy" and "one of the best things in the pantomime." Conversely, when Mrs. Rousby guested, Harriet played the Duchess of Norfolk in *Twixt Axe and Crown*.

When French opéra-bouffe reached England, Harriet found an ideal vehicle in its unparalleled combination of burlesque humor and fine singing. When Charlie Head floated an English *Giroflé-Girofla* at the poor old Philharmonic, with the starry Julia Mathews in the dual title-role, Harriet was given the superb "heavy lady" role of Aurore, and won enthusiastic notices. When the Phil put up *The Waterman*, she was a plump little Mrs. Bundle. She also appeared at the Charing Cross Theatre in comedy (Mrs. Toodles, Mrs. Wellington de Boots, etc.), played Mrs. O'Kelly in London's first *The Shaughraun* at Drury Lane, took part in Gilbert's *Pygmalion and Galatea* at the Alexandra Palace, and returned to the Charing Cross to play Mrs. Winkle in *Young Rip van Winkle* and Mrs. Grimley in *20 Pounds a Year*. She toured with Joseph Eldred, appeared with the Strand Theatre company, and then she was hired to play Mrs. Partlett, the pew opener, in the new British "opéra-bouffe" *The Sorcerer* at the Opera Comique. It was a triumph for her ("Miss Everard was excellent"; "incomparable"), but it was also, probably, the death of her. From *The Sorcerer* and its companion, *The Spectre Knight*, Harriet went on to create the role of Little Buttercup, especially written to feature her, and wrote herself into history. And then came *The Pirates of Penzance*. The part of Ruth was played originally (in America) by Alice Barnett. Miss Barnett was very tall and decidedly Amazonian. In London, that part was to be launched by lovable, roly-poly Harriet. It wasn't, because she suffered a rehearsal accident that effectively ended her career, and maybe her life. She died on 22 February 1882 while *Patience* was playing at the Savoy. There was no cuddly contralto role for her in that one. I guess Carte knew she would not be returning.

I'd better tidy up the ends. In 1879, Harriet married (again?) a gentleman—well, a commission agent—seven years younger than she, by the name of George William Darley Beswick. The marriage was, of course, of short duration. He remarried after her death, but died himself 6 July 1904. As for the brothers and sisters, the members of the Woollams family were the delight of the Hammersmith, Brook Green, and Richmond amateur dramatics for years, before both Percy and Walter turned professional. Adela didn't, but after a curious marriage (yes, another) to a chap called Paul Xavier Hubert—who was supposed to be a naval attaché from Livorno but seems to have been the son of a Woollams Wallpaper employee—took, as her second husband, Mr. William Lauderdale Maitland. Mr. Maitland was a florist of Irish sources, and he too had been involved in showbiz. Under the pseudonym of "the brothers Mansell," he and his dotty brother Richard had been responsible for bringing the groundbreaking opéra-bouffe *Chilpéric* to England. William was the smart brother who got out of the theater and back into flowers.

Aeneas Dymott (Bob Beckett)

Another *Pinafore* actor whom we sha'n't see again is Mr. Dymott, who played the role of sailor Bob the Carpenter to the sailor Bill the Bo'sun

24. Aeneas Dymott (Bob Beckett): "A British Tar."

of Fred Clifton. Always just Mr. Dymott. No first name, no past, no future . . . Well, I thought that needed to change, so I sat down and . . .

Aeneas Joseph Dymott was his full name, and he was born in Southampton, around 1830, the son of James Dymott, a tailor, and his wife Sarah (née Frith). In 1841, the couple can be seen living in Parsley's Court, French Street, with daughters Nancy and Julia Mary and our lad. The girls would go on to be schoolmistresses, and Aeneas established himself as a woodcarver. Well, that was his day job. But young Mr. Dymott had a big bass voice, and when he wasn't carving, he sang. However, before I spot him singing, I spot him breeding. He had a daughter, Julia Frost Dymott (1853), by a young lady named Eliza Frost, whom he married four years later when a second daughter, Eliza Nancy, arrived. He fathered a Mary in 1858, an Aeneas Frank in 1860 (replaced by another in 1862), and lost his wife when she was but thirty-five. He would quickly remarry, one Ann Cress[e]y, daughter of a carpenter from Templecombe, Somerset, and have yet another daughter, Celia (Cecilia Annie).

By this time, Mr. Dymott, installed with his family at 4 Hanover Place, was carving wood only part-time. He was a part of the all-male ensemble at Evans's famous Supper Rooms. Evans's wasn't often covered by the press, so I don't know when he began working there and when he ended, but the vocalists at that celebrated Covent Garden venue tended to be long-serving, and I see him in 1863, and again in 1868, as "second [i.e., low] bass" with Messrs. John Whitwell (baritone, later to join the Carte chorus), Barrett, Ball (tenor), Walton, J. Hogan (baritone), Smith, and Matt Cooper, intoning "The Old Church Bell" to the late-night chop-and-porter audience.

But, between times, Dymott had also been seen further afield. In 1867, he appeared as a soloist ("Down among the Dead Men") at both the Canterbury Hall—with Emily Soldene and Alfie St. Albyn, no less—and at the Oxford, where he took the bass solo in a selection from *The Ruins of Athens*. I suspect there were many, many more such unrecorded occasions. In 1871, Dymott (with Hogan) was on the program at Store Street Rooms for the concert of George Allen of the Philharmonic Music Hall, and in 1877, he went on the musical stage. The occasion was the amateurish production of a Macbethish "opera" titled *Biorn*. Its cast was as unusual as its text, and our Aeneas was featured alongside the author's wife and an indifferent Italian baritone, who played the Norwegian thane and his bloody wife. Future Savoyard Gerard Coventry and the young Giulia Warwick were part of the wreckage, along with a bunch of (probably phony) Signors.

Giulia, as we know, went on to play in *The Sorcerer*. I wonder if Aeneas was in that chorus; I think, probably, he was. He was nearly fifty, and in the next census he would describe himself as "woodcarver and chorus singer." But, for HMS *Pinafore*, a real bass voice was needed for the bottom line in the memorable glee "A British Tar," and so our hero got the part that would make us, 150 years later, remember him and write about him. So, please, commentators, now you know that Mr. Dymott did not come from nowhere. By the time of *Pinafore*, he'd been known as a low bass singer in the Covent Garden area for at least fifteen years.

Dymott's future was not so happy. He was one of the losers in the split that occurred between Carte, Gilbert, and Sullivan, and their backers. The split is one of the most-written-about elements of Cartesian history, so I will cover it only briefly. Carte had tied up the production rights for HMS *Pinafore* rather cleverly. His investor-directors had already shown themselves friable and unadventurous, and—in the early days of the run of the new show, before its momentum gathered—had several times wanted to pull the plug. When it became a huge success, of course, they wanted to be as "in" as possible, but their interest in the show and the production had a contractual stop-date to it. When that date was reached, with sails a'flying, they, unbelievably, invaded the theater with some hired roughs midshow, to carry off "their" scenery and props. Apparently, it was Little Buttercup (yay! Harriet!) who led the action to repel these intrusive boarders, and the foolish "pirates" were set to flight and into court. The result was that the directors mounted a rival production across town, while Carte, Sullivan, and Gilbert retained the Opera Comique production. In spite of some fine casting, the rival version sank, while the Carte production ran on, as the original Comedy Opera Company sank into oblivion and the D'Oyly Carte Opera Company of the future decades rose into being.

When the split happened, Dymott chose to leave the Opera Comique and go with the moneymen to the Imperial and the Olympic productions of *Pinafore*. If he were looking for security, he backed the wrong team. But it didn't really matter. He played in *Pinafore*, in the succeeding *Marigold*, filled in his 1881 census papers, and, weeks later, died at the age of fifty-one.

All Aboard the HMS *Pinafore*

During the long run of HMS *Pinafore* at the Opera Comique, there were, naturally, folk who temporarily or subsequently played the by then celebrated roles. George Temple and Frank Thornton were among the most remarkable. Temple (né James George Rexworthy, b. Bedminster, 1842; d. Clifton, 8 December 1899) took up Barrington's role, and would still be playing in G&S for Carte as late as 1896.

Thornton (né Frank Thornton Tubbs, b. London, 16 May 1845; d. London, 18 December 1918), who had been in the chorus of *The Sorcerer*, as Grossmith's understudy, afterward played his roles on tour and was still with Carte in 1892. Rosina Brandram and Emily Cross, who took turns at Buttercup, and Lilian La Rue of whom we have already

25. George Temple as Samuel.

spoken, were among the replacement ladies, along with eight Josephines of more or less durability. The eight included Fanny Holland (b. 11 Ratcliff Highway, London, 14 September 1847; d. 45 Alum Chine Road, Bournemouth, 18 June 1931), a fine concert singer who specialized in the Jewel Song from *Faust*, was longtime soprano at St. George's Hall, and, in many ways, the prototype Gilbert and Sullivan heroine; pretty Alice Burville (b. 24 Nelson Street, Mile End Old Town, Stepney, 11 July 1856; d. The Convent, East Street, Littlehampton, 4 July 1944), who had been the little Duchess to the little Duke of Alice May for Carte; the beauteous Blanche Roosevelt ("the best thing about her singing was her looks"); the interesting Elinor Loveday (née Ellen Jane Hodgkinson, b. Ashton-in-Makerfield, Lancashire, 9 May 1850; d. Hampstead, 14 February 1927), wife of Henry Loveday, stage director to Henry Irving, and a sister-in-law to Annie Tremaine; and the once mysterious "Miss Duglas Gordon." Mysterious no longer—well, not wholly.

Miss Duglas Gordon (Josephine)

Sitting in my seaside retreat one recent wine-stained evening, I was able, joyously, to write, "Today, I have solved one of the biggest 'who was . . .' mysteries in the Gilbert and Sullivan canon." Yes, it really was as big a mystery as Fred Clifton, and it's been puzzling me and others for many decades, just as Fred did. Who exactly *was* that little lady who scored so wonderfully, all round Britain, right at the beginning of the era of Cartesian musico-theatrical domination, as Aline and Josephine? Who was Miss Duglas Gordon? Well, now, finally, I know.

Obviously, the lady wasn't any kind of a Duglas Gordon; the moniker was just another of those pseudoaristocratic stage names so popular at the time. Lord Duglas Gordon was a well-known inhabitant of Burke's peerage. The lady's birth name was Ellen Louise Thomas, and she was born in Camden in 1858, the eldest of what seem to have been the six children of Edward Henry Thomas of the Wellington Iron and Coal Company, and his wife, Minnie, from Barnstaple. Mr. Thomas was the son of Moy Thomas, son of Moy Thomas, solicitor, so I think they were "comfortable." Edward and Minnie bred Ellen Louise, Edward Moy, Herbert Moy, Amy Blanche, Rhoda Mary, Martin Moy, Walter Bernard Moy, and Florence E.—you can see the up-to-date family in the 1871 census living at Clifton Villa, Acre Lane, Brixton—before Edward's death in 1878.

26. Nellie Duglas Gordon as Josephine.

It was at this time that daughter Nellie, with the lovely soprano voice, put on her new name and went on the stage, seemingly without any public preparation, playing Brigitte in Charlie Head's misguided attempt to bring back the Philharmonic Theatre's huge hit *Geneviève de Brabant*, under the aegis of Mr. D'Oyly Carte. Alice May, star of *The Sorcerer*, had the unenviable task of trying to "be" Emily Soldene, Alice Burville played the title-role, in the place of Dolly Dolaro, and nineteen-year-old Miss Gordon was cast in the third female role. Mr. Carte was evidently pleased and, from the Phil, little Miss Gordon was plunged straight into his first provincial touring company, singing Constance to the Aline of a confirmed star, Pauline Rita, in *The Sorcerer* and in *Trial by Jury*. When Madame Rita decided, pretty soon, to move on, Nellie was quite simply promoted to prima donna—and she remained thus. When HMS *Pinafore* set out for its first provincial tour, Nellie was outer England's first Josephine, winning nationwide notices of the ilk "[She] looks, acts and sings the part well-nigh perfectly."

Between *Pinafores*, Nellie visited Nottingham to play Maid Marian in Tom Charles's *Babes in the Wood* (featuring "I Know That My Love Loves Me") for the festive season. She gave her Josephine at the Standard Theatre ("a pleasing appearance on the stage and an excellent voice") and, finally, in early 1880, at the Opera Comique.

But now things get tricky. Nellie, amazingly, seems to be out of work. Had she offended the Carte club? Had enough for a bit? Was she out of work purposely? Pregnant? My next sighting of her is in the 1881 census, at 87 Ferndale Road, listed as an "actress, disengaged," along with Mama Minnie Thomas, Edward, Rhoda, Martin, and Walter; brother Herbert is just "visiting." But the curious thing is that Nellie is listed as Nellie Morgan, twenty-two, widow. Really? There is no sign of a marriage in the British records.

Well, Nellie reappears in Dublin in September 1881, at the Queen's Theatre, playing in dramas (with interpolated songs such as "Come Back to Erin") and burlesque ("left nothing to be desired in her singing"). She went on the road in *La Mascotte*, *Geneviève de Brabant*, and *La Fille de Madame Angot* (as Lange rather than Clairette) in a less-than-top-notch company, and ended up at the Liverpool Rotunda at Christmas playing Cinderella for eight weeks; 13 February 1883 was her Benefit. She and Constance Moxon (née Smith) gave the "Balcony Scene" and the Gens d'armes duet from *Geneviève*. And that is the last time I see Nellie.

In 1891, Minnie is still housing Martin ("stockbrokers clerk"), Walter, and Rhoda; in 1901, it is Walter ("hay merchant"), Amy ("actress"), and Florence ("engineer's clerk"). Edward got into advertising; Herbert became a kitchen engineer; Martin a "commission agent and share dealer"; Amy apparently married Mr. Chaplin; Walter and Rhoda (Mrs. Graddon), they all stay in view. But where did Nellie go? I've cracked the nut, but I can't get the kernel out. Help, somebody!

A Little Bit of Pi-ra-cee: HMS *Pinafore* in America

If HMS *Pinafore* was a hit of major proportions in England, it proved a sensation in America. Boston won the race to produce something under the celebrated title, with a mediocre cast, a female Ralph, Mr. W. Melbourne as Tom Bowlin, and someone named Little Gertrude as the Midshipmite. On the West Coast, Alice Oates produced her habitually approximate version with a definitely superior cast: the First Lord was the same James Gould Taylor who had played in *Thespis* at the Gaiety; the producer was Rackstraw; Bob Graham, the future Tony of *My Sweetheart*, was Bill; and, since Alice had pinched his part, the company's fine English tenor, Dick Beverley (né Edward Dickinson, b. Beverley, Yorks, 1838; d. Flushing, New York, September 1880) was interpolated as a character named Dick Trunk—singing what, I wonder. Maybe the real music—because Alice was liable to ladle in the odd pop song.

As productions of more but usually rather less accuracy proliferated around America, James Duff brought HMS *Pinafore* to New York's Standard Theatre. Tom Bowlin was still in the lineup, but Ralph was now played by a male, and the rest of the cast boasted some fine names: Tom Whiffen (b. Chatham, Kent, 1 June 1834; d. Hertford, 10 October 1897)—ex-of St. George's Chapel, Windsor, and the Gallery of Illustration—was a capital First Lord; his wife, née Marion Fanny Blanche Galton (b. Islington, 12 March 1845; d. Bedford County, Virginia, 26 November 1936), a splendid actress-contralto, was Buttercup; the role of Corcoran was taken by a tenor ("Fair Moon, to Thee-he I-yiy Siiiiing"). But the problem role was, again, Ralph. I have written a pretty comprehensive piece about the gentleman who played the role; it is titled "Ralph Wreckstraw, or A Tenor and His Troubles." Here it is.

Henri Laurent (Ralph Rackstraw)

Henri Laurent: it is a matter of decades since I first bumped into this fellow. I've written about him a bit a few times since, because slices of his story collide with not only that of Emily Soldene but that of the great dramatic soprano Rosa Csillag, with the tale of the Gilbert and Sullivan operas in America, and the history of the very special San Francisco Tivoli Opera House of the Kreling family. So, I thought: let's put the story of "America's Ralph Rackstraw" together as coherently as possible, for the sake of the Great Goddess Clio (muse of history), and the family historians on ancestry.com who have got his tale hilariously wrong and kill him off a quarter of a century early, at a time when he was still on the stage.

For yes, "Henri," the man who must have got a record number of "can't sing, can't act" notices in his life and career, worked steadily—or, more accurately, unsteadily—on the stage for a thirty-five years. How? Why? I have no idea. He was a tenor, which helps: a light and often, it seems, effortful tenor. He was tall, with a good figure and clearly some sort of physical charm, judging by the number of wives and "wives" he went through. Also, he didn't seem to mind for whom he worked or for how little time, and, when there was no work to be had, he mounted his own companies, which lasted anything from a few days to, if he were lucky, a month or two. Anyway, I'll tell the story as I've found it.

First of all, who actually was this "lanky tenor" who claimed sometimes to be French, occasionally English, and ultimately (and correctly) a naturalized American? Well, he was actually born in Brighton, Sussex, of an English father and an allegedly French-born mother. I know nothing about mother. The family historians modestly put "private" in the place where her name should be, so I imagine there's some irregularity in the tale. Anyway, his mother, Henrietta, appears in only one census, because at some stage, in the 1850s, the family relocated to Paris.

Henri's father was born, in Brighton, as John James Hayward Ghislain, on 19 August 1816, son of "surgeon" Alexander Ghislain (which sounds pretty Belgian to me) and his wife Anne (née Lloyd). Fast-forward: my next sighting of John is in 1841. He's in Brighton, with his wife, and producing their first child. So is he the John Hayward "Geshing" who was married the previous year in London? But to whom? The registers list three possibilities Elizabeth Hornsby, Jane Polkinghorne, and Sarah Todd; but she's supposed to be a Henrietta. More mystery.

There seem to have been about eight children born to the couple in the next decade or so, all surnamed "Gesling," all born in or around Brighton, and latterly at the Shakespeare Inn, Howard Place, West Hill, and an address in Montpelier Road. Both addresses were pubs, and father was a "licensed victualler." And in the 1851 census, the family's name was given as "Hayward." "Hayward" was the middle name of most of the children, too. More mystery.

In the 1850s, father had another career change. The family at some stage moved to Paris, where, in 1856, John James was working for

27. Henri Laurent . . . "Ralph Wreckstraw."

John Arthur, an English agent and wine merchant. He then set up as an independent "English Agency Office, wine merchant, general agent," at Faubourg Saint-Honoré 30. His employer dragged him to court, where he was fined twenty-five thousand francs for breach of contract and obliged to cease trading. Then, in 1858, he turns up as "clerk to the Rev Archer Thomas Gurney," the vicar of the official Parisian English Church in the rue d'Aguesseau. In 1862, he was appointed to raise money from British residents of Paris for the Albert Memorial.

But it was younger members of the family who made the splash. Reginald and Harry became sculling champions, and the Brighton press reported, in 1865, "several very valuable prizes, amounting to between 50 and 60 pounds, were carried off by the sons of Mr. Hayward Gesling, formerly a much-respected (really?) resident of Brighton." Reginald "of the Paris Rowing Club" indeed became, for a number of years, sculling champion of France, then president of the Cercle d'aviron. He, of course, had a day job, too. I see him referred to as "chaplain of the British

Embassy," but it appears he was, specifically, the funeral officer of the embassy, responsible for the repatriation of strayed Anglican corpses to the motherland. One of those bodies was that of Oscar Wilde. Later he would make a second appearance in the headlines when he was involved in a celebrated and complex lawsuit (Viditz vs. Gesling) concerning an inheritance from a maiden Irish lady. Reginald's younger brother, Rowland, later became his adjoint.

But Harry, as we shall see, was vowed to a very different kind of life. In 1868, Harry won the French junior sculls (ah! that physique again), and in the same year John Ghislain-Gesling died. By the 1871 census, Harry was back in London, staying in a hotel and described as an "agent"—for whom or what it is not said. But within months, the "agent" had got himself a job as a chorister with the Gaiety Theatre company, as one of those useful men that Hollingshead employed to play all the little bits and pieces and make up the vocal choruses. He (the physique?) played Achilles in *La Belle Hélène* on tour. During the 1872 summer, he went on tour with the Liverpool Prince of Wales Company in *Geneviève de Brabant*, playing the little part of the Hermit, and later one of the gens d'armes, and when he returned to the Gaiety tour he was promoted to the role of Grog in *La Grande-Duchesse*. The tour company appeared for a while in London, and Harry was cast to play *Lischen and Fritzchen*, as a forepiece, with Claliah Albertazzi, and the bit part of Count Screwem in the burlesque *Snae Fell*, at the Gaiety itself. But the understudy got his chance: Augusta Thomson, principal boy in the burlesque, went "off" and Harry stepped in to her breeches for the nonce.

Harry toured some more, played a bit part in *Guy Fawkes MP* at the Gaiety, and, on 16 February 1874, got married. Lizzie Wright (1850–1936) had been, for several years, one of the most appreciated British principal dancers around London. Emily Soldene recorded that she was "a brilliant dancer." Her real name was Elizabeth Macintyre, she hailed from Glasgow, and the marriage turned out to be a horrid mistake, but I will recount the scandals in their place!

Harry finished at the Gaiety, after three years' service, and joined up with Emily Soldene's company as an understudy, in which capacity he replaced Violet Granville as Charles Martel in *Geneviève de Brabant*. Emily's next date after London was New York, and Harry, as the second or third tenorino of her troupe, got to make the trip. He appeared as Martel, as Pomponnet in *La Fille de Madame Angot*, and as Landry in

Chilpéric on the left-hand side of the Atlantic, and when the rest of the company went home, he didn't. The rest of his career, and most of his life, would be spent in America.

The Soldene company and their shows had been decidedly successful, and others leaped to imitate them. One of these was the rather down-market Robinson Hall and, even though Harry had been only a very minor player with the Soldenes, he was cast, billed large, in the title-role in the Hall's production of *Chilpéric*. He lasted less than two weeks. But something like two months later, he was hired as leading tenor by America's touring comic-opera sweetheart, Mrs. Alice Oates. It was a fair company: Australian baritone John Howson, Charles H. Drew, Gus Hall, Annie Kemp Bowler, and, at least to start with, Henry's wife, Miss Lizzie Wright. Alice played a large repertoire of rather personally botched versions of the opéra-bouffe repertoire—*Giroflé-Girofla*, *La Fille de Madame Angot*, *Le Prés St. Gervais*, *La Grande-Duchesse*, *La Jolie parfumeuse*, *La Princesse de Trébizonde*, and even *Trial by Jury*—and Harry was the leading man in each and every one.

He was also, soon, rather obviously, leading man to pretty Alice in more than one way, and, on 4 December 1877, the merde hit the machine: "On December 4, in this city, the wife of Henri Laurent, first tenor of the Oates troupe, instituted proceedings for divorce, alleging grave improprieties with a prominent lady member of that troupe." This was the beginning of a longish period in which Harry featured more in the gossip columns than the music ones. He sued the *Cincinnati Times* for twenty thousand dollars; Alice had dismissed him because managers wouldn't book the troupe because of his immorality (what, asked the paper, advisedly, about *her* immorality?); and then he had sailed for Le Havre. How deliciously *scandaleux*!

In a few months, though, Harry was back, in what could have been the job of his career: James Duff was staging what would be New York's first sighting of a fairly rightish version of *HMS Pinafore*, and Harry Laurent would be the city's first Ralph Rackstraw. The show, and particularly Tom Whiffen as Sir Joseph, were immediate hits, and then the jiggery-pokery started. *HMS Pinafores*, or shows sailing under that title, went into production all over the place, while those that had got in on the ground floor started squabbling among themselves. Duff had, apparently, signed his Gotham cast—or Harry, anyway—for the eight weeks he counted on the piece running. Two weeks before the contract lapsed, Harry sniffed a better opportunity and a better deal up at the Fifth Avenue Theatre, so he gave notice.

At his last performance for Duff, Harry refused to go on for act 2 until his salary was paid. The manager had foreseen this, and had Alonzo Hatch standing by, but Harry—wearing the all-important costume—refused to leave until paid. Duff called the police, Harry spent the night in the cells, and then he sued Duff for false imprisonment . . . and lost. Anyway, Hatch stayed on at the Standard, Harry played night one at the Fifth Avenue and, on legal advice, stayed off on night two. The Josephine—Blanche Corelli—played Ralph. Then the courts ruled that Harry could play until everything was sorted out, as *Pinafores* began to flood the nation, and everything and anything to do with the show flooded the columns of the nation's newspapers. The *Chicago Tribune*, in its usual *National Enquirer* style of journalism, headlined "*Pinafore* Is Getting Stale" before inventing a tale about Harry hiding in a cupboard in Alice's room and a resulting fight with Edward Connell.

Harry put together his own company, allegedly with financial help from Alice, and "Henri Laurent's Fifth Avenue *HMS Pinafore* company" duly set out on the road, with Blanche Corelli as his leading lady. The press took violent sides, pro- and anti-Alice, published the usual amount of fiction, and then, for heaven's sake, Lizzie got in on the act waving a bundle of love letters. Alice accused her of blackmail (and it's pretty clear that Lizzie was after, and got, money), but both girls were already out of the picture. It was bye-bye Alice, bye-bye Lizzie; hello Blanche. "Mdlle. Corelli" was actually a German, *eigentlich* Eva Dorothea Hermann, the daughter of the magician Carl Hermann and the great Hungarian soprano Rosa Csillag (née Goldstein), and her story (see *Victorian Vocalists*) is as colorful as Harry's.

The couple's *Pinafore* company folded in Canada in July 1879, and they joined up with a troupe playing *Fatinitza*, *Giroflé-Girofla*, and an unfortunate piece by the young Gustav Kerker titled *Cadets*. The partisan press sneered, "The vivacious Oates will probably pour ashes on her head when she hears that the Laurent-Corelli party has come to grief in the bleak northwest."

But work was not lacking. The stage spectacular specialists the Kiralfy brothers had mounted a production titled *Enchantment* at Niblo's Garden. *Enchantment* featured two English vocalists, our versatile Charley Campbell and little Rose Lee, as some vocal relief to the piles of scenery and dances that were the raison d'être of the show. Now the piece was going on tour, and Harry and Blanche were hired for the singing roles. When summer came, they went to St. Louis and made three attempts at presenting their comic operas there, but they were saved from the wreckage when *Enchantment* was revived for a second run at Niblo's. After the Niblo's season, the couple set off for Boston to launch "Henry Laurent's Original Fifth Avenue Company" in *Pinafore, Trial by Jury, Olivette*, and so forth. Blanche had rewritten the libretto of *Olivette* so as to combine the roles of Valentin and Mérimac into one (Zeus knows what she had done to *Pinafore*), and the whole affair was desperately amateurish, but that didn't stop Harry, who had been greeted by his usual "he can neither act nor sing" notices, from launching a number-two company. At Newport, Rhode Island, the twenty-three members of the company each had a warrant for his arrest taken out, for wages unpaid. But they plodded on, around Massachusetts and environs, with the standard repertoire—*Billee Taylor, Olivette, Fatinitza, La Mascotte*—and intermittent announcements of new works.

They were in rehearsal for Albert Grisar's *Les Poupées de l'infante* (*Puppets*) in Boston when, on 14 September 1881, Lizzie was said to have been brought to bed with twin daughters; oddly, one is registered in New York, and one in Boston. Wow! How did she manage that? The press had once dubbed Harry "the Gander-Legged Tenor"; it seems that Lizzie was of the opinion that what was good for the gander was good for the goose! The family historians list these daughters (if there were, indeed, two) as being surnamed Laurent. Harry is named as the father in each registration, but I'll guarantee he had nothing to do with them. He and Lizzie hadn't been near each other for rather more than nine months. And Blanche and Harry had actually gone through a marriage ceremony in Boston on 12 June 1881. Anyway, Harry was likely flying somewhere over the moon: he had had a good notice! One Boston critic had said that he was "by far the most deserving of praise" of the artists in *Puppets*.

And on it wandered. Harry played the Duke in *Patience* for Rice; returned to the Boston Gaiety for *Pinafore, Patience,* and *The Pirates of Penzance*; and then ventured to New York for more *Pirates* ("in one or two sentimental moments [he] managed to be quite effective, but generally he so forces and strains what is left of a tenor voice [that was never of much account] that he becomes far from pleasant vocally in the better part of the score . . .") and *Billee Taylor* ("a bad Billee both in vocal and dramatic way"). All in all, Harry's acting was, these days, getting better notices than his singing. So, on he went. He appeared at Tony Pastor's as Pippo in *La Mascotte* and then as the Colonel in *Patience*; he undertook a tour with Catherine Lewis, took part in a disastrous local piece called *Uncle Sam*, at Chelsea, Massachusetts; and spent a season at the Spanish Fort, New Orleans, followed by another with the quickly folding Acme Company. In November 1884, he was still in New Orleans, playing *The Merry War* and *The Little Duke* under the banner of "Laurent's Ideal Comic Opera Co." "Mrs. Laurent" is listed as its choreographer; which Mrs. Laurent is *that*? Lizzie!?

The year 1885 brought more indifferent employment: Harry appeared with Fay Templeton at Memphis, and with Amy Gordon till she got a better job; and he undertook a tour with Teddy and Fred Solomon and Lillian Russell, which lasted only a few weeks. In 1886, he was booked for an imploding season at Minneapolis. An engagement for summer at St. Louis and the one-night stand circuit with "Yank" Newell followed, while, at the same time, Blanche's last try at a Blanche Corelli Opera Company collapsed in Baltimore. Blanche went home to Vienna, and . . . well, she's another story.

In 1887–88, Harry can be seen trying one more Rackstraw in the boondocks, and pushing his luck by hopelessly suing one more management (Emily Soldene! How very dare he!), before, finally, floating ashore in San Francisco, engaged for an interesting season at the Orpheum. Well, it was interesting on paper: the repertoire they played, before the management ran out of funds, included *The Old Guard*, *Amorita*, *The Queen's Lace Handkerchief*, *The Marquis of Rivoli*, *Boccaccio*, and *The Merry War*. They down-marketed to the Wigwam Theatre, but then Harry got lucky; Arthur Messmer was struggling with the tenor workload at the Tivoli, so Laurent was hired to supplement him. He made his first appearance as Gaston in *Donna Juanita* with Ethel Lynton, then as Grosvenor in *Patience*. When the Krelings presented grand opera instead of the comic variety, he and Messmer alternated Manrico and Faust, and he sang Arturo to Messmer's Edgardo and the Lucia of . . . don't ask! Harry appeared as Lionel in *Martha*, Jan in *The Beggar Student*, in some role in *A Night in Venice*, and in *La Fauvette du Temple* (*The Nightingale*) . . . and then, as usual, he fouled up. He sued the Kreling management for back salary, they countersued, and he got two weeks' wages, the boot, and a ticket to New York. In June 1889, I see that he was engaged at Herzberg's West Brighton Pavilion on Coney Island. He is not only performing but also stage directing.

Now, I have not been so naïve as to think that Harry had been living a monkish life since the seemingly indifferent-all-round wandering-off of Blanche. Well, he hadn't. He had allegedly married (?) again, and he had had a son. Well, I suppose it was his. Anyway, the young lady concerned was a soubrette soprano by the name of Julia Glover, said to have been born in 1870, and to have been married to him in 1886. To this one he, and his fading charms, would, at last, stick.

In 1890 Harry was hired, alongside no less a star than Giuseppe del Puente, for the Gustav Hinrichs's opera company, but he quit and instead meandered back to Boston (where his notices were often less unfavorable than elsewhere) to join what was billed as Colonel Foster's Boston Ideals. He was—ideally—cast as Saint-Angénor, the broken-down tenor, in *La Fauvette du Temple* ("[he] has apparently lost his voice but being a comedian of ability does not seem to need it in his part"), but the cast roster resembled in no way the quality of that of Miss Ober's original Boston Ideals, and the venture came to grief nastily in Louisville. Harry wandered on through the Able Opera Company, the Shackford Opera Company in *Said Pasha*, the Sargent Aborn Opera Company, and the *City Directory* company, and so it went on.

In 1894, Mr. Laurent actually played at New York's Casino Theater, in an English version of the hit German musical comedy *Der Corner Grocer aus der Avenue A*. Alas, New York was not ready for a genuine American musical comedy, and the piece folded in a month. But Harry was on the right track: he was now a comedian who sings a bit. As such, he joined Nellie McHenry's company, playing John Potipher in *The Bicycle Girl* (Julia was chorus), but allowed himself to be tempted back to comic opera in an attempt to run a Tivoli-type house in Chicago. When he played a summer season at Rock Island, Illinois, the local paper protested, loudly, at their theater being palmed off with such poor singing. Julia, now promoted to solo parts, had at least the virtue of freshness. Harry was clapped out.

Harry played in *The French Maid* on tour, in vaudeville, in Edward Rush's "naughty" *Sappho*, in potted operas, and in something called the Murray Lane Opera Company. Then, somehow, when it seemed he was all washed up, he got hired by the fashionable actor Richard Mansfield to play supporting roles in his company. For some three years, Harry appeared with Mansfield, playing François, the comedy servant, in *Beaucaire*, Artemidorus in *Julius Caesar*, Michael Nagoy in *Ivan the Terrible*, Scholorman in the English version of *Old Heidelberg*, and in *Beau Brummell*, *A Parisian Romance*, *Dr. Jekyll and Mr. Hyde*, and the like. And when his time with Mansfield finished, Harry joined Charles Hawtrey, playing Dr. Chapman in *A Message from Mars*. A new career, as a character actor, seemed to be blossoming for him, but it didn't happen.

My last sighting of sixty-year-old Harry, on stage, is with Hawtrey in an Actors' Fund Benefit in May 1905. He died at 3 Deans Road, Merstham, Surrey, on 4 January 1920.

Pinafore, Pinafive, Pinasix . . .

America got all sorts of *Pinafores* or sort-of-*Pinafores*: Edward Rice presented one where Buttercup was played by popular burlesque dame George K. Fortescue, with the grand comic opera contralto Rose Leighton—New York's original Plaintiff in *Trial by Jury*—as (for goodness' sake!) Hebe;

28. George K. Fortescue as an American travesty dame of a Little Buttercup.

Gorman's Philadelphia Church Choir gave one with Emma Howson reprising her Josephine alongside a lot of folk whose names mean nothing, even to me; the Germania Theatre gave it in German; there was a Pennsylvania Dutch edition, a Yiddish version, and a kiddie troupe one in which Bob Beckett sang "Nancy Lee," Bobstay played the concertina, and someone else sang "La Marseillaise"; while the Globe Theatre welcomed a racially-limited version by "the Colored Opera Co." And that is without counting the "burlesques," which featured Sullivan's score and dumbed-down and broadened versions of Gilbert's plot and characters.

It was December 1879 before Carte, helpless in the face of all the thoroughly legal "piracy" going on, finally staged a "proper" *HMS Pinafore* in New York. Unfortunately, he too made a couple of awful casting errors: particularly unfortunately, among an otherwise fine cast, they were his tenor and his soprano. *HMS Pinafore* played only for a month, because Carte was here to fry other fritters, and the *Pinafore* dollars had already flown. But as they had flown, they had established *Pinafore* as a phenomenon . . . and the dollars would come.

I could write for a long, long time about *HMS Pinafore* and what it is and what it was, and what folk did with and to it . . . but this book is already getting too fat. Confidence: if I could have only *one* G&S opera, this would have to be it. I wonder why: my first *Pinafore* was an all-schoolgirl affair at Nelson College for Girls—I still remember Miss Marianne Jaray in breeches as Sir Joseph—and my nearly most (not very) recent was at Sadler's Wells, a colorless job which, I think, featured Nickolas Grace. I remember being particularly bored by the Josephine. And, then, hurrah! A dazzling production from Dublin, with Australian (again!) Fred Evans as a *désopilant* J. P., Paul Bentley as an hilarious Corcoran, Michelle Todd a deliciously sweet-singing Josephine, and marvelous staging by Mavis Ascot . . . Ahhhh, but that was a few decades ago. Nowadays, I read it, I play it, I sing it (not very well, at seventy-five . . . "Fair moo-oo-ntowoops"), or listen to it, think of Dublin, and I fall in love, all over again . . . just as folk have been doing for going on a century and a half.

5

The Pirates of Penzance, or The Slave of Duty

Melodramatic opera in two acts
Fifth Avenue Theater, New York, 31 December 1879

The main problem with having a major international success, in literature, the theater, in anything—apart from collecting coin that is due you, and preventing the piracy and plagiarism of your work—is coming up with an equally or almost as good work to follow it.

Well, Messrs. Gilbert and Sullivan, with amazing aplomb, did the second of those things, and Mr. Carte tried really hard to do the first. In an attempt to prevent the American theaters from plundering the profits from *The Pirates of Penzance*, as they had from *HMS Pinafore*, he arranged to produce it, first, in New York.

The new piece—a burlesque of melodrama, prematurely titled *The Bold Burglars*—was based on a merry conceit that Gilbert had used previously in his German Reed piece, *Our Island Home*: the accidental pirate. "When Frederic was a little lad," he was apprenticed to a seafaring career. Unfortunately, his nurse, Ruth, was a little hard of hearing, and took her orders to bind him "to a pilot" to be "a pirate." But now he is of age, released from his indentures, and ready to join the Cornish constabulary, sworn to wipe out his former brethren. And, to top that off, on day one of his freedom he has discovered Woman: Mabel Stanley, daughter of a major general—a naughty major general, too, with a chorusful of daughters, all seemingly the same age, who has told "a terrible story" to prevent the pirate band helping themselves to a conjugal soprano or a contralto apiece. Frederic will save them! But a dreadful discovery has been made: Frederic was born in leap year, on the 29th of February: he is still a pirate apprentice, for "he is a little boy of five." He is obliged, by Duty, to swap sides. But the police have a trump card: the name of Queen Victoria! And Ruth reveals that pirates "are all noblemen who have gone wrong." Once again, things are seldom what they seem, and all can end in the approved "parsonified" style.

The Pirates of Penzance had a slightly more difficult birth than had had *HMS Pinafore*. The authors and producer were in New York, but the management team, headed by Helen Lenoir, was in London. Material was sent back and forth across the Atlantic. The piece was, allegedly, subjected to additions, excisions, and alterations. "Signor Brocolini" (John Clark) related to the press, in later years, that he hadn't liked the original "Pirate King's Song," so another had been manufactured for him. Maybe. But all seems to have been pretty well in place by opening night. The review in *The Brooklyn Eagle* mentions, first "Hail Poetry," "the Chattering Chorus," the "Paradox" trio, the "almost ecclesiastical" "Ah, Leave Me Not," the "excruciating" Policeman's Chorus, the "burlesque romanza" and patter-song of General Stanley, and the "several airs" of the Sergeant of Police. Several? "Oh, Is There Not One Maiden Here," is noticed elsewhere, and Mabel's "fascinating waltz" is there in the first night notices. So, it seems any postpremiere alterations were in the detail, rather than in the substance.

The Pirates of Penzance might have been a pain to get on, but the result, when it opened at the Fifth Avenue Theatre, was stunning. The critic of the *New York World* regaled, "The text is excruciatingly funny . . . the subtle wit of the author of *Pinafore* and the true musical humor of the composer of that most popular of comic operas, have again been united successfully. . . . Compared with *Pinafore*, it is infinitely superior in plot, language and humor, while musically there can be no comparison, the airs and choruses of last year's wonderful success being mere trifles. . . . The humour of the music lies, in fact, in its serious imitation of grand opera, the outrageous perversions of common sense being treated with the [ut]most solemnity." Of course, much of what America had seen as *HMS Pinafore* had been mightily approximate, but this gentleman had got the message, and he was one of the many so to enthuse. *The Pirates of Penzance* did not, however, settle in for a statistically long run at the Fifth Avenue. It was time for Carte to tie up those financial ends in the rest of America, and therein lay a world of trouble. Not that the production hadn't given the three partners enough trouble already. As usual, it was those actors and singers. Carte, Gilbert, and Sullivan had shown a real adroitness in casting "outside the square"—most of the time. This time was, mostly, no exception.

Several of the leading men would become prominent figures on the musical stage: former music hall "Dancing Quaker," John Handford Ryley (né John Riley, b. 12 Cooper's Terrace, Camden Town, 11 September 1841; d. 216 Portdown Road, London 28 July 1922) would become, in a vast career, America's outstanding G&S comic player; Signor Brocolini [né John Clark b. Cork, 26 May (?) 1842; d. Brooklyn, 7 June 1906) would be a baritonic feature of the American theater for decades; and John Furneaux Cook (b. London, 1839; d. West Kensington, 10 January, 1903), a scion of a well-known British operatic family, had a long and

29. An Irish King Hildebrand: John Brocolini né Clark.

successful career as a basso character man until blindness struck him. Of the ladies, the *Pinafore* girls, Misses Bond and Brandram, were started on their long lease of Cartedom. And then there was the memorable Alice Barnett . . . to whom we will come at her greatest moment.

But the mistakes came in the usual places: the society amateur tenor and, oh dear, the third-rate last-minute prima donna. Oh, yes, she was stunning-looking, but oyyy!!!! I suffered, in my time as a musical casting director, from authors and directors casting roles, as the theatrical term goes, "by their cock." It drove me mad. I don't know which of our boys was responsible for this glamorous disaster—Gilbert has been blamed, but I suspect sexy Sullivan—anyway, whichever it was: idiot!

Blanche Roosevelt (Mabel)

Theatrical mythology has been curiously and undeservedly kind to some folk. Blanche Tucker (b. Sandusky, Ohio, 2 October 1853; d. 25 Montague Street, London, 10 September 1898) went from failure to failure as a performer—and from photographer to photographer as a beauty.

She should have stuck to the latter. Miss Tucker—otherwise known as Miss Roosevelt, Madame Rosavella, Madame Macchetta, and as Countess or Marchesa Allegri—was a decidedly striking woman. And that was, in truth, largely the trouble; as one writer quipped, "the best thing about her singing was her looks." The "exceedingly fair American with magnificent red hair," as Frank Harris described her, was time and again given opportunities beyond her vocal capabilities because of her physical appearance. And the results were just what might have been expected.

Blanche Tucker was the eldest of the three daughters of William H. Tucker, a Virginian lawyer and politician who, in the 1850s, made his home in La Crosse, Wisconsin; he was later elected to the US senate, as a representative for his adopted state. Her mother was Elizabeth Letitia Roosevelt, known as Lizzie, a daughter of Nelson Roosevelt, "one of the New York Roosevelts." Blanche preferred, for some reason, usually, to say that she was born in Chicago ("and lived through the fire"). And, usually, she gave a date something like five years after the actual date of her birth. But truth and the published history of Blanche Tucker very often don't go hand in hand. Not even her red hair—which was dyed. For when, in 1873, Blanche took out her first passport, in order to go to Europe to study, she admitted to being nineteen years old, 5 feet 4 1/2 inches tall, and blonde. The mythmaking hadn't begun yet.

30. Blanche Roosevelt: "The best thing about her singing was her looks."

Nineteen-year-old Blanche Tucker left America for Paris in 1873. She later said she was sixteen and went as musical correspondent for the *Chicago Times*. A local paper reported at the time "Miss Blanche Tucker of Chicago, a young amateur vocalist, has arrived in Paris bearing warm letters of introduction from Pauline Lucca to Madame Viardot Garcia who is to have entire charge of Miss Tucker's musical education." Apparently, Madame Viardot was not in charge for very long, for Miss Tucker is next heard of in Italy, a pupil of Antonio Trivulzi, where she is said to have appeared in concert in Milan, while writing copy for the *Chicago Times*. Somewhere along the way, the fair young American came to the eye and/or the ear of Mr. Ernest Gye of London's Covent Garden Opera, and the said Mr. Gye engaged her for his 1876 season. Blanche said the engagement was for eight years; it ended up being less than eight performances.

Blanche made her operatic debut on 15 April 1876, as Madame Rosavella, singing Violetta in *La Traviata*. "She is extremely good looking," remarked the review the next day. "Avant tout une beauté," echoed the French press. That was not enough for Mr. Gye, who dropped her from the Covent Garden bills after three performances. Blanche worked out her engagement, instead, with one more Violetta at the Alexandra Palace (15 May 1876), at the parallel Floral Hall concerts, and, later in the year, in the theater's promenade concerts. She later promulgated the vain canard that she was "the first American to sing Italian opera" at Covent Garden. However, Adelina Patti, Canadian-American Emma Albani, and New York's Zare Thalberg had all been on the Garden bills in 1875, and even Emma Abbott would sing later in this season.

During 1877, Blanche was again seen in concert in London, before heading out on a tour in Holland and Belgium, and ending up in Italy, where, toward the end of the year, she became the wife of one Agosto Macchetta, later to be titled Marchese d'Allegri. Madame Macchetta, Countess d'Allegri, was, of course, "socially interesting," and the press duly gobbled up the bits of "information" concerning her that were liberally flung its way. She was reported as performing at, or more often "going to perform at" the Vienna Hofoper as Filina in *Mignon*, in *Faust* at Versailles, or in Rossini's *Otello* somewhere or other. Maybe, but I think not. Certainly, she was announced by Jules Brasseur of the Paris Théâtre des Nouveautés to appear as Lydia, in the Paris production of Franz von Suppé's *Fatinitza*. But she didn't. She was replaced, for incompetence and unprofessionalism, before opening, and of course she sued noisily. Brasseur went to court and said that her French accent was lousy and that she kept skipping rehearsals, but, predictably, he lost four thousand francs all the same.

Following the *Fatinitza* incident, Madame Macchetta left Paris and—amid paragraphs declaring she would be starring in her own productions of *La Traviata* and *Otello*—crossed to London, where she encountered another susceptible (male) theatrical writer. In double-quick time, "Miss Blanche Roosevelt" had become the latest Josephine in *HMS Pinafore* at the Opera Comique. The consensus was that she was "a new and attractive representative . . . very young . . . has much to learn . . . manifest talent and promises well . . . when she has time to become familiar with the character, and the requirements of the stage . . . grace and sweetness." Mr. Sullivan came in to conduct for the occasion. Miss Roosevelt played three weeks, and that should have been it. But . . .

Helene Crosmond, whom the team had hoped would play Mabel, ultimately put herself financially out of their court, and the triumvirate turned, in extremis, to Blanche. A few weeks later—with their American prima donna and an otherwise British company in tow—they arrived in

New York. They opened at the Fifth Avenue Theater on 1 December 1879 with HMS *Pinafore*, with Blanche again playing Josephine, alongside Hugh Talbot and J. H. Ryley. The local press was not impressed: "[She has] a small soprano voice of limited register in which there is much of amateurish indecision and she was decidedly disappointing in a vocal way. She has a very handsome presence, however, and tried to act, although with little success." But, when *The Pirates of Penzance* opened on 31 December, it was Miss Roosevelt who was Mabel.

Messrs. Gilbert, Sullivan, and Carte did not persevere long with their association with the "weakest member of the company"; a Brooklyn chorine stepped in as Mabel, in the first weeks! But another light opera producer, their American ally John McCaull, took their place and put up the backing for what was dubbed the "Blanche Roosevelt English Opera Company." The company launched a Broadway version of Alfred Cellier's successful British comic opera *The Sultan of Mocha* (14 September 1880), which failed in thirteen nights, and subsequently, in Boston, his new *The Masque of Pandora* (10 January 1881). Cellier's *Nell Gwynne*, with Miss Roosevelt in the title-role, was also announced. Amateurish and underprepared, the whole affair came quickly apart, and Miss Roosevelt's retirement from the stage was announced. In fact, she was not yet quite finished.

In 1881, Blanche appeared in New York in the odd concert and a regular number of newsworthy carriage accidents (she had previously made the papers as having had a hotel ceiling collapse on her while in bed), and, ultimately, she was picked up by Moritz Strakosch for his touring opera company. She opened as Marguerite in *Faust* at the French Opera House in New Orleans ("a splendid looking woman . . ."), and was promptly replaced by the French soprano Maria Leslino. She even returned to Broadway in a repeat of her *Pirates of Penzance* role, but the reaction was the same: "A beautiful girl, somewhat uncouth in her gestures, with a well-taught, but bodiless, voice which gives promise of effect but, alas, breaks the promise to the ear."

And so, after a career of pretty undiluted failure, Blanche Roosevelt bowed out, and Madame Macchetta returned—as an author. The career of Madame Macchetta, authoress and *journaliste*, however, was doomed to last not very much longer than that of Bianca Rosavella, vocalist. The sometime Blanche Tucker died in London in 1898. Her death registration said she was forty-two years of age. Her gravestone apparently makes her thirty-eight. She was, in fact, a little less than a month short of her forty-fifth birthday. Before her affairs could be settled, a creditor attached her estate for a debt of 107 pounds. The Marchese d'Allegri, whom she seems to have shed, said he wanted nothing. But the creditor didn't get his money. Blanche, so it eventuated, had nothing to her name but a few clothes and three trunks containing the manuscripts to her books. And no one wanted those.

Hugh Talbot (Frederic)

Blanche mightn't have caused too many problems before opening night, but her tenor did.

A middle-aged San Francisco Italian singing teacher died in Stockton's Detention Hospital on the last day of October 1899, and the news made the national and even the international press. "The famous tenor . . . once well-known as an operatic tenor in the companies of Adelina Patti and others," rattled on the obituaries, without getting too precisely factual. "Signor Ugo Talbo" had nurtured his myth well. He wasn't, of course, Italian. And, truthfully, he'd only intermittently pretended to be. "Famous" he had never been—not even for five minutes.

Hugh Brennan was born at Portobello Barracks, near Dublin, on 15 October 1844, the son of Edward Brennan and his wife Margaret. He is said to have been a youthful choirboy. In the 1861 census, he is described as a lawyer's clerk. It was while he clerked that he began his career as an amateur tenor. My first sighting of him as such is in January 1868, when he turns up in a performance of Barnett's *The Ancient Mariner*, given at the Royal Institute of British Architects. Later, he is referred to as "one of the Moray Minstrels." Ah, the Moray Minstrels; the cradle of Sullivan's *Cox and Box*.

By the time of my next sighting, Mr. Hugh Brennan is gone for good: he has disappeared into the northern part of Italy and metamorphosed into Signor Ugo Talbo. It is September 1872 and he is singing the Duke in *Rigoletto* at Treviglio. He is nebulously mentioned, also, as having appeared at Livorno in *Faust*, which seems to have been in 1871, as well as Alvaro in *La Forza del destino*. Later the same year, someone inserted a little paragraph in the press that was duly picked up by a bundle of those journals of the world with nothing better to fill their columns: "Milan is in ecstasies over the 'beautiful and robust voice' of a new tenor, Ugo Talbo." Some papers clearly took the piece at face value, but the *Era* was having none of it: "In London amateur circles he used to be plain Hugh Brennan," it sniffed. The *Musical World* was kinder with its description of "the former popular amateur tenor of the fashionable Moray Minstrels."

Later Ugo would claim to have sung all round Europe, alongside just about any star soprano you care to pick, during the mid-seventies. Really? I spot him in late 1873 and early 1874 doing a run of operas at Nice, where he sang *Rigoletto* inter alia alongside the Borghi-Mamos, mother and daughter, and back there again in 1875 in concert ("Une charmante voix de ténor, son succès a été complet"), but that's all. A fellow singer who later worked with him on a number of occasions commented that Talbo had "sung in Italian opera in Europe and one season at Her Majesty's Opera, London." Nebulous. And if he was a primo tenore in Europe between 1872 and 1876, why was it never reported in the music journals? Give or take a *Rigoletto* at Treviglio. In 1877, however, Ugo Talbo drew the prize that every British tenor sought: a contract as a principal tenor at Her Majesty's Theatre with Mapleson's Italian Opera. I imagine, from what followed, that it was a typical five-year contract, even though it fizzled out well before five years was up.

The 1877 Italian opera season at Her Majesty's opened on 28 April, and on 4 June, Ugo Talbo was put up as the Duke in *Rigoletto*. The new Irish tenor shared the limelight with Canadian Alwina Valleria (Gilda), and he apparently did all right. The *Era* dubbed him "a new tenor of considerable merit" and continued, "Signor Talbo may be congratulated upon the possession of no ordinary qualifications for the post of first tenor. He has an excellent voice, of good compass, and sympathetic in quality. It is brilliant and effective especially in the upper portion and what is to be mentioned with satisfaction is that Signor Talbo does not indulge in the vibrato which so distresses the ear of the auditor and wears out the voice of the artiste. Signor Talbo has, besides, a good stage presence and his acting is characterised by earnestness. Altogether the new tenor made a decidedly satisfactory debut." Not all were so sure: "Signor Talbo has much to learn, and can only be regarded, at present, as a first-class amateur." It doesn't sound as if he had been running around Europe as primo tenore to the likes of Adelina Patti, does it?

A few days after Hugh's debut, impresario Mapleson rolled out the tenorial big guns of the season: Theodor Wachtel, Enrico Tamberlik, et alia. But then, on 13 July, Ugo Talbo was given a crack at the title-role of *Faust* to the Marguerite of Christine Nilsson. After Nilsson, came another great prima donna for Ugo's scalp belt: Etelka Gerster arrived and succeeded to the role of Gilda and, on 24 July, Signor Talbo appeared for one night as Mantua, alongside her and the splendid Rigoletto of del Puente. And that was it. Three *Rigolettos*, three *Fausts*, and one act of *Rigoletto* at the Crystal Palace (21 July) on the occasion of Mapleson's Benefit. The *Musical Times*, having encouraged his *Rigoletto* ("a really good tenor voice, and a very fair stage presence, the 'high C' being as usual the passport to the favour of a large portion of the audience"), summarized at the season's end, "Signor Talbo must be mentioned as a vocalist who has gradually worn out the welcome accorded to him on his debut." But Ugo continued his onward soar, and in August he went on a two-month concert tour in Denmark, Sweden, and Norway with Zélie Trebelli, Conrad Behrens, and Alwina Valleria.

When the Mapleson company—without its international stars—went out on tour, Signor Talbo was not, however, included in the team. But he did play one performance. While the team was in Dublin, the tenor took a night off. *Martha* was due to be played and it appears the other tenors were unable to cover it. Signor Talbo was summoned, and the hometown critic cheered for Mr. Brennan on his "first appearance in his native country."

When the company returned to Her Majesty's Theatre, there was still no Signor Talbo to be seen, but on Boxing Day Mapleson mounted a season of English opera, played by a group of singers most of whom could not, normally, have aspired to the heights of a Mapleson company. George Perren was the most consequent of the tenor team, and Rose Hersee, Tillie Bauermeister, and Helene Crosmond headed the ladies. The feature of this "short winter season" was the production of an English version of Friedrich von Flotow's *L'Ombre*, otherwise known as *The Phantom* (12 January 1878). Miss Bauermeister (Vespina) and Mr. Talbo as Fabrizio were the soprano and tenor. The tenor was well enough liked, and the *Era* volunteered, "Mr. Talbo, the young English tenor who was recently a member of Mr. Mapleson's Italian company, appeared with considerable success as the hero. When he has made himself completely familiar with the opera he will be a very satisfactory representative of the character." Hmm; didn't know his part? When the season at Her Majesty's was done, and the company went back on the road, Ugo was given a crack at the part of Carlo in *Linda di Chamonix*. Manchester nodded, "A tenor new to us acquitted himself well."

The prospectus for Mapleson's 1878 town season included Signor Talbo among the tenors of the company, but it seems as if he appeared, on stage, only at the Crystal Palace (20 July) for Mapleson's Benefit, playing Don Ottavio in *Don Giovanni* alongside Valleria, Trebelli, Crosmond, and del Puente. And that *Don Giovanni* was Signor Talbo's last performance under his Mapleson contract. Over the next twelve months, I have spotted him singing in the odd concert, but otherwise it appears that he sat around—like so many of Mapleson's long-term-contract-but no-more-needed players—doing nothing, until he was released or loaned out.

When our tenor turned up again, he had gone back to being "Hugh Talbot." He had been released or loaned out by Mapleson to Mr. R D'Oyly Carte to create the principal tenor role in *The Pirates of Penzance* in New York. It appears that he owed his new job to his *Faust* partner, Helene Crosmond, who had been offered the role of Mabel. She didn't accept, but, so a kind of interoffice memo from the Opera Comique tells us, "she recommended a tenor, Hugh Talbot, who sang under the name of Talbo. He wants to go and would be cheap. I know of no one. Power or anyone like that w[oul]d not be listened to in New York. Helene Crosmond says that Talbo is the best Faust she has ever played with." So he wanted to go, did he? I wonder why. Anyway, thanks a heap, Helene. When the company opened with *HMS Pinafore*, *The Clipper* criticized, "Mr. Talbot's singing as Ralph was quite unsatisfactory—his voice is a small tenor, not without sweetness, but of so limited a range that he is unable to cope with the upper notes of his score." This of a man who had been encored as Mantua at Her Majesty's Theatre?

As the team worked to get *The Pirates of Penzance* on to the stage, they encountered a few hiccoughs, no little thanks to Mr. Talbot. John Brocolini, who played the Pirate King, recounted many years later in an interview:

> He was [good] so far as his singing went, but he was an indifferent actor and as for his committing the lines of his part to memory, it seemed to be an impossibility. It came to the day before the performance of *The Pirates* at the Fifth Avenue Theater, New York. The other principals had been "letter perfect" in their dialogue for a week, and had discarded their manuscript parts days before, but Talbo still clung to his and had to refer to it in nearly every speech. We all began to feel anxious as to the result, and Gilbert, who had evidently been doing his best to control his temper, could stand it no

longer. Talbo stopped in a speech and then consulted his manuscript. Gilbert got up from the table at which he was sitting, conducting the rehearsal. "Mr. Talbot"—he never called him Talbo—"are you ever going to know your lines?" "I hope so Mr. Gilbert but this is new business for me and I suppose I am rather slow at it." "We are to play this opera tomorrow night and you know no more of your lines than you did on the first day you got them."

Talbo was a quick-tempered Irishman, and Gilbert's brusque manner irritated him. He looked up and replied with a dangerous flash in his eye. "Suppose we go on with the rehearsal, Mr. Gilbert, and we can talk it over later." The rehearsal was resumed but, in a few minutes, the same trouble with Talbo occurred again, and as he stopped to read his lines from the manuscript Gilbert's patience gave way. Throwing his hands up over his head he exclaimed: "Great heavens, when God made a tenor he spoiled a man!"

Talbo threw down his manuscript and made a rush at Gilbert with his fists clenched and in a towering state of anger and with threats that he would smash his Scotch head in. The women shrieked and ran to the back of the stage, but the men jumped in between the maddened tenor and the author of the libretto, who stood quietly looking down at his antagonist with an immovable countenance. Several of us got Talbo away at last and with an apology to the women for his display of temper, he turned and calling out to Gilbert, "You can get another tenor to sing your opera," left the theater and went home.

They were obliged to cozen him back or postpone the production, and, in the end, Brocolini and Ryley learned his lines and eased him through the first night. But he did not go down well. A seemingly measured review in the *Clipper*, which was devoted, naturally, more to the new work than the players, found everyone except the tenor and the soprano "deserving of praise" and shook its head "Mr. Talbot impresses one most unfavourably as to his capabilities either as an actor or a singer." The *New York Dramatic Mirror* let loose with pure abuse, accusing him of "effeminate bearing and [a] simpering manner that no doubt would be charming in a young miss straight from the confines of a select boarding school, but on the stage they are loathsome and disgusting" and describing him as possessing a "weak, uncertain voice of nasal quality and limited volume" as well as of not knowing his lines. A couple of weeks later, the Brooklyn press commented "it is rather singular . . . that after so many performances he should have tripped in his lines."

Gilbert and Sullivan history says that Talbot was sacked from the *Pirates of Penzance* company after arguments with Gilbert and/or Carte. But although this was certainly envisaged—and a letter written by Sullivan soon after opening night confirms already that "we shall have to get rid of him"—it wasn't yet true. He did, however, quit the Fifth Avenue Theatre, as he was deployed to the B company, introducing the piece to Philadelphia, and then to John Stetson's company, which was presenting the Boston premiere, with the whole original Broadway cast of principals. *The Mirror* nodded, "Although a little awkward [he] worked into the music and business with considerable cleverness. His voice is not very strong, but it is consistent with itself and sufficient for the general demands upon it here made."

Soon after, Talbot was advertising himself as a "primo tenore in English opera," and that he "will rejoin Mapleson's Opera Company in January 1881 . . . in the interval he will accept engagements in English opera, oratorios, concerts . . ." Talbot didn't rejoin Mapleson. In fact, he never again returned to Britain. But he did return to the opera, to give at least a handful of the advertised fifty-two roles in his repertoire. His first engagement was as principal tenor with a little troupe organized by the baritone Giovanni Tagliapietra and featuring the young Marie Litta as its lead soprano. Columbus, Ohio, credited him with "a clear, pleasing voice" in *Il Trovatore*, *Faust*, and *Martha*. But elsewhere the press reported, "The people of Memphis did not like Ugo Talbo's singing, but they hold on to his private baggage with a fond attachment." Tagliapietra's company ground to a halt in New Orleans in December, just in time for Talbot to head back to Boston and Blanche Roosevelt.

Miss Roosevelt had spent some of her time, during their last Boston date, chatting up the aged poet Longfellow. As a result, she was producing an operatic version of his *The Masque of Pandora* with music by the Carte conductor, Alfred Cellier. Blanche, of course, played Pandora, and Hugh Talbot was Epimetheus. He was condemned as "almost as lifeless as he was as Frederic."

However, if Mapleson didn't need Signor Talbo, others did. Moritz Strakosch and Clarence Hess had been touring an English opera company around the United States with some success and more quarrels. It had come to tenor versus tenor fisticuffs, and the loss of one tenor. Ugo Talbo and his "52-opera repertoire" were hired as a replacement. He got to give his Faust and Mefistofele ("passable . . . a robust tenor but very stagey") and maybe one or two more roles for a few weeks, before the company faltered at Akron. Strakosch did a hasty up-class of his team, before the important date in Philadelphia, replacing Signor Talbo with Italo Campanini and Pasqualino Brignoli.

In August of 1881, Signor Talbo headed west to San Francisco to join another opera company, under the direction of Inez Fabbri, which was announcing the first Californian production of *Carmen* in English. A certain Fiorenza d'Arona (née Sarah Elizabeth Thompson) was to be the Carmen, and Signor Ugo Talbo would be Don José. There was "a large and fashionable audience" for the premiere ("Signor Talbo . . . a clear strong voice which he used with excellent effect but his acting was scarcely up to standard"), but for the second performance so few customers turned up that Inez canceled the performance. The "season" was soon over. But the Fabbri engagement turned out to be a good thing, because Signor Ugo Talbo stayed for the rest of his life in California. He gave concerts from time to time, and it appears that he was well liked. The *Chronicle* reported, "His full, sympathetic tenor is beginning to ring through our social circles and he is fast acquiring a pleasant popularity." The "social circles" proved decidedly useful allies, for, in the years that followed, Talbot established himself as a fashionable West Coast singing teacher.

When Talbot died, the American press, coast to coast, wrote, "He was a noted singer in England thirty years ago and has prominent relatives there. He was once an officer in the English army"; and "a celebrated tenor and leading man for Patti. He was well-connected in England." Well connected? Elizabeth was a milliner, Anne a draper's saleswoman, Sarah a schoolmistress, and Richard a teacher.

Taking the *Pirates* Back Home

Getting *The Pirates of Penzance* profitably established in America proved a Cartesian cauchemar. Everyone wanted to see the new show, and Carte and his company couldn't be everywhere. Brooklyn, Boston . . . fair enough . . . but Carte touring companies couldn't be concocted quickly enough to take the new hit to other regions. In the end, it didn't matter, give or take a few hundred thousand dollars in lost royalties, because *The Pirates of Penzance* would eventually establish itself, with all the vigor of HMS *Pinafore*, until, in the twenty-first century, it is now one of the most oft-played operas of the G&S canon, all around America.

Meanwhile, Britishers watched and waited—and very agreeably, too, because HMS *Pinafore* still had her flags aloft at the Opera Comique. There'd be time enough to play the ace of diamonds when the ace of hearts had finished trumping the town. *Pirates* had been copyrighted for Britain by a soi-disant production staged, almost simultaneously to the US opening, by members of Carte's touring *Pinafore* company. Text and music were of the most approximate, and the forty-five people who watched the "staged reading" had no idea what it all was, but they were not wholly being short-changed, because the cast for the occasion was a top-notch one. The Mabel, Emilie Petrelli (née Emily Mary Jane Peters, b. 12 Upper Wellington Street, Covent Garden, 30 September 1859; d. 17A Derwent Road, Anerley, Kent, 23 January 1925) would go on to take over the role in London, and could have become the Savoy's resident soprano had she not turned down the title-role of *Patience* as being a "soubrette part." Tenor Llewellyn Cadwaladr (b. Ruabon, 1857; d. London, 7 February 1909) had a fine career on both sides of the world; contralto Fanny Harrison (née Frances Harris, Mrs. Isaac Cohen, b. Westminster, 1838; d. 1 Grosvenor Place, Margate, 13 February 1909) played comic opera—much of it G&S—for a decade, while bringing up a theatrical dynasty; comedian Richard Mansfield would remake himself as a highly fashionable actor in America; Fred Billington (b. Lockwood, 1 July 1854; d. London, 2 November 1917) was to become a four-decade Savoyard; John Le Hay (né John Mackway Healy, b. Hackney, 25 March 1854; d. London, 2 November 1926) was long a successful comic opera player, both with Carte and others; and "Fred Federici" would later play the Mikado (where he'll be given his due). It was a provincial cast largely worthy of any city.

But the Opera Comique had its "A" team, and several of the folk there playing in HMS *Pinafore* would walk straight into roles in its successor. The most important, George Grossmith and Richard Temple, were to become major vertebrae in the Savoy Theatre team, remaining with the Carte company through many years and many of Gilbert and Sullivan's operas. Grossmith, of course, had been on the team since *The Sorcerer* and he would remain so for a dozen years, creating most of the famous comic roles of the Savoy repertoire.

George Grossmith (Major General Stanley)

George Grossmith (originally billed as "junior"; b. London, 9 December 1847; d. Folkestone, 1 March 1912) began performing in his early twenties, like his father, as a solo entertainer at the piano. He made his first regular professional appearances—while keeping up his day job as a court reporter and shorthand writer—at the Polytechnic Hall with such pieces as *Human Oddities*, *The Yellow Dwarf*, *The Silver Wedding*, *The Bunkum Penny Readings*, and *Theatricals at Thespis Lodge*, and subsequently on the road, sometimes in tandem with his father or, occasionally, with the Howard Pauls, and performing *Jottings from the Jetty*, *Mrs. Mayfair*

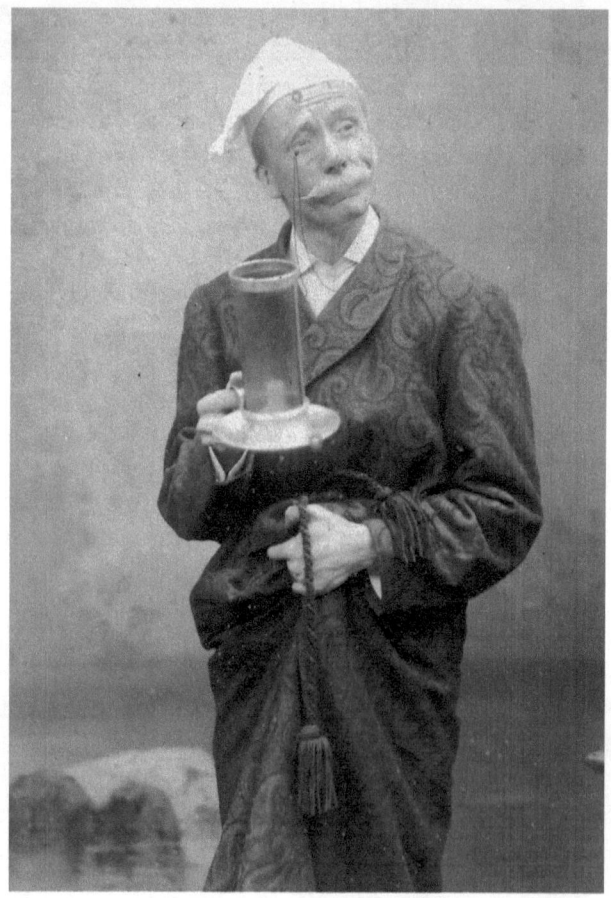

31. George Grossmith: "Yes, yes, he is a Major General."

at Home, In the Stalls, The Christmas Pantomime, Seven Ages of Song, Our Choral Society, and others such. In 1876 he toured a two-handed entertainment, *Entre Nous*, in tandem with Florence Marryat, which featured a tiny musical duologue, adapted from Ernest d'Hervilly's *La Céramique*, as *Cups and Saucers*.

Grossmith first crossed paths with W. S. Gilbert when he played the role of the Judge in a minor London performance of *Trial by Jury*; as a result, he was, against considerable protest from the backers, given the leading comic part of John Wellington Wells, the sorcerer of *The Sorcerer*. His tentativeness and nerves were forgiven by first-night critics who did not, at the time, expect to see anything like a finished performance at a première, and Grossmith worked up his courage and his part successfully enough, through the run, to be retained for the following piece. He, thus, created the role of Sir Joseph Porter KCB in *HMS Pinafore* ("When I Was a Lad"; "Never Mind the Why and Wherefore"), and played the Major General in the London version of *The Pirates of Penzance* ("I Am the Very Model of a Modern Major-General"). Thereafter, now confirmed at the very top of the musical-comic profession, he created the principal comedy roles in each of the Gilbert and Sullivan works of the next decade—Reginald Bunthorne (*Patience*), the Lord Chancellor (*Iolanthe*, "Nightmare Song"; "The Law Is the True Embodiment"), King Gama (*Princess Ida*, "If You Give Me Your Attention"), Ko-Ko (*The Mikado*, "Tit Willow," "I've Got a Little List"), Robin/Ruthven (*Ruddigore*), and Jack Point (*The Yeomen of the Guard*, "I Have a Song to Sing, O"; "A Private Buffoon")—establishing himself as a comic-opera institution and a huge public favorite. Throughout this time, he continued to write and perform his solo entertainments, and, on several occasions, such of his pieces as *Cups and Saucers, A Musical Nightmare*, and *The Silver Wedding* were played as afterpieces on a Carte program.

After *The Yeomen of the Guard*, Grossmith retired from the stage and returned to his old form of entertaining at the piano, purveying such pieces as *Society Up-to-Date; Homburg, or Haunted by the Mikado; The Tide of Fashion;* and *Do We Enjoy Our Holidays?* through Britain and America with lucrative results. On the few occasions on which he allowed himself to be lured back to the theater through family or financial considerations—with *His Excellency* (1894, Governor Griffenfeld), the Savoy Theatre's *His Majesty* (1897, Ferdinand V), and *The Gay Pretenders* (1900, Lambert Simnel)—his natural nervousness and friability of memory, which he had largely conquered at the Opera

Comique and the Savoy, got the better of him, and each experience was less and less successful.

Having throughout his career as an entertainer provided himself with monologue material and songs, Grossmith also contributed the music to a number of little operettas of which the most successful was *Mr. Guffin's Elopement*—played for many years by J. L. Toole and including the popular song "The Speaker's Eye"—and the most substantial, a full score for a musical version of *Un Chapeau de paille d'Italie* as *Haste to the Wedding*. He was also the author of several books, of which *The Diary of a Nobody*, written in collaboration with his brother, Weedon, was the most successful.

Richard Temple (Pirate King)

Richard Barker Cobb (b. London, 2 March 1846; d. London, 19 October 1912) made his first appearance on the stage in May 1869, as Count Rodolfo in a performance of *La Sonnambula* at the Crystal Palace. He spent most of his early career as a baritone vocalist in touring opera (Stanley Betjeman's Company, Crystal Palace Company, Rose Hersee's National Opera Company at the St. James's Theatre, the premiere of T. Luard Selby's *Adela*, etc.) playing such parts as Figaro, Conte di Luna, Mephistopheles, and Devilshoof. He also appeared in comic opera, at the Alfred Theatre (*Lost and Found*, 1871), in Manchester (W. C. Levey's *Punchinello* 1871, Marquis), with Fred Sullivan's touring company (1871) in *Cox and Box*, *The Rose of Auvergne*, and *Breaking the Spell*, and in opéra-bouffe, first in the provinces (Cocorico in *Geneviève de Brabant* at Liverpool) and then in London in *Le Roi Carotte* (1872, Pippertrunk) and *L'Oeil crevé* (1872, Gerome). In 1873, he toured with Julia Mathews and the Gaiety Theatre company, and got his best London opportunity to date when cast as Larivaudière in the original English production of *La Fille de Madame Angot*. His range was evidenced when he stepped up to deputize for the tenor Dick Beverley as Ange Pitou, in Emily Soldene's production of the same show, at the Opera Comique.

Temple subsequently appeared in the burlesque *Ixion Re-wheeled* (1874, Jupiter) at the same house, played Rhododendron Pasha in the Islington production of Offenbach's *Les Géorgiennes* (1875), directed and played in Sullivan's *The Zoo* on the same program, and appeared as the Sultan in *The Sultan of Mocha* at Liverpool, as Buckingham in Cellier's *Nell Gwynne* at Manchester, as Carlo Maloni in Solomon's *A*

The Pirates of Penzance, or The Slave of Duty

32. Richard Temple: An orphan Pirate King.

Will with a Vengeance at the Royalty, and toured with François Cellier's opéra-bouffe company, performing his own adaptation of *Geneviève de Brabant* and *Cox and Box*.

And then Temple joined Richard D'Oyly Carte's Comedy Opera Company to create the role of Sir Marmaduke Pointdextre in Gilbert and Sullivan's *The Sorcerer*. He remained with Carte to create Dick Deadeye in *HMS Pinafore* (1878) and was London's first Pirate King in *The Pirates of Penzance* ("The Pirate King") and Colonel Calverly in *Patience* ("When I First Put This Uniform On") at the same house. However, when Carte moved his operations to the new Savoy Theatre, Temple remained at the Opera Comique to play for Hollingshead in his revival of Gilbert's *Princess Toto* (1880, Portico) and, thereafter, at the Gaiety in Solomon's *Lord Bateman* (Ephraim MacDallah).

Temple returned to Carte, however, to create further Gilbert and Sullivan roles as Strephon in *Iolanthe*, as Arac (with his mock Handelian aria) in *Princess Ida*, the title-role of *The Mikado* ("A More Humane Mikado"), the ghostly Sir Roderic in *Ruddigore* ("The Ghosts' High Noon"), and Sergeant Meryll in *The Yeomen of the Guard* (1888). When it came to *The Gondoliers*, however, it is said that he declined the limp role of Luiz, allegedly written for him, and, after more than a decade of playing little else than the works of Gilbert, attempted, with no more success than other departing members of the company, to take his Savoy popularity into other fields.

Temple appeared in the operetta *The Silver Trout* (1889, Jack Lacy) at a Benefit, then made an attempt at management by taking out a tour of Gounod's *The Mock Doctor*, starring Effie Chapuy, in 1890. It was an expensive failure. His later ventures as a performer and director similarly held few highlights: he played in the disastrous *Miami* (1893); succeeded Colin Coop as Sid Fakah in the variety musical *Morocco Bound* (1893); directed and played Dick Fid in Howard Talbot's maiden *Wapping Old Stairs* (1894); and performed in *The Geisha* in St. Petersburg. He later directed the touring musical *The Red Spider* (1898), toured as John Ironsides in a khaki-updated *Fille du Tambour-Major* (1900), appeared as Henry VII in the unfortunate *The Gay Pretenders* (1900), played in the children's musical *Little Hans Andersen* (1903), and made his final West End appearance in 1906 as Mr. Burchell in Liza Lehmann's comic-opera version of *The Vicar of Wakefield*. During the later part of his career, Temple also did some teaching, but in his last years he became an invalid, and he ended his days in Charing Cross Hospital in "dire poverty."

Temple was married to the soprano Bessie Emmett (b. 43 Store Street, London, 3 August 1846; d. 96 Lyndhurst Road, Peckham, 9 May 1875) and, later in life, to Anne Marie Davis. His son, who worked as Richard Temple Jr. (b. 96 Lyndhurst Road, Camberwell, 25 October 1872; d. New York City, 14 October 1954), had a successful musical theater career.

Emily Cross (Ruth)

Two other *Pinafore* veterans who continued on into *Pirates* did not last the length. George Power retired from the company and, pretty much, from the profession, partway through the run, to be replaced by another ex-Italian opera tenor, "Signor Leli." Poor Miss Everard didn't make it to opening night. The accident she suffered in rehearsal meant that she couldn't take up the role made for her, and Ruth was played on first night, and until she returned, by her *Pinafore* standby, Miss Emily Cross (Mrs. M. E. Jobling). Family was the only reason Mrs. Jobling was standby for anyone: she had had and would have a fine career as an actress.

Emily Cross was born in Lyme Regis, Dorset, and baptized there on 2 November 1845. A few years later, her family removed to Saint Peter Port, in Guernsey, where her father worked as a "bath chair man." It was in the Channel Islands that Emily made her first appearances as a teenage vocalist, before, in 1862, she was apprenticed to Mr. Edward Dean Davis, actor-manager of the Newcastle Theatre Royal company. I see her first giving songs between the shows and attracting much attention, with her "Merry Is the Greenwood," "Come into the Garden, Maud," "Kathleen Mavourneen," and "La Manola" ("an attractive person and an excellent voice . . . encored"). In October, I spy her billed to play the bass role of Hecate in *Macbeth*. From then on, for more than four years, under the wing of Mr. Davis, she was a featured favorite on the Newcastle stage, and there was general mourning among Novocastrian playgoers when it was announced that she was leaving. But she was going to Drury Lane.

Emily's "first appearance in London" is oft described. In fact, it was a bit of a mess. The cast announced for *Rob Roy*, for 16 March 1867, was topped by Sims Reeves as Osbaldistone, Phelps as Nicol Jarvie, and Mr. Powrie as the outlaw, but it didn't happen. Mr. Reeves, for the thousandth time, was "ill." It finally got on a week later (23 March), with Reeves being hurriedly replaced by William Harrison. The *Era* reported that Emily was

> a debutante whose claims to favour are of a strong kind. Very prepossessing in person and manner, her acting is easy and graceful and her reception was of the most cordial description. She sang the usual songs with much taste and expression and has a sweet voice of no great power but which she manages with considerable skill. Her first introduced song was encored, and in the unaccompanied duet with Mr. Harrison, "Though You Leave Me Now in Sorrow" and "A Highland Lad My Love Was Born," Miss E Cross established her position with the audience. . . . The Diana of the play is the palest possible reflex of the Diana of the novel. Miss Cross, however, infused

new spirit into the performance, and threw a grace of her own round the part. Her voice is a full, round mezzo-soprano, and her singing proved that her voice had been turned to no indifferent account. She sang "From Morn to Eve, So Bonny-O" and "John Hielandman" and was encored in both.

When manager Chatterton later sued Reeves for breach of contract, it came out in court that it was the star tenor himself who had been responsible for Emily's hiring, specifically for that one role, specifically to play opposite him!

Emily was swiftly on her way to other major engagements. The first was at Liverpool, where Phelps was to play Bottom in *A Midsummer Night's Dream*. Emily was cast as Oberon and "created an immense impression by the superior nature of her vocal qualities." She played with the Wigans in *The Poor Noblesse* and *The First Night*, and, when

33. Emily Cross: A piratical maid of unexpected work.

manager Alexander Henderson's Benefit came round, she actually played opposite him (not known as an actor!) in *The Leap Year*. Then it was on to Bristol for the opening of the new theater. *The Tempest*, with James Bennett as Prospero, was the opening attraction, and Miss Cross was Ariel. She stole the show: "one of the choicest bits of acting we have seen"; "it is but rarely that we hear such vocalisation on the stage"; "beautiful singing." Manager Chute promptly mounted *Rob Roy*, and *The Little Rebel, Loan of a Lover, Macbeth* (Hecate), and *Hamlet* with Emily as Ophelia, before bringing out, again, *Rob Roy*. She repeated her Diana to the Osbaldistone of a future singing star, "Frank Crellin" (later "Celli"). Extending her engagement, she starred in *The Colleen Bawn* (with songs), played Josephine in *The Child of the Regiment*, and principal boy in the Christmas *Aladdin*, until she had become as great a favorite in Bristol as in Newcastle. Shortly after, she was recalled to Bristol for a special engagement as Julia in *Guy Mannering*. Chute himself played Dandie, and the hero was Sims Reeves.

Miss Cross returned north to play twelve nights at South Shields and also to get married. Her husband was a Newcastle man, [Mark] Ernest Jobling, son of a local solicitor, and later a mining engineer. They would have some thirty-five years of married life together. Back in London, Emily was engaged to repeat her Ophelia at the Princess's Theatre, but this time, circumstances were against her. The Hamlet was a "gentlemanly, amateurish" actor named Allerton, and Emily was pregnant. She gave birth to a daughter, Lily, slightly too soon, in the privacy of Bodmin, Cornwall, on 13 October 1868.

Emily Jobling returned to the stage at the Prince's Theatre, Manchester, at Christmas, then—no juvenile now but a confirmed star—to Mr. Davis, for another run at Newcastle, Carlisle, Edinburgh, and at Liverpool for Christmas, playing Jack Frost in *Queen Bee* ("acted and sang in a style seldom witnessed in this kind of performance"). The year 1870 was spent, again, largely with Davis, largely in Newcastle, largely en famille, and in March 1871, a second child, a son, Ernest Nathaniel Lambert Jobling, was born. The baby was put in the care of a nurse while Emily continued to follow Davis to Blyth, York, Whitby, Sunderland, and back to Newcastle, but on 21 August 1871 small Ernest died, at the age of five months. Emily carried on: trouping around the north, playing everything from *East Lynne* to *The Colleen Bawn*, *The Power of the Heart*, and *Charles II* to a musical comedy drama written by Cunningham Bridgman with music by one amateur Frederic Clay. *Shipmates* was produced by Davis at Sunderland (1873) with Emily featured, and making a success of a Clay song, "Lover Mine." In 1874 a second daughter, May, was born.

Emily seemed to have given up theatrical ambition for family life, and her appearances over the next years were almost all in the north. But when the famous Compton Benefit *Trial by Jury*, with its cast of London celebrities, was given in March 1877, Emily was among the starry bridesmaids. A pregnant bridesmaid, for in May she gave birth to her third daughter, Emily Alice Jobling. She still continued to take the odd job. She sang Madame Lange to the Clairette of Connie Loseby in a production of *La Fille de Madame Angot* mounted by Alfred Cellier and she sang Siebel in *Faust* back in Guernsey, but she was, seemingly, at this time, concentrating on being a wife and mother. So a comfy little job in London would be just the ticket.

Thus, Emily turned up at the Opera Comique, playing opposite Temple as Mrs. Nankeen Worcester in *Cups and Saucers*, and, as usual in such situations, covering the ladies' roles in the principal attraction of the evening. During the run of *HMS Pinafore*, she deputized not only for Harriet Everard as Buttercup but also for Emma Howson as Josephine. And now, with Miss Everard injured, it was the versatile Emily who was called on "pro tem" to introduce the role of Ruth, the "piratical maid of all work" to London. The opening night reviews mostly concentrated on her "jump in" rather than her performance ("acquitted herself remarkably well"; "much spirit and drollery"), but Emily proved herself more than a jump-in, and played the role of Ruth for several months before Miss Everard took over. The management presented her with a suitably inscribed bracelet of thanks. I wonder where that is now.

Emily was instead hired by John Hollingshead for the revival of *Princess Toto*, and stayed on at the Opera Comique to play the character role of Mrs. Pounceby in the hit comedy *The Mother-in-Law*, with its Aesthetic Quadrille. She appeared, sporadically, during the early 1880s, before, in 1886, she was cast in the production of Arthur Wing Pinero's *The Schoolmistress* at the Court Theatre. It was the same story again: cast in the supporting character role of Mrs. Admiral Rankling, she jumped in for Mrs. John Wood in the title-role of the hit play. Her new "fach," playing vinegarish spinsters, was established for the last dozen years of her career, during which time she played with Olga Nethersole, in Rutland Barrington's *Bartonmere Towers*, and in his failed attempt to revive the German Reed establishment (Daphne in *Happy Arcadia*), in burlesque at the Gaiety, as well as starring in Pinero's *The Amazons*, and playing long seasons in *The Strange Adventures of Miss Brown* and *Jedbury Junior*. She died at Rock Park, Barnstaple, on 4 January 1904.

Rutland Barrington (Sergeant of Police)

If Emily was a "Pirate" who was not originally scheduled, what to say of the Sergeant of Police? The story has been told, albeit by Rutland Barrington, that he was originally not needed for *The Pirates of Penzance*, that the "little" Sergeant's role was intended for Fred Clifton or another of that ilk, and that Barrington petitioned for it . . . well, maybe. Clifton was still playing the part, with its hit song, in America, when London's edition opened. Anyway, whatever the circumstances, it was Mr. Barrington who played the Police Sergeant at the Opera Comique; who made a hit, in his "seventeen-minute part," with the same number with which Clifton had scored in New York, and who went on to become a backbone Savoyard.

The young "Barrington" (né George Rutland Fleet, b. Penge, 15 January 1853; d. St. James's Infirmary, Balham 31 May 1922), son of John Fleet, a "wholesale dealer in colonial produce," and his wife, Esther (née Faithfull), worked as a clerk in the city before, in 1874, securing his first engagement as an actor with Henry Neville at the Olympic Theatre (*Lady Clancarty*, Lafleur/Marquis de Presles in *The Two Orphans*; Mr. Porcelain in *Family Jars*, etc.). He ventured into the musical theater playing the little *Lessons in Harmony* with Ella Dietz, and singing E. L. Blanchard's musical sketch "St. George and the Dragon," in the touring Entertainment of his aunt, Miss Emily Faithfull. He took his sketch, thereafter, to Mrs. Howard Paul's Entertainment, and he remained with that lady, through 1876 and 1877, on the road, playing Cuthbert Vane's *By Return of Post*, a sketch by George Grossmith Jr., and doing a Charles Santley imitation to the lady's famous Sims Reeves impersonation, until she disbanded her company to take up the role of Lady Sangazure in *The Sorcerer* (1877). Mrs. Paul, it is said, suggested that the company hire her decidedly effective twenty-four-year-old colleague as well, and Barrington thus created the role of the curate, Dr. Daly, in Gilbert and Sullivan's piece, with its favorite number, "Time Was When Love and I Were Well Acquainted." He remained with Carte to become the first Captain Corcoran in *HMS Pinafore* (1878, "I Am the Captain of the Pinafore"; "Fair Moon, to Thee I Sing"; "Never Mind the Why and

Wherefore") and, when it seemed that there would be no role for him in *The Pirates of Penzance*, Cartesian maybethology (i.e., Barrington) relates that he suggested that he be given the "comparatively small" part of the Police Sergeant. Well, as we can see, maybe.

Barrington continued as a key member of the D'Oyly Carte Company for more than a decade, creating the parts of Grosvenor (*Patience*), Lord Mountararat (*Iolanthe*, "When Britain Really Ruled the Waves"), King Hildebrand (*Princess Ida*), Pooh-Bah (*The Mikado*), and Sir Despard (*Ruddigore*), before leaving the company to set up in management on his own account. When this venture bankrupted him, he ended up on the road with the operatic company run by one Mme. Ilma Norina (née Josephine Muntz), performing a second-rate piece called *The Rose of Windsor*. He was pleased to return to the Savoy, where he appeared in such latter-day D'Oyly Carte productions as *The Nautch Girl* (1891, Punka, the Rajah), *The Vicar of Bray* (1892, Rev. William Barlow), *Haddon Hall* (1892, Rupert Vernon), *Jane Annie* (1893, Proctor), *Utopia (Limited)* (1893, King Paramount), and, in his last return, *The Grand Duke* (1896, Ludwig).

In 1894, Barrington again left the Savoy, this time to join George Edwardes's company at Daly's Theatre, replacing Harry Monkhouse in the senior comic role in *A Gaiety Girl*. He began another fruitful run of parts, which saw the now stout and jowly Barrington introducing for Edwardes the character/comedy roles of the Prince Regent/Nils Egilson in *His Excellency* (1895); Marcus Pomponius in *A Greek Slave* (1898, "I Want to Be Popular"); the Mandarin, Yen How, in *San Toy* (1899, "Six Little Wives"); Quinton Raikes in *A Country Girl* (1902); and Boobhamba in *The Cingalee* (1904), and succeeding Monkhouse as Marquis Imari in *The Geisha*.

In his fifties, Barrington continued his series of large comic creations, featuring in such pieces as *The White Chrysanthemum* (1905, Admiral Sir Horatio Armitage KCB) and as a ridiculous Pharaoh in *Amasis* (1906, Amasis IX). Between appearances in the music halls (*The Tramp*, *The Silent Way*, *The Moody Mariner*) and in the nonmusical theater, he repeated his Gilbert and Sullivan roles in revival and took comedy parts in some of the new wave of continental musicals: Lucas van Tromp in *The Girl in the Train* (1910, *Die geschiedene Frau*), the Major Domo in *Baron Trenck* (1911), and Max Somossy in *The Joy-Ride Lady* (1914, *Autoliebchen*). He was forced into retirement by a stroke in 1919.

Barrington wrote the texts for several small operettas, including *Quid Pro Quo*, played as a forepiece to *Princess Toto* at the Opera Comique,

34. Rutland Barrington as Pooh-Bah, the Lord High Everything Else.

and *A Knight Errant* (1894), played as a curtain raiser to Gilbert's *His Excellency*. He also authored the children's musicals *The Water Babies* (1902) and *Little Black Sambo and Little White Barbara* (1904), played as Christmas entertainments at the Garrick Theatre. Barrington married, during his time at the Opera Comique, Ellen Louise Jane Stainer.

Marion Hood (Mabel)

And what of the ladies? The twenty like-aged daughters of our Pythagorean military man and his Babylonic cuneiform? Edith, Kate, Isabel, and . . . so the American notices tell us . . . the *youngest* of them all, Mabel. Well, Kate ("far away from toil and care") was played by none other than Miss Jones from Cincinnati: "Lilian La Rue"; Edith ("let us gaily tread the measure") was Julia Gwynne (née Putney), more famous as Mrs. George Edwardes than for her tidy career as a comic opera singer; Isabel was Neva Bond, sister to Jessie. But, Mabel . . . ah! " 'Tis Ma-a-a-a-a-a-bel . . ." For Mabel, the triumvirate dug up a soprano who was infinitely superior to their American prima donna. She'd had a couple of stage names (and would have a couple of married ones) since starting her career, very young, in Liverpool, but she had been a highly successful professional singer, in a sphere different from that of Messrs. Gilbert and Sullivan, for over a decade.

"Marion Hood" was born as Sarah Ann Isaac, at 57 Fleet Street, Liverpool, on 1 April 1854. I (and others) have often called her "the Jewish soprano," but a great-grand-relation has objected. Maybe he is

35. Marion Hood: "Yes! 'Tis Mabel."

one of Marion's maternal Rawlinson family "of Lynn." I am, possibly, being too sweeping: maybe Sarah was Jewish as I am Jewish: by the father, not by the mother. Just wanted to clear that up. Sarah started her singing life as a musical-hall kiddie soprano—a nineteenth-century Julie Andrews. Here's my brief summary of her grand career.

The story handed out by Richard D'Oyly Carte, when he put his new leading lady before the public, went thus: "The elegant, blonde, twenty-two-year-old Miss Hood was studying at the Royal Academy of Music when she accompanied Harriet Coveney to a rehearsal at the Opera Comique and was given the opportunity to audition for Gilbert and D'Oyly Carte. She sang the Shadow Song from *Dinorah*, and found herself cast, for her 'first appearance on any stage' as the original Mabel of London's production of *The Pirates of Penzance*." Bosh. It was—like so many Cartesian cast biographies—so much rhubarb. Mrs. Sarah Ann Hunt was knocking twenty-six, a widow of several months, and she'd been earning her bread as a soprano vocalist, with plenty of "appearances on the stage," at the age of twenty-five and twenty-six, for fourteen years.

"Marion" Isaac, daughter of a Liverpool shipwright by the name of George James Isaac and his wife Mary (née Rawlinson, who signed her daughter's birth certificate with an illiterate "X") seems to have made her first appearance on the stage at the age of twelve, singing and dancing the role of Irish Moll in the ballet *The Rigs of Donnybrook Fair* ("nightly encored") at the Rotunda, in her native Liverpool. She took her remarkably fine, agile soprano voice into public, as a stand-up vocalist, at that same venue the following month, and, thereafter, she traveled widely in Britain, performing ambitious soprano music in the country's better music halls, and venturing, come Christmastime, on to the pantomime stage. The "exquisite, youthful soprano" was seen particularly frequently at Hull's Alhambra Music Hall, managed by Charles Henry Hunt, and, at the age of seventeen, she became Mrs. Hunt. She continued to cover the halls of the British provinces, and occasionally of London, with regular success until, in 1879, Carte came into the picture and Sarah Ann stopped being "Marion Isaac" and became the less Semitic and more yo-ho-British "Marion Hood."

At the end of her noticeably successful engagement in *The Pirates of Penzance*, Marion remarried and announced her retirement from the stage. But she returned, after just six months' absence, and was seen as Constance to the *Claude Duval* of Frank Celli in Solomon's comic opera (1881), starred as Casquette in *The Golden Ring* (1883) and as Laura in the first London production of *The Beggar Student* at the Alhambra, and took Florence St. John's role of Girola in a revival of *Les Manteaux noirs* (1885). Having attempted Gounod's Marguerite at the Crystal Palace, and found its operatic demands too strenuous, Marion returned to the musical theater, playing the star role of Phoebe in *Billee Taylor* at the Gaiety; in her first burlesque role, as Winifred Wood in *Little Jack Sheppard* (1885); and then, when "Gaiety George" Edwardes switched genres temporarily, created the title-role in Cellier's *Dorothy* (1886). However, when that show transferred to the Prince of Wales, for what would be the most famous part of its vast run, she remained behind, to become the leading lady of the Gaiety new burlesques, taking over as Mercedes in *Monte Cristo Jr.* (1887), and creating the roles of Tartina in *Frankenstein* (1887), Esmeralda in *Miss Esmeralda* (1887), and the Queen of Spain in *Ruy Blas and the Blase Roué* (1889), alongside Nellie Farren and Fred Leslie. She toured with the Gaiety's two megastars through Britain and on to America and Australia.

Marion later took over the title-role of the burlesque *Joan of Arc* in London, and in 1892 made another trip to Australia with the Gaiety company, playing Carmen (*Carmen Up-to-Data*), Marguerite (*Faust Up-to-Date*), and *Joan of Arc* for George Musgrove. On her return she took over the title-role of Alma Somerset in Edwardes's tour of *A Gaiety Girl*, before she went into retirement as the wife of a comfortably-heeled stockbroker, bringing to an end a dozen years as a leading lady in the musical theater, during which she had been at the front end of all the most active elements in the theater of the time: the Gilbert and Sullivan operas; the Alhambra Operettes; the record-breaking *Dorothy*; the Gaiety new burlesque; and the new-style musical comedy. Mrs. Frederick Beaumont Hesseltine died at 3 Prince's Avenue, Margate, on 10 August 1912.

Launched, nicely perfectioned after its New York tryout, with this cast of splendid talents, *The Pirates of Penzance* ran on at the Opera Comique for a year before taking off to the provinces, the colonies, and even the Continent, establishing itself as a classic for all time.

6

Patience, or Bunthorne's Bride

Aesthetic opera in two acts
Opera Comique Theatre, 23 April 1881

The "British Tar" burlesqued, old-fashioned melodrama burlesqued . . . what would Mr. Gilbert and Mr. Sullivan come up with, as the fun-target for their next English opéra-bouffe? The wide world of the English-language musical theater was all agog for its "next helping."

The difficulty was that the gentlemen concerned were, themselves, not quite sure. Gilbert had turned back to his comic magazine writings and selected a piece titled *The Rival Curates* for comic-operaticizing. It was a rather backward-looking idea, partaking more of the older English flavor and world of *The Sorcerer* than of the subsequent well-bred hilarities of *HMS Pinafore* and *The Pirates of Penzance*. Partway through the writing of his libretto, Gilbert found that "the necessity of respecting things ecclesiastical hamstrung his humour" and he junked the idea. Instead, he turned his rival curates (after all, what is more dull than "a pale young curate"?) into rival . . . rival . . . what?

Well, one of the more luxurious fads of the time was "aestheticism": the cult of The Beautiful. Or, rather, what its devotees perceived as the beautiful, in something of the same way that, today, California's bleach babes, seven-packed musclemen, and plastic furniture are perceived as "beautiful." The cult of aestheticism was a little more tasteful than today's obsession, with its rather yearning leanings toward the "pure" mediaeval age, and "art for art's sake," and it became, for the nonce, a fashion. Ladies (particularly) and gentlemen, with nothing better to do, became followers of the fad and of its figureheads: Walter Pater, Algernon Charles Swinburne, James McNeill Whistler, Dante Gabriel Rosetti, and, of course, Oscar Wilde. Oscar Fingal O'Flahertie Wilde was not the first, nor the most effective of the "aesthetes" (the movement, of course, brought forth some wonderful furniture and other physical artifacts), but he was one of its most visible adherents, and he used the movement of the moment to promote his profitable lunchtime lectures and his tours. Sadly, because of Wilde's homosexuality, the aesthetic movement has, today, become viewed as a "gay thing." It was nothing of the sort. The star gents of the play that Gilbert finally wrote are the descendants of "the rival curates," aesthetes for the momentary fashion: two men competing, even if they must ridicule themselves with mediaeval poses, to win the love of a lady-ee!

Well, the lady in question, and the show, were named, a bit ordinarily, *Patience*. On a monument? But the *Rival Curates* backbone remained, featuring two men—Mr. Reginald Bunthorne and Mr. Archibald Grosvenor—trying to outdo each other in the most fashionable of "stained-glass" attitudes, in order to win the favor of a soprano—a mere milkmaid named Patience! At the same time, the trendily devoted ladies of the local aristocracy are pursuing the two fake aesthetes . . . and the forsaken military men are pursuing *them* . . . Well, there's your comic opera! So, it was curates "out" and aesthetes "in"; mildness out and mockable mannerisms in military uniforms and burlesque-aesthetic costumes in. The preproduction press whispered, "As everyone knows, it deals with the aesthetic movement, and it resembles a comedy more than any of Mr. Gilbert's other pieces at this house. It is intended as the final stroke to Maudle, Postlethwaite & Co," before adding, less correctly, "Mr. Barrington plays the principal part . . . Mr. Temple is not in the cast." Messrs. Maudle and Postlethwaite were cartoon characters invented by George du Maurier and featured by him in the pages of *Punch*. They were a couple of humorously pretentious arty gents who had a curious resemblance to Whistler and Wilde—something like the Julian and Sandy of the 1950s radio series *Round the Horne*. And oh! so ripe for burlesque. And burlesqued they duly were, and in double-quick time. By F. C. Burnand in *The Colonel* and by W. S. Gilbert in the tale of "Bunthorne's Bride."

Every Lady of the village is sighing mediaevally at the tootsicums of the aesthetic poet Reginald Bunthorne, rebuffing the officers of the 35th Dragoon Guards, who were their last year's swains. Only the milkmaid, Patience, remains innocently aloof. She equates "love" with the feeling one has for a great-aunt, until she is informed, by the more experienced Ladies, of the sentiment's sublime unselfishness. Dutifully, she determines to experience love. But to love her handsome childhood sweetheart, Archibald Grosvenor, cannot be considered unselfish, so she regretfully agrees to love the smitten Bunthorne, who has secretly admitted to her that his poetic persona is nothing but an attention-grabbing sham. But, now that Reginald has declared a preference for Patience, the other lovesick maidens promptly desert him to adulate Grosvenor instead, and Bunthorne becomes morbidly miserable at being insufficiently admired. He forces the usurper to deaestheticize and become commonplace, and he himself takes up his rival's blithely poetic and agreeable manner. Bunthorne being now perfectly agreeable, Patience feels duteously able to desert him for Grosvenor, and, as the other ladies return to their neglected dragoons, rather than to dear Reginald, the foolish fellow is, at the final curtain, the only one left without a partner.

It was a plot that involved Gilbert's "things are seldom what they seem" motif, as Bunthorne switched personas to suit circumstances, and also the theme of "the slave of duty" that had motivated the plot of *The Pirates*. However, it did not particularly seem designed for the company of the previous piece. I wonder if, as was rumored in the press, Temple was truthfully not to have been in the cast. I have always found it a little odd that Colonel Calverley, the role he took, has two numbers, closely together, in act 1 and then zilch. Also, that the only tenor role was not that of Grosvenor but the lesser role of the Duke of Dunstable, who, nevertheless, was given the final plot twist.

The central role of Bunthorne went, naturally, to the "lion" of the company, George Grossmith. The writers supplied him with some splendidly characteristic lines and a principal soliloquy to equal any of his previous songs, as he detailed his credo, how to become a successful aesthete ("If You're Anxious for to Shine"). And the role of his rival, Archibald the all-right . . . had he been begging again? . . . was cast with Rutland Barrington, whose main number was a nursery-rhyme parody ("The Magnet and the Churn"). Richard Temple got two lively martial solos ("When I First Put This Uniform On"; "If You Want a Receipt for a Popular Mystery") as the Colonel of the Heavy Dragoons, and that was about it, for the men, apart from a small (but enjoyable) ditty for the tenor Duke. Bunthorne and Grosvenor—naturally, given the story outline—dominated the script, but neither was exactly an operatic singer, so Sullivan was forced to sidewind his more substantial music into Temple's role.

36. Wannabe aesthetes: Messrs. Thornton, Lely, and Temple.

In a similar way, the lioness's share of the ladies' music fell to the "prima donna," if one can thus dub the lady in the affair. There was none of the operatic burlesque of "The Hours Creep on Apace" or "Poor Wand'ring One" in the role of Patience. Her little solos ("I Cannot Tell What This Love May Be"; "Love Is a Plaintive Song") were principal girl numbers—delightful principal girl numbers, but not in the style of a Josephine, an Aline, or a Mabel. And, for that very reason, the Cartesian company underwent a very important change in its personnel. Emilie Petrelli, who had succeeded Marion Hood in the role of Mabel, and who was asked to carry on into the new work, turned the part down. Patience, she declared, and with reason, was a soubrette role. So, the Opera Comique had to look for yet another lead soprano—and they got a stayer.

Leonora Braham (Patience)

Leonora Abraham (b. London, 3 February 1853; d. London, 23 November 1931) would fill the star soprano spot in the company in the next five "Savoy Operas."

Born in London, the daughter of Philip Abraham, a professor of the Hebrew language, and his wife, Harriet (née Boss), Leonora began her working life as a teacher, in Gower Street, but by 1873 she was appearing in concert. I wonder, could she be the "Miss Braham" singing "Non più mesta" and "Se m'abbandoni" with the highish society amateurs from Woolwich to Ryde to St. George's Hall, in 1869–72? I see her, definitely, at St. George's Hall (as "Miss Leonora Braham") sharing a bill with Florence Lancia, J. W. Turner, and Jessie Royd (26

37. Leonora Braham as Patience: "I Cannot Tell What This Love May Be."

April 1873), in an English Glee Union concert, and at St. James's Hall with Theodore Distin, before, at the age of twenty-one, she joined Mr. and Mrs. German Reed's company at the St. George's Hall. She would appear there, continuously, in the juvenile soprano roles of their highly popular four- or five-handed musical playlets, for more than four years.

Leonora's first ventures into the regular theater were in the Americas, where she and her husband, Frederick Edwin Lucy Barnes, formerly secretary to the composer George Macfarren, had gone soon after their marriage. While Barnes was employed as assistant organist at Trinity Church, Leonora starred in the New York productions of the British comic operas *Princess Toto* (1879; "a most excellent performance, both vocally and histrionically. She has a sweet, light soprano, finely cultivated and executed very effectively") and *Billee Taylor* (1880). Otherwise, the trip was not a success. A handsome son was born, and some months later, Barnes committed suicide.

On returning to Britain, Leonora was hired by D'Oyly Carte to create the title-role in *Patience*, and for the next six years she held the position of leading lady at the Savoy Theatre, through the memorable creations of *Iolanthe* (Phyllis), *Princess Ida* (Ida), *The Mikado* (Yum-Yum, introducing "The Sun Whose Rays" and "Three Little Maids"), and *Ruddigore* (Rose Maybud), and the first revival of *The Sorcerer* (Aline). In 1887–88 she and her new husband, Scots Cartesian tenor James Duncan Young (b. Dunkeld, Perthshire, 1854; d. London, 12 December 1932), spent a season with Williamson, Garner, and Musgrove's Royal Comic Opera Company in Australia (*Dorothy*, *Erminie*, *The Mikado*, etc.) but, on their return, she did not, in spite of her old position in the world of comic opera, succeed in finding appreciable work. She appeared in London only as a replacement in *Carina* and in the short-lived *Gretna Green*, and on tour in the title-role of *Nanon*, in Edward Jakobowski's *Paola* (1889, Paola), and in the burlesque *Miss Esmeralda*.

In 1890, she went to South America as leading lady with Edwin Cleary's comic opera company, then produced and starred in a tour of a small comic opera, *The Duke's Diversion*, on her own account, before again leaving Britain to spend two years touring British comic opera in South Africa. During this tour she also made a venture into heavier waters and appeared as Santuzza in *Cavalleria rusticana*.

Leonora's only subsequent West End appearance of note was in the comedy role of Lady Barbara Cripps in George Edwardes's musical comedy *An Artist's Model*, although she continued to make appearances around Britain (Julia Jellicoe in *The Grand Duke* and the Carte repertoire, Nora in *Shamus O'Brien*, Bathilde in *Olivette*, Madame Michu in *Les P'tites Michu*, Widow Melnotte in *Melnotte*), and appeared as Donna Adelina Gonzales in New York's *Because She Loved Him So* (1899), until after the turn of the century. Mr. and Mrs. Young had a quarter of a century of stage-retired married life, but Young, sometime secretary of the Actors Association, latterly suffered from mental alienation and spent his final years in an asylum.

Lady Jane and the Tenor

There was, however, one other important role in *Patience*. A role that would leave, perhaps, the most indelible mark of all of the show's characters in the panoply of G&S creations. Even though it had, truthfully, precious little to do with the show's main plotline. After the little rolypoly Buttercup of Harriet Everard, and the tall, angular Ruth of Emily Cross, the writers returned to the Lady Sangazure style of contralto, and they invented the character of the Lady Jane: the oversize, overage devotee of everything (and every man) aesthetic. For me, the abiding image from *Patience* is that of Lady Jane, opening the second act, alone on the stage but for her violoncello, giving forth with her paean to the pains of the ageing woman, "Silvered Is the Raven Hair," in a perfect burlesque of the Victorian contralto parlor song. The role of Lady Jane was created by the tall, and massive, Alice Barnett, who had played Ruth in America, and subsequently in London. Here, she made the first of what would be two outstanding, successive Savoy successes, both in character and with song. A character who, in wonderfully burlesque fashion, finished the opera in the arms of . . . the tenor!

The latest tenor of the organization, although he had a slight role here, was another who would become a solid link in the Cartesian chain. Although "Durward Lely" had spent a successful decade singing in opera, he was not a society amateur, nor even an Englishman. And he *had* dipped into comic opera, albeit comic opera with the flag bearer of the standard of opéra-bouffe in England: Emily Soldene. His last job had been in Soldene's productions of *Carmen* and *The Naval Cadets*. Durward Lely would, like Miss Braham, be a stayer, and introduce the tenor roles in five Savoy operas.

And, from 10 October 1881, they could rightly be named Savoy Operas. Carte had built the Savoy Theatre, largely on the profits from his Gilbert and Sullivan productions, and now the shabby, smoke-stained old Opera Comique could be left behind, in favor of the new theater on the Strand and . . . its electric lights!

Given the huge trouble employed to protect *The Pirates of Penzance* from the royalty rippers-off of the former colonies of America, it was a little surprising that nothing was done to protect *Patience* in a similar way. But *Patience* aroused little interest beyond the Atlantic. Doubtless, the exploits of Messrs. Maudle and Postlethwaite were not familiar to the average American in the way that the nautical drama and the melodrama were, and there is little that is duller than a burlesque when you have no understanding of what is being burlesqued. As it ended up, Australia saw *Patience* before New York did. But then Oscar Wilde turned up in America, on a lecture tour under the management of—guess who: Mr. D'Oyly Carte—and America soon knew its Maudle from its Postlethwaite. The official American production, when it did arrive, in 1882, with Carte at its helm, was, on the whole, a good one. The splendid Jack Ryley was Bunthorne, with comedian James Barton and later baritone William T. Carleton playing Grosvenor. But it was Lady Jane who stole the show.

Augusta Roche (Lady Jane)

Mary Augusta Darvell (b. St. James, London, 16 August 1849; d. New Orleans, 18 October 1893), known as Augusta Roche, was born in London, the daughter of a commercial traveler. She said she had her musical training under Manuel Garcia at the Royal College of Music, or was it the Royal Academy of Music, but, since the program for an 1866 professional students' concert at the more modest London Academy of Music features her name, I imagine that, in fact, it was there that she was educated.

Augusta seems to have started performing in public in 1868, when her name turns up as a replacement for Clara Lacey in the Bijou Operetta Company at Chatham ("Miss Augusta Darvil") "with the greatest possible success." In 1869, she can be seen on the programs of such lesser institutions as the Schubert Society, the Bow and Bromley Institute, and the Chatham Choral Society, as well as at the modest concerts given by the pianist W. Bollen Harrison, where she shared the bill with one Miss Pimina Hayes, "chamber singer to the Princess Poniatowski," and with a young baritone by the name of Richard Temple.

In 1871, Augusta was married to surveyor Roderick Edward Cherrill, but by June 1873 she can be seen back on the platform, now no longer

38. Augusta Roche as Lady Jane: "There Will Be Too Much of Me, in the Coming By and By!"

"Augusta Darvell" but "Augusta Roche." Between 1874 and 1877, she was featured on a variety of other, mostly lesser, concert bills, although when she performed with Edith Wynne for the British Orchestral Society, a critic dismissed her with "[her] qualifications are not yet obvious at a first hearing." The society must have disagreed, because in 1875 she subsequently sang at a series of concerts for them, including a performance of *The May Queen* in one of which her colleagues was none less than Sims Reeves.

She spent the summer of 1874 singing at Ramsgate ("a charming voice and a decided vein for emulation"), visited Brighton for John Cheshire ("Una voce"; "The Green Trees Whispered"), appeared with the Albert Hall Amateur Orchestra and the Schubert Society, at the Brighton Aquarium and the Royal Aquarium, and shouldered grander company when she appeared at St. James's Hall for the 1875 St. Patrick's Day concert ("Dermot Asthore"; "She Is Far from the Land"; "Savourn Deelish") alongside Kate Santley, Edward Lloyd, Antoinette Sterling, and Edith Wynne.

Miss Roche sang at Arthur Wilford's concert, and when that gentleman launched his new Schubert Society of Brussels, she was the featured vocalist at the inaugural concert ("Nobil signor"; "Felicia marianis"; "L'ultimo pensiero"; Beethoven's "Mélodies Ecossaises"), billed as "of the Covent Garden Promenade Concerts." She appeared with the British Orchestral Society (Sullivan's "Thou Art Weary"), at the Alexandra Palace with Julius Benedict's lectures, and in 1876 and 1877 at the Aquarium ("C'est l'Espagne"; "Nobil signor"; "The Sailor Sighs"), the Eyre Arms, Langham Hall in Birmingham, and in dates from Hastings to Middlesbrough.

At the end of 1877 (19 October), Mrs. Cherrill gave birth to a daughter, Rose, and the following year, another, short-lived child, Lillian (3 October 1879), but on her return—her voice apparently now deepened since the days when she had trilled "Una voce poco fa" and the like—she took the turn that would lead her to her hour of glory. She turned to the light operatic stage. Her stage career didn't begin all that gloriously; her first engagement was at the Alhambra, playing the little part of the Abbess, and understudying Fanny Edwards, in the successful London production of Offenbach's *La Fille du tambour-major*. However, things soon got better. In October 1880 she was hired by Carte to play the part of Ruth in *The Pirates of Penzance*, alongside Laura Clement, Gerard Coventry, George Marler, and Walker Marnock, on the British road, and then, when Carte organized the company that would take his latest London success, *Patience*, to America (22 September 1881), he deployed Miss Roche, on a three-year contract at forty dollars a week, to play Alice Barnett's role of Lady Jane.

The American critics went wild with delight: Miss Augusta Roche was a huge theatrical success, and soon, on the heels of that success, she started culling something of a significant social success as well. And that pair of successes brought with them discord: Miss Roche now decided that she was worth more than the forty dollars a week she'd signed for, and she demanded a raise. Surprisingly, Carte doubled her salary. But that was just the beginning. After *Patience*, she was moved to a revival of *The Pirates of Penzance* at the Bijou Theater, where, once again, she was adjudged to be the show's outstanding feature, then, at the end of that season, Carte summoned her back to England. But Miss Roche didn't want to go back to England. She wanted to stay where her theatrical and social triumphs had been won, so she refused to go. Carte insisted. So she called in sick. Carte again insisted, and Miss Roche took to writing anti-Carte missives to the newspapers. And she didn't go.

Instead, she went to Newark's Park Theatre, where she appeared as the star of the show in an amateur charity concert, giving, of course, her Lady Jane. The director of the Benefit had a special costume made for her for the occasion: "A dress of black satin with dead green Japanese silk draperies looped up and hooked on with large dead-gold bullion buckles and ornamented with sundry cords and tassels of the same material would of itself look pretty aesthetic. But upon the front breadth of the dress is embroidered in green and blue silk a life-size peacock made of real peacock feathers . . ." At the end of the concert she was interviewed: "Miss Roche lives with her husband and children in a fashionable quarter of the city and her apartments would form a capital illustration for the aesthetic apostle's discourse on Household Decoration." The interview ended, once again, with her stating her determination under no circumstances to return to England. And she didn't. She stayed, and she joined John McCaull to play Lady Jane in a revival of *Patience*.

In November 1882, the newest Gilbert and Sullivan comic opera, *Iolanthe*, was brought to America, and for the Alice Barnett role of the Fairy Queen, Carte cast . . . Augusta Roche. So, all was mended? Far from it. Miss Roche opened with the show, but before two months of the run had gone by, she was sacked. Helen Lenoir, the company manager, had had enough of her star's behavior, and when Madame decided, unilaterally, to take a night off and go to another theater, Miss Lenoir made her move. The Fairy Queen was dumped. Miss Roche sued. She lost.

It was a bad year for Augusta altogether, because things weren't going very well up at the fashionable apartment either. It seems that Mrs. Cherrill had been casting glances at a certain Dr. Frederick W. Jennings, and her husband, who had for several years been living comfortably off her earnings, was mighty wrath. His retort was to "kidnap" daughter Rose, and to refuse to return her until Jennings was out of the picture. Augusta went to court and to the papers, and Cherrill demanded twenty thousand dollars for "alienation of affection" and sued for "crim con." This time, Augusta won, and within a few months she had also won a divorce, with custody of the child—followed by a new husband.

Back in the theater, things would, similarly, go downhill. In 1883, Augusta repeated her Lady Jane at the Standard Theatre (26 March) and then took the role of Public Opinion in Edward Rice's rather peculiar version of *Orpheus and Eurydice* at the Bijou, but thereafter the winners became harder to find. She joined up with Barnett's "New York Ideal Company," a third-rate outfit that wasn't "ideal" for long; she also toured with the unimpressive Thompson Opera Company, and appeared in a second attempt by Alfred G. Robyn to get his comic opera, *Manette*, off the ground. Light glimmered only a little, in 1885, when she was allowed back into the Carte fold to tour Canada and New England as Katisha in *The Mikado*.

Augusta appeared on Broadway as the Marquise in the American version of *Serment d'amour* known as *The Bridal Trap* (1886) for its four-week run. She took part in the not very classy out-of-town production of Richard Stahl's original musical *The Sea King* (1890), and, in 1891, she appeared for what would be the last time on Broadway playing the role of Samarantha in the twelve-performance run of a minor musical titled *The Khedive* mounted by the ludicrously named "Imperial Opera Company." It was a far cry from her Lady Jane days. In February 1893 she was reported as being "of the Deshon Opera Company," another minor touring musical company, but there was also something positive to say. Miss Roche, the press announced "will retire from the stage in May and return to the UK, after 15 years on the US stage." And this time she did want to go. For, so it was reported, Dr. Jennings had "inherited $60,000 from his father." She wanted to go, but fate wasn't going to let her. Mrs. Augusta Roche Jennings (properly, Mrs. Mary Augusta Jennings) died, in New Orleans, in October 1893, at the age of forty-four. The *Daily Picayune* gave her a mention in its "Green Room Gossip" column. "Her success in *Patience* was so pronounced," it reported, "that, even to the time of her death, she was known in the profession as 'Lady Jane.'" Lady Jane was a bit of a pain . . .

John Handford Ryley (Bunthorne)

Although Miss Roche made the sensation, the backbone of the American company was "the American Grossmith," Jack Ryley. The *Clipper* described him as ""a little man, with a thin voice, serious face and very active legs who raises sunflowers at his tasty little New Rochelle villa and takes a great interest in public affairs."

39. Jack Ryley as Bunthorne: "Ultra-poetical, super-aesthetical."

Jack Ryley (né John Riley, b. 12 Cooper's Terrace, Camden Town, 11 September 1841; d. Edgware, Middlesex, 28 July 1922), son of a solicitor's clerk, began his performing life as a "comique" in the music halls ("Mr. Riley a new aspirant for comic fame sang and danced with tolerable spirit and humour," Deacon's Music Hall 1863). I see him on the bill at Sheffield in 1864 alongside Irish ex-kiddie performer, Marie Barnum (née Maria Elizabeth Crome), with whom he formed a double act, performing a mock-serious routine as the "Dancing Quakers" to a selection of Offenbach music. They also became husband and wife.

Ryley, however, found more significant and sustained success when he switched, in his thirties, from the halls to the musical theater. He made his earliest such appearance in the Gaiety burlesque *Ali Baba à la mode* (1872), performing his act as known, then on tour with the Gaiety company (*A Mere Blind* with Fred Sullivan 1873), and, over the next few years, went on to a whole succession of fine roles in the musical theater. He played with Emily Soldene's company at the Opera Comique (Trénitz in *La Fille de Madame Angot*; *Le Leçon de chant*, 1873), in *Melusine the Enchantress* (1874, *Les Chevaliers de la table ronde*) at Holborn, and with Kate Santley in *Cattarina* (1875, Fernando), in Lecocq's *Le Prés Saint-Gervais* (Nicole), in Gilbert and Clay's *Princess Toto* (Zapeter), and in *Madame l'Archiduc* (1876). During a period as first low comedian at Manchester's Prince's Theatre, he played in comedy with Toole (Bungs in *Tottle's* etc.), in pantomime with Mrs. John Wood, and in the Manchester musicals *The Sultan of Mocha* (Flint) and *Nell Gwynne* (Amen Squeak), taking time out to take over in the London production of *The Sultan of Mocha*. At Easter 1877, he joined the company at the Alhambra to play in *Orpheus in the Underworld* (Mercury), *King Indigo* (Babazouk), and *Wildfire* (Baron Hey Derry Downe), and it was from there that he went on to join the D'Oyly Carte establishment (1878), with which he played the principal comic roles (John Wellington Wells, then later the Learned Judge and Sir Joseph Porter) in the British provinces.

Following what was to be his last British Christmas, playing Dame at Leeds, Ryley was taken across to America with Carte's company to play Sir Joseph Porter in the "official" Broadway production of *HMS Pinafore* (1879). Thereafter, Jack spent most of his time in America, performing frequently as Carte's principal comedian, and introducing to America such British characters as the Major General (*Pirates of Penzance*, 1879), Flapper (*Billee Taylor* 1881, 1885), Blood-Red Bill (*Claude Duval*, 1882), Bunthorne (*Patience*, 1882), the Lord Chancellor (*Iolanthe*, 1882), the King then Don José (*Manteaux Noirs*), King Gama (*Princess Ida*, 1884), John Wellington Wells (*The Sorcerer* Boston 1885), Ko-Ko (*The Mikado*, 1885), General Bangs (*Polly* 1885), and Jack Point (*The Yeomen of the Guard* 1888). He also appeared in a long list of other leading comic roles in American versions of French and German musical pieces in the course of a high-profile career as perhaps the classiest comic opera comedian of the era.

Ryley latterly toured with Duff's company and Lillian Russell (*Gasparone*, *A Trip to Africa*, *Iolanthe*, etc.), and with Rudolf Aronson's company as Cadeau in *Erminie* in 1888–89. In the 1890s, he was seen playing Baron Otto von Piffleseltzer in the unfortunate *The Robber of the Rhine* (1892); Sir Lionel Ravenswood in the Boston musical *Westward Ho!* (1894) and in *Zip* (1894–95), as well as in Broadway's version of André Messager's *La Basoche*; and in the "romantic comic opera" *Leonardo* (1895, Fra Patchouli), before returning home to Britain for some less-exacting engagements and what turned out to be a long retirement. He was seen in the 1913 silent film of *Hamlet* as the Gravedigger.

Ryley's marriage with Marie fizzled out, and he instead married the English vocalist Madeleine Lucette (née Madeleine Matilda Bradley, b. London, 26 December 1858; d. Alvaney Gardens, Hampstead, 17 February 1934). Madeleine was subsequently to make her name as a successful author and playwright.

Carrie Burton (Patience)

Carrie Isabella Burton (b. Cambridge, Massachusetts, 10 September 1858; d. New Jersey, October 1931) was the daughter of Edward Burton, a brass finisher, and his wife, Nancy M. Dunlap. She made what seems to have been her stage debut in 1877 as the mezzo-soprano in Anna Granger Dow's little opera company, with Adelaide Randall, Herbert Brown, Louis Pfau, John E. Brand, and Edward Payson. The following

40. Carrie Burton: A less innocent-looking Patience.

year, Mrs. Dow, Carrie, and Miss Randall played with "L. M. Ruben's company," which visited the Grand Opera House (Buda in *The Bohemian Girl*; *Maritana*).

However, in 1879, when *Pinafore* mania hit America, Carrie found herself in her comic-opera element. She appeared in *HMS Pinafore* as, variously, Hebe and Josephine, alongside the star musical-comedian Digby Bell, then featured in a season at the Bijou Theatre playing Susan Bumpus in *Charity Begins at Home* and Viola in *The Spectre Knight* (1880) before going on tour with E. E. Rice's Bijou company (*Pirates of Penzance*; *Charity Begins at Home*, etc.). In 1881 she took the star role of Phoebe in *Billee Taylor* and the title-role of *Patience* at the Standard Theatre, and in 1882 she was Constance in *Claude Duval*, and Phoebe again. However, she turned down the part of Constance to the Aline of Lillian Russell in *The Sorcerer* and, instead, went on the road with James Barton's company playing *Iolanthe*, with Walter Pelham.

Thereafter, Carrie played Alexina in *Falka* at the Casino Theatre; appeared in *Zanita* in Boston (1884); and, in 1889, played Florina in McCaull's production of *Clover* at Palmer's Theatre and on the subsequent tour before, seemingly, putting an end to her career. She married a widowed Hungarian ex-army captain (otherwise a beef packer and a real estate agent), Theodore G. Korony, and had two children.

Patience after the Aesthetic Days

Patience has flourished like the green bay tree since its first production. It has been played on the Continent in German and Hungarian, with the delightful subtitle of *Dragoner und Dichter* (Dragoons and Poets). It has even—this, probably the least "operatic" of G&S works—reached the odd opera house. It has gone to places, in the modern age, where the British aesthetic movement, Pater, and Whistler have never been heard of. Does it then stand on its own merits as a stage piece, without its burlesque context—despite its less-than-drawing title, Gilbert's least interesting heroine, and Sullivan's least "operatic" score? Yes, it does.

But I think that the blubber-lipped Oscar Fingal O'Flahertie Wilde, who has become as much a simplistic icon for the twenty-first century as Attila the Hun, Jeanne d'Arc, and Che Guevara have, may still be the piece's best publicist, 140 years on . . . Mr. R. D'Oyly Carte knew his business!

7

Iolanthe, or The Peer and the Peri

Fairy opera in two acts
Savoy Theatre, 25 November 1882

Apart from the final effluvium of spirits from the underworld in *The Sorcerer*, and the little cupid twinkling above the plighted judge's head in *Trial by Jury*, Gilbert had, a little surprisingly, steered clear of using fairies, elves, and goddesses as characters in his collaborations with Sullivan. And he had proven, by the ingenuity of his characters and his delightful deus-ex-machinal twists, that he had no need of "magic" of the old-fashioned *Devil to Pay* type to shape his plots. And he proved it all over again in *Iolanthe*. Yes, all the female characters of the piece are fairies . . . well, bar one, and that is made up for by the fact that one of the men in the cast is of the spawn of fairyland. But, improbably, he is only a half-fairy . . . and therein lies the nub of the plot.

Long, long ago in fairyland, a little boy, Strephon, was born. His mother was the mezzo-soprano fairy, Iolanthe, and his father . . . shock, horror! was a mortal man. The Queen of the Fairies could nothing do but banish the wayward fay, who has since dwelt (on her head) at the bottom of a stream. Strephon has grown up, as 50 percent fairy-boys do, as an Arcadian shepherd, and he is, naturally, in love with Phyllis, who is, naturally, an Arcadian shepherdess—even though we never see a sheep. Unfortunately, Phyllis is also a Ward-in-Chancery (I didn't know Chancery accepted shepherdesses, Arcadian or otherwise, did you?). She's also so pretty that she is sighed over by the whole House of Lords, including the Lord Chancellor, who is having a deuce of a job convincing himself (in his official position) of the suitability of himself (in his private position) as a husband for his ward. Peripeteia strikes when Iolanthe is pardoned, and Phyllis spies her shepherd saying "Good morrow" to this beautiful young lady in an unnecessarily osculatory fashion. Mother, schmother! The wedding is off! Off! Phyllis plights herself to any peer who pleases. Strephon calls his fairy aunts to his aid. Revelations are the order of the day, and the Lord Chancellor, "an old equity draughtsman," makes a tiny amendment—no magic needed, just a little legal chicanery—to Fairy Law that allows all to end happily.

In spite of the usual guesswork paragraphs in the gossipy press, there seems to have been little doubt as to the nature of the new Gilbert and Sullivan work for the Savoy Theatre. The *Era* newspaper published an almost accurate plot summary many months before the production. And the music? Sullivan had Arcadia, the House of Peers, and a burlo-dramatic Queen—O! shades of *The Bohemian Girl*—to set to music, and he grabbed the opportunities therein fully. The finale to act 1 of *Iolanthe* is one of his finest. I should know: it's been blu-tacked in my brain for seventy years! How often, out of nowhere, do I find myself cooing "Go away, madam . . ." and "Bearded by these pu-hoo-ny mortals."

However, copyright details ruled, and once again, while the piece was being referred to as *The Princess Pearl* or *Perola* to put goodness-knows-whom off the track, Carte organized a double-headed premiere, one on each side of the Atlantic. And thus, give or take half a handful of hours, *Iolanthe* had a double "first night cast."

The piece's two principal protagonists were, quite simply, on each side of the Atlantic, the stars of *Patience*. The deliciously funny character of the Lord Chancellor, with his three memorable numbers ("The Law Is the True Embodiment"; "When I Went to the Bar"; and the extreme patter of "The Nightmare Song") was Grossmith in England and Ryley in America. And, as his antagonist, the vast, imperious (but, nevertheless, susceptible) Queen of the Fairies, were cast the two champion Lady Janes: Alice Barnett (in the United Kingdom) and Augusta Roche (in the United States).

Alice Barnett (Fairy Queen)

Miss Barnett was born at 2 Bucklersbury, Cheapside, on 17 May 1846, a descendant of a famed theatrical family: not on her father's side—Charles Barnett was a stationer—but on her mother's. Elizabeth Fanny Barnett was née Kemble, as in Henry Kemble, Charles Kemble, Adelaide Kemble, and Mrs. Sarah Siddons: theatrical royalty, one and all. Both Alice and her elder sister, Fanny Kemble Barnett (Mrs. William Ebenezer Poole) followed

41. Alice Barnett: "Who taught me to curl myself up inside a buttercup?"

Adelaide's way and trained as vocalists, and both were fine contraltos, but fate and physique were to lead them in different directions. Madame Poole was, for fifteen years, a useful concert and oratorio singer. The tall and massive Miss Barnett started out on the same rails, but, after some eight years, performing in mostly modest concerts, she took a branch-line labeled "this way to D'Oyly-Carteland" and everything changed.

Alice studied with the excellent contralto Mrs. Natalia Macfarren and made her public debut in 1871 (27 May) at a concert given by Mrs. Raby Barrett. The future Fairy Queen sang "Voi che sapete." Thereafter, I see her singing at Crouch End, Wood Green, Sussex Hall, Shoreditch, Camden Town, Chelmsford, the Schubert Society, and at the classy concert lectures of Mrs. John Macfarren, as well as at Leamington, Blackheath, Swindon, and further afield—Middlesbrough, Southport, and Portsmouth—occasionally in a *Messiah* or an *Elijah* with local unknowns. Mostly she sang ballads, sometimes a bit of Schumann or Handel . . . and then came *HMS Pinafore*.

In 1879, Alice was cast as Little Buttercup in one of Carte's touring companies, to such good effect that she was taken to New York to repeat the role and to create the part of Ruth in *The Pirates of Penzance*. On her return to England, she took up the role of Ruth in the London production, and segued into two of the greatest G&S contralto roles: the Lady Jane of *Patience* with her silvered hair and her violoncello, and the imperious Fairy Queen of *Iolanthe*.

In October 1883, however, Miss Barnett (now Mrs. John Thanet Dickins, wife of a retired coal merchant) suffered an illness ("Kemble rheumatism") and had to withdraw from the Savoy cast. She was replaced by one "Rosa Carlingford," under which pseudonym apparently sheltered a society semiprofessional who had scored a hit with her "basso" performance as Peronella in *Boccaccio*. It was a pro tem arrangement only. When the new opera, *Princess Ida*, was mounted, the role of Lady Blanche, which would doubtless have been Alice's, was given to Miss Brandram, who had been with the company since *Pinafore* days. Since there was no question of demoting the long-serving Miss Brandram, the revivified Alice went out with the touring company, and then with what might be termed the semiopposition. She joined Edward Solomon, composer of the megahit *Billee Taylor*, and his paramour, divette Lillian Russell, as, first, the "heavy woman" of their London production of *Pocohantas*, and then in the same position in their *Polly* and *Billee Taylor* in America. And, while she was in America, she was engaged to go even further; Alice sailed for Australia, under contract to Williamson and Garner. She and her husband remained down under for three years, Alice appearing in mostly G&S roles as well as such as Martha in *Faust* and Mrs. Privett in *Dorothy*, before they went back to Britain, where she picked up her career as a very tall, very popular, contralto.

Alice featured in *Dorothy*'s successor *Doris* (Mistress Sheldon) at the Lyric, toured for Auguste van Biene as Martha in *Faust-up-to-Date* and Micaela in *Carmen up-to-Data*, and with the Burns-Crotty Light Opera as an ugly sister in *Cinderella*. She played the Duchess of Duffshire in *In Town*, Dame Hecla Courtlandt in *His Excellency*, and served as a replacement for poor Lillie Belmore as the nonheiress of *The Shop Girl* in the West End before again voyaging to America to repeat her *His Excellency* role. Her next engagement was as Miss Berry McNab in *The Telephone Girl* on the English road, but she was, again, forced to leave the company by illness. This time it was her husband's; Dickins died on 24 August 1896, at the age of sixty-one.

Alice made one more American trip, to play in *The Mandarin* (Sing Lo), then settled back into her role in the long-touring *The Telephone Girl* until Christmas 1897, when Arthur Collins called on her for his pantomime. And thus, the original Fairy Queen and Lady Jane ended up at Drury Lane, playing Miss Gertie Girton in *The Babes in the Wood* alongside Dan Leno and Ada Blanche. And after little Dan Leno came even smaller Little Tich! Alice was cast opposite (or, more precisely, "towering over") the little comedian in his Osmond Carr musical comedy, *Billy*. She towered again in the "heavy" Gladys Homfrey role of Melanopis in *A Greek Slave* on the road, and then went back to play her umpteenth *Telephone Girl*.

To all evidence, purely as a contralto vocalist, sister Fanny was the more competent of the two. But while Fanny pursued a classical career at the second level and was content as the wife of a medical registrar, Alice got herself on that yellow-brick road to the Savoy, capitalized on her physique and her comic ability, and won lasting fame.

The family's connection with the Cartesian world would continue. Fanny's son, Harold Poole, rather swankily adopting, latterly, the stage name of "W. H. Kemble," spent a good half dozen years under Cartesian colors. He married a fellow Cartesian, Nancy Pounds, of the many-branched Pounds family of singers, thus adding another few pages to a family tree into which, yes, I have delved, but that's another (rather long) story.

W. T. Carleton (Strephon)

So, who played the lightsome, fairy-mortal crossbreed, Arcadio-sheepherder hero? In olden days, it would have been Nellie Farren or Madeleine Clary in tights, but G&S had forsworn all that. In a hilariously grotesque turnaround, they cast the part with chunky, baritonic Richard Temple in London, and in New York with another of precisely the same breed, who had, over the years, shared many a bill and many a stage with his contemporary: Mr. W. T. Carleton.

The baritone who called himself William Turnham Carleton was born as plain William Standing, at 3 Batten's Terrace, High Street, Peckham, on 23 August 1848. But there was nothing "plain" theatrically about his family. He was one of three brothers, the sons of a London customs-house clerk, each of whom would make himself a deservedly prominent name in the Victorian theater.

42. W. T. Carleton: But half a fairy, and a member of Parliament.

The eldest, Frank, started his singing life as Frank Standing, then switched to "Frank Crellin," but, with the Italian opera in view, finally became "F. H. Celli" (b. Dalston, 8 April 1845; d. London, 27 December 1904). Frank was a splendid baritone singer with a splendid baritone moustache and splendidly wavy baritonic locks who sang in operetta, comic opera, opera (both the Italian Maplesonian kind and the English type with Carl Rosa), musical comedy, and even, latterly, in the music halls. In his forty-some years as a singer, he covered everything from the creation of the title-role in Sterndale Bennett's *Thorgrim* to singing "Jack's the Man" at the Alhambra.

The youngest of the three baritonic brothers, [James] Herbert Standing (b. Peckham, 13 November 1846; d. Los Angeles, 5 December 1923), although he played leading roles in the musical theater (*La Vie parisienne, Nell Gwynne, Chilpéric, The French Maid*), made his name, both in England and in America, as an actor. And the middle brother, our William, had a career that rivaled—if not excelled—them both.

In spite of his half-century career, it doesn't seem that William has been much written about. I can't even find a university thesis about him and his brothers. And I, shamefully, bundled the three lads together in one article in my *Encyclopaedia of the Musical Theatre*. It is time to give William Standing—otherwise Mr. Carlton, otherwise Mr. W. Carlton, otherwise Mr. W. Carleton, and, finally, thanks to concurrence, Mr. W. T. Carleton—his due. And what better place than here for America's second Archibald Grosvenor and everyone's half-first Strephon.

My first sighting of "Mr. Carlton" is in Doncaster. He's singing with Mr. D. Morley's Entertainment *The Two Eras*, alongside the teenaged Miss Pauline (recte Mary Ann) Grayston. A year later, he has been "discovered." Edwin Villiers of the South London Music Hall (etc.) has picked up the "admirable bass vocalist" and is featuring him and his "Will o' the Wisp," "The Vagabond," "The Friar of Orders Grey," and so forth, south of the Thames. But the stalwart baritone was soon spotted, also, by the theater guys: in April 1870, he toured with John Russell of Covent Garden playing *Bluebeard* with the amazing Augusta Thomson, apparently playing the tenor role of Bluebeard! Or has the reviewer made a muddle? He sang for Villiers in south London and in his summer season at the Margate Assembly Rooms. However, when he, Cicely Nott, and William Terrott played the little *Rose of the Auvergne* at the Bedford Music Hall, the beastly boys of patent theaters dragged them to court. The trio lost, but only technically, and I see that William's next shop was with the leaders of the "plays in music halls" movement, Charles Morton and Emily Soldene, at the Philharmonic, Islington, playing their law-skirting "scena based on" *Chilpéric*.

After a turn at the Canterbury Music Hall (where Villiers had succeeded manager Morton), Carleton was hired for another production of *Bluebeard*, this time at the Alhambra, and this time in the comical role of Popolani, after which he went to the Opera Comique to play a little operetta with Edward Cotte and Emmeline Cole. The piece was titled *Dr. Ambrosias, His Secret*, and the composer was Mr. R. D'Oyly Carte. When the young composer, who was also a high-flying musical agent, published his "special opéra-bouffe" client list shortly after, the bass-baritone section of the said list was headed by Mr. R. Temple and Mr. Carlton.

Mr. Carlton didn't lack for work. He appeared with the short-lived National Opera at the St. James's Theatre as Florio in *The Rose of Castille* (Temple was Pedro); he sang Bide-the-Bent in *Lucia di Lammermoor* with Sims Reeves and Hermann in *Letty the Basketmaker* at the Gaiety;

and he joined Fred Sullivan and Dick Beverley to play *Cox and Box* at a Benefit. At Christmas 1871, he set out for a seven-month Gaiety tour, with England's original "Grande-Duchesse," Julia Mathews at its head. Mr. Carlton was her General Boom, Agamemnon to her *Belle Hélène*, Popolani in *Barbe-bleue*, and played a theatrical *The Rose of the Auvergne*. When that tour ended, Carleton went straight back to Villiers, at Margate, giving such baritonic hardies as "Will o' the Wisp," "The Yeomen's Wedding," "Heart of Oak," and the *Cox and Box* "Rataplan" as "a welcome relief to the surfeit of comicalities" on the summertime programs.

When the new Gaiety tour set out, Carlton was again featured, this time alongside Annie Tremaine of *Thespis*, now a full-blown leading lady. He added Pietro in *The Brigands*, Matt o' the Mint (*The Beggar's Opera*), and the Viceroy in *La Périchole* to his repertoire. The Gaiety seemed to regard him as a comic, rather than a straight baritone. Other folk had other ideas. There was to be no summer at Margate Sands this year. When Clarence Hess, manager of the Kellogg Opera Company, returned to America from a talent-spotting mission, in August 1873, he brought with him two tenors—Joseph Maas and Wilford Morgan—and one baritone: William Carleton.

Carleton would play no comic roles for Hess; he was Don José in *Maritana*, Ashton in *Lucia di Lammermoor*, Luna in *Il Trovatore*, and Almaviva in *The Marriage of Figaro* while Henry Peakes played the ex-barber. At the end of his contract he returned to England and I see him in the Crystal Palace operas (Valentine in *Faust*, Hoel in *Dinorah*) and in Hervé's season of Covent Garden proms. He was billed as "the new baritone," giving his old favorites, and he took the baritone part, to Lewis Thomas's King Koffee, in the composer's topical "Ashantee Symphony." However, within months, he was back in America, re-signed by Hess for more of the same. Over the following four seasons, he played the full star-baritone repertoire with the company: Luna, Rigoletto, Valentine, Escamillo, Danny Mann, the Flying Dutchman, Plunkett, Amonasro, Richard the Lionheart in Balfe's *The Talisman*, *e tutti quanti*.

But another change was coming. He was signed to play the role of the Drum Major in *La Fille du tambour-major* at the London Alhambra, and—although he returned, thereafter, to America to give his Escamillo to the *Carmen* of Marie Roze—his new way had been set. He quickly became one of America's top musical-theater baritones, appearing in the first half of the 1880s in such important pieces as *Patience* (Colonel Calverley), *Claude Duval* (Duval), *La Mascotte* (Pippo), *The Merry War*

(Umberto), *Les Manteaux noirs* (Don Luis), *Rip van Winkle* (Rip), *Iolanthe* (Strephon), *The Queen's Lace Handkerchief* (Cervantes), *The Beggar Student* (Symon), and *Nanon* (D'Aubigné) before, in 1885, leaving the baritone slot in *Amorita* to brother Celli and taking out his own traveling comic opera company. He toured for a number of years, around America, during which he produced and starred in *Erminie*'s successor, *Mynheer Jan* (1888, Karl). For a number of years, the Carleton company had a reputation second to none for quality, but latterly there was something of a falling off, and, finally, Carleton disbanded his troupe.

He returned to Broadway to play in a long list of further musicals—from Danny Mann to Gilfain in *Florodora* to Lt. Berner to the Mdlle. Mischief of Lulu Glaser (1908); and—after a series of nonmusical roles—again, as late as 1919, when he took over from DeWolf Hopper in *Everything* at the Hippodrome. He also appeared in some thirty silent films between 1914 and 1920, notably as Zamaliel in the spectacle *Fantasma*.

In contrast to his brothers, William appears to have a settled private life. He married Margaret Propert James at twenty-two, and sired a son, William Propert Standing (aka Carleton). This son became a musical theater juvenile man, and married the miniature soubrette Harriette Mary Kavanagh (aka "Toby Claude") and . . . well, the Standing family tree fills an entire page in *Who's Who in the Theatre*, but I'll leave it there.

Jessie Bond (Iolanthe)

The storyline of *Iolanthe* resulted in one minor lady member of the company being allotted an altogether more important part than heretofore. *Iolanthe* is the only Gilbert and Sullivan work where the jeune premier has a mother. Mrs. Rackstraw? Mrs. Poo? Lady Fairfax? And, of course, because this is a fairy opera—better still, a burlesque fairy opera—by inexorable (except when bent slightly by an old Equity Draughtsman) Fairy Law, she must if not "be" then at least "seem" to be younger than her big, baritonic son. The role of pretty Phyllis being, after Patience, the next of the "soubretty" Savoy ladies, was clearly made to measure for Miss Braham . . . so, who was to be the errant fairy? If I had been the casting director, it would have been the so-far wasted Rosina Brandram, but no. Miss Brandram's time was not just yet; instead, the part was given to the eight-years-younger Jessie Bond. Perhaps she had less voice, but she had more youth. Prettier? In whose eyes? "Taradiddle, taradiddle, tol lol lol."

Miss Bond had been solidly employed by Carte since her hiring for the remnants of the role of Hebe in HMS *Pinafore*. She and her sister had been two heads of that Cerberusian creature known in the Gänzl family as EdithKate'n'Isabel in *The Pirates of Penzance*, and she had again been featured as part of the *Patience* trio of Ladies AngelaSaphir'n'Ella—supporting ladies with a few lines to sing solo and snatches of dialogue but no real character to play. And now she was to have a key role—the title-role indeed!—in the new Savoy opera.

We should know all the whys and wherefores of Jessie Bond's career and life. After all, she wrote an autobiography. Alas, I think G&S scholars the world over would agree that Jessie's book is the most disingenuously unfactual of all Savoyard autobiographies. Just as Carte tried to remake her biography when she joined the Opera Comique company, Jessie tried to reremake it in her soi-disant memoirs. But Jessie Bond would spend the better part of her career as a well-loved Cartesian. Post-Savoy, she proved a disappointment. And pre-Savoy . . . well, here's the bit of her life and career that Mr. Carte "forgot."

Jessie Charlotte Bond (b. Pratt Street, London, 10 January 1853; d. Worthing, 17 June 1942) was the daughter of John Bond (Jr.), a hereditary piano maker, and lawyer's daughter Elizabeth (née Simson); she was the third child of a family that included two elder brothers and, soon after, two younger sisters. The family moved to Liverpool when Jessie was three, and she studied piano with Isouard Praeger, making what appears to have been her first appearance at the Hope Hall in his concert of 18 May 1865, "aged 11," alongside another local pianistic teeny aged twelve.

Subsequently, Jessie studied voice with local music master Ferdinand Alexis Schottländer, and made her public debut as a vocalist on 18 November 1869, at a concert of his pupils, singing "Ah, quel giorno" (*Semiramide*) and her teacher's ditty "Oh, Do Say Yes." In 1871 (30 January), she made her "second appearance in public," singing "O Thou Afflicted" (*St. Peter*), the *Dinorah* goatherd song, and Schottländer's "The Spanish Beggar Girl." We are told that the teacher was a bad egg, that he seduced the teenager and forced or bamboozled her into a marriage. A child was born, and died, Ferdinand was allegedly unfaithful, and the marriage ended in divorce in 1872. Weird story; I'd like to hear his version. Anyhow, Ferdinand whisked off to Ireland, remarried, had more children, and lived long enough to see his ex-wife become a starlet.

Jessie was seen quite frequently in the Lancashire concerts during the next few years: with Mr. and Mrs. Howard Paul at the Royal Alex-

43. Jessie Bond: Iolanthe, thou drippest!

andra and the Queen's Hall; in her first *Messiah* with the Liverpool Società Armonica; or singing "Ah, quel giorno," "Nobil signor," and two of Horton C. Allison's songs at the young pianist's concert (1872). She appeared at Birkenhead with Edith Wynne and Montem Smith in *The May Queen*; at Oswestry and the Liverpool Institute in more *Messiahs*; and sang in a number of Edward de Jong's classy concerts, in Liverpool, Bradford, and Manchester (*Dinorah*, "The Sailor Boy's Farewell," "Looking Back," "Ah, quel giorno," "Auld Robin Gray," Randegger's "Sleep, Dearest, Sleep," "The Sailor Boy's Return" in a "quiet unassuming manner . . . a contralto or mezzosoprano of good quality, not however distinguished by power, and each effort was warmly received").

The credits mounted steadily: the Liverpool Saturday Concerts ("Terence's Farewell," "Wapping Old Stairs," etc.), the contralto music in *Elijah* at Birkenhead (1873, "very far above the rank experience has taught us to look for in local singers"), and a "careful and finished rendering" of *The Messiah* at the Liverpool Amphitheatre on Good Friday. She appeared in various miscellaneous concerts, another *Messiah* at Oswestry, *Jephtha* at Birkenhead, at Southport with Edward Lloyd, and at the Liverpool Ballad Concerts, and then, in 1876, Jessie enrolled at the Royal Academy of Music. The oft-repeated statement that she "went to the RAM [as a pianist] and discovered a voice" is so much nonsense, as are all other versions of her career that elide the first half dozen years of her career as a vocalist into almost nothing. In fact, she passed a modest time at the Academy and very quickly stopped advertising herself as "RAM."

In 1877, Jessie sang with the Liverpool Philharmonic Society; at Jules Rivière's proms at the Queen's Theatre; at the Scarborough Aquarium; at the Glasgow Saturday Evenings; at Kilburn (Balfe's "Killarney"); with Helen Taylor's lectures at Sadler's Wells (*Elijah*); and with Thurley Beale in the concertina concerts at Langham Hall. On Good Friday 1878 she sang one more *Messiah* with Fred Packard. Miss Jessie Bond seemed promised a nice, little career, in minor and provincial concerts, with which to supplement her teaching activities. And then Mrs. Howard Paul got terminally ill. And the tale of Jessie Bond, Savoyard—which is related in detail in many, many books (including mine, and hers)—began.

Jessie played several other engagements, away from the Savoy, in later years (the musical comedy *Go Bang*; Gilbert's *His Excellency*), and she even pops up singing with Madame Konss-Baylis's Gipsy Revellers in 1890, before retiring to a rather more satisfactory second marriage.

Durward Lely (Lord Tolloller)

Since *Iolanthe* had a half-fairy baritone hero, what was to become of the traditional tenor? Sullivan had solved that situation already in *Patience*. With his title-soubrette paired off with the Barringtonic Grosvenor, he had simply swung the tenor music into the role of the Duke of Dunstable, who was the "pair-off" for the heavy lady! It worked marvelously. (Today's writers of musicals might take heed: how tired are we all of acoustically exaggerated "heroes" striving up beyond the stave.) The *Patience* example was most successfully followed. The tenor music was

Iolanthe, or The Peer and the Peri

44. Durward Lely as Lord Tolloller: "Spurn not the nobly born."

the lot of one of the rejected suitors, Lord Tolloller. And it was sung, in England, by the same tenor, the Scots Durward Lely, who had played Dunstable in the earlier piece.

James Durward Lyall was born in Arbroath, on 2 September 1852, the son of an estate factor and farmer. He took his first musical steps in his hometown of Blairgowrie as "Mr. Durward," before, sponsored by the cattle breeder Patrick Allen Fraser, Esq., of Hospitalfield, he went to Milan to study with (of course) Francesco Lamperti. He was heard in public, apparently for the first time, in concert at Rome's Teatro Argentina. "News" from Italy was inclined to be a bit approximate, but he allegedly played his first opera role at Rimini: Manrico in *Il Trovatore* (not, at that stage, played by a tenor robusto). The first dates I have provenly picked up for "Signor Dorvaldo Leli" are at Sassari in November 1876 and Cagliari in February 1877 (*Barbiere di Siviglia, Don Pasquale, L'Elisir d'amore*), where he was adjudged to have a "voce soave e patetica," at the Teatro Martinetti in Garlasco (*Il Trovatore*), at Intra (*La Favorita, Il Barbiere*), Lago Maggiore (*Maria di Rohan*), and at the Politeama Umberto, Oneglia (*La Sonnambula*), all in 1877. In March 1878, he was hired to go to Krolls Theater, Berlin, as fourth primo tenore with an Italian opera company. The producer bankrupted and scarpered after the first night; the other three got to sing *La Traviata* and *Linda di Chamonix*, but I think Signor Leli may not have sung anything. Anyway, that was the end of his European adventure.

Back in England, he was hired for Her Majesty's Theatre and, in February 1879, he was cast to play Don José to the *Carmen* of Selina Dolaro in the first English-language performances of Bizet's opera. He was subsequently snapped up by Emily Soldene to be Don José to her Carmen. First time around Britain, he played *Carmen* only, with all the other tenor roles being taken by Henry Nordblom, but he softened his implacably operatic mode sufficiently to sing Florio in *The Naval Cadets* and the Defendant in *Trial by Jury* on Soldene's second tour, and then chucked it altogether—along with the Italian name. He took over the role of Frederic in *The Pirates of Penzance* with Mr. Carte's company at the Opera Comique.

Durward Lely, as he had now become known, was to stay half a dozen years with Carte, as leading tenor in *Patience, Iolanthe, Princess Ida*, the revival of *The Sorcerer, The Mikado*, and *Ruddigore*. However, when he withdrew from the Savoy company, he was still only in his mid-thirties. There was plenty more career to come.

A large part of Lely's subsequent career was devoted to concerts, singing Scottish songs with his wife at the piano, and appearing in that favorite vehicle of the slightly clapped-out tenor, *Rob Roy*, where, in the role of Osbaldistone, one could include a virtual concert of Scots material. Both Marie Roze and, especially, Adelina Patti made use of his good (but not *too* good) tenor voice and used him regularly as a support act. However, he had not abandoned the theater. Lely appeared at the Opera Comique as Don Felix de Tornado in *Carina*, and toured as Hildebert in *La Girouette* with Giulia Warwick. However, when he appeared with the Carl Rosa, during their 1890 London season, singing Rudolph in *Lurline*, his voice was reckoned "too small"; Barton McGuckin was given the role of Don José. Lely was recalled when the company went on tour, for more Don Josés and a share in the other tenor roles along with Agostino Montegriffo, John Child, and Wilbur Gunn, and, when Augustus Harris mounted a matinée series of *Carmen*, Lely retuned to Drury Lane to give "his" role opposite Daria Farini and later Zélie Trebelli, and to sing Thaddeus in *The Bohemian Girl*, and Don Cesar in *Maritana* with Marie Roze.

Lely sang at the Boosey Ballad Concerts and in northern *Messiahs*; he appeared in *Zampa* and *Norma* with northern amateurs, and in the unfortunate *Nydia, the Blind Girl of Pompeii* at the Crystal Palace. He sang Ebenezer Prout's *Red Cross Knight* here, *The Spectre's Bride* there, and the Rossini *Stabat Mater* with Amy Sherwin, and Augustus Harris recalled him one more time to Covent Garden, in 1892, for one more Don José with Trebelli. It was, actually, not wholly his last. Oscar Hammerstein imported him to the United States for an 1893 opera season. The experience was not a happy one, and the Lelys hurried home.

From here on, his theatrical jobs—except for repeated *Rob Roys*—were few: a couple of weeks as a takeover in Goring Thomas's *The Golden Web*; Adelina Patti's friendly showing of *Gabriella*; and a Scottish opera based on *Cramond Brig* (*Holyrood*). By and large, Mr. and Mrs. Lely simply toured their concert show, through Britain, America, Canada, Australia, and New Zealand, and returned home to their nice mansion in the highlands of Perthshire. Lely died at Queensborough Gardens, Hillhead, Glasgow, on 29 February 1944, at the age of ninety-one.

Charles Manners and Lithgow James (Private Willis)

Jack Ryley, Lyn Cadwaladr (New York's Tolloller), Jessie Bond, Durward Lely, Leonora Braham, Rutland Barrington, Augusta Roche, Richard Temple, and others were all (or would be) recidivist Cartesians, but there were some in the cast of *Iolanthe* who were not.

In London, Charles Manners played the part of the sentry, Private Willis, whose final-curtain fate it is to become a Fairy King. His opening solo to act 2, alone in his sentry box, unaware that six-foot fairies are nigh, was another gem: a fit follower, as a curtain raiser, to Lady Jane's violoncello number in *Patience*. He tells us "When all night long a chap remains on sentry-go, to chase monotony, he exercises of his brain, that is assuming that he's got any" before coming to the logical conclusion that "every boy and every gal that's born into the world alive, is either a little Liberal or else a little Conservative." Fa-lal-la. Charles Manners (né Southcote Mansergh, b. Hoddesdon, 27 December 1857; d. Dublin, 3

45. Lithgow James: six feet four inches of sentry or sailor.

May 1935) was a proper bass. And Sullivan had, inspirationally, written the "Sentry's Song" for a plunging bass. Fa-lal-la! So Mr. Manners (bass) came off tour, into the Savoy, and created the part of Willis. His future is well-known. From *Iolanthe* he moved on the Carl Rosa company, Covent Garden, and thence to his own company, the Moody-Manners Opera Company, with his wife, Fanny Moody.

In America, Willis was played by baritone Lithgow James (né James Smith, b. Pulman's Yard, Barnard Castle, 1846; d. Queen St., Barnard Castle, 27 February 1900). "Lithgow" was unlucky. He seemingly had everything going for him: talent, a fine voice, acting ability, good looks, six feet four inches . . . but, in the end, he is best known for having married, and, justifiably, divorced, a twenty-one-year-old widow named Maggie ("Jack") Greig. Maggie was to become England's "Queen of Comic Opera" as Florence St. John.

James was born in Barnard Castle to William Smith, a metalworker, and his wife Mary (née Lithgow). While his brothers took up the family trade, he started his working life as apprentice to an iron founder. However, he soon swapped life in the foundry for music and, by 1871, I see him in Westminster's Purbeck Place billed as "musician." I don't know if and what he had done to date. (I did look round the Yorkshire concerts ... but how to sort out a James Smith?). It is November 1872 before I spot him first: on a program at the Albert Hall, alongside no less a star than Ann Banks, supplying the musical illustration to Julia St. George's reciting of *The Tempest* and *As You Like It*. I don't see him again, thereafter, till 1875, when he surfaces in the Crystal Palace opera season (*Il Trovatore*, *Un Ballo in maschera*), then singing *The Creation* in concert at the Sunday Evenings for the People, before joining the Durand Opera Company as a principal baritone alongside Annie Tonnellier, Sophia Mariani, William Parkinson, and, oh dear, Florence St. John. He sang in Dublin and Liverpool with a company headed by Parkinson and Blanche Cole, and at Ashton-under-Lyne he married Miss St. John.

They toured together in 1877, appearing in concerts in Edinburgh, in opera with the Blanche Cole company and at the Crystal Palace, and also on the road with Rose Hersee's company. They sang in the Manchester pops, played a five-week season at Cork over the holidays and James gave his Malatesta at the Alexandra Palace and the Crystal Palace, before they went out on the road again, he playing Henri to Jack's Germaine in *Les Cloches de Corneville*. The couple played in the Brighton panto together, and all seemed well, but soon after Lithgow advertised for work, saying he had "no objection to overseas" engagements—what! without the wife? Well, the wife had changed in status. After that tour, Alexander Henderson had called on Miss St. John to play her *Cloches* role in town, and then cast her in the very important title-role in *Madame Favart*. She had caused a veritable sensation and was on her way to becoming London's biggest musical-theater star.

So, James joined Carte, and—as soon as that engagement finished—he did, indeed, sail for America, to join Emma Abbott's company (1880–81). When he came home, it was to find that Mons Marius, the musical comedy star, and his wife had been unashamedly profiting from his absence; big James ended up in court when Marius took refuge from the cuckolded husband's fists in the law. James went back to America. In 1881–83, he found plenty of work: *La Mascotte*, *The Snake Charmer*, *Patience* for Comley and Barton and for Haverley, *The Merry War*, and as a six-feet four-inch Private Willis in America's first *Iolanthe*. But the spies back home had been taking notes and, in 1882, he sued his wife for divorce, citing Marius as corespondent. That relationship was *un secret de Polichinelle*, and he won his case.

James rejoined Carte for a few months, playing Corcoran and the Pirate King ("looked the part to the life and acted and sang splendidly"), then headed back to America, singing with a Strakosch concert party, and appearing as Arac in *Princess Ida* in Boston. When he returned home, however, he merely sang in a few concerts around Sunderland. He visited America again in 1887–88, but then returned home for good. It seemed his career had ended. But fellow Barnard-Castellian Valentine Smith co-opted him for his staunchly touring opera company and, thus, Lithgow was seen, around Britain, for several years more singing Luna, Don José, Plunkett, Devilshoof ("the requisite physique, abandon and voice"), and Arnheim. In the 1891 census, he can be seen sharing a home in Queen Street, Barnard Castle, with his unmarried sister, Alice, labeled slightly prematurely "retired vocalist." He didn't make it to the next census: He died in his hometown in 1900, leaving his 2,111 pounds, ten shillings, and sixpence to Alice. What a waste of a man and an artist!

Iolanthe's Legacy

Iolanthe as we know it in the twenty-first century isn't quite the *Iolanthe* of its first showings. While the principal numbers—notably the dancing trio of the three noble lords, "Faint Heart Never Won Fair Lady"—were immediately and sublimely popular, elsewhere Gilbert had gone on, just a little bit too much, hitting the same political button. So, a song for Strephon, who has been metamorphosed into an MP, and is ready to wreak havoc on parliamentary customs (information already supplied by the Queen), was quickly excised, and a set piece for Barrington soon went the same way. And thus made less jabbing and more joyful, *Iolanthe* went on to become one of the favorite comic operas of the nineteenth, twentieth, and twenty-first centuries.

8

Princess Ida, or Castle Adamant

A respectful operatic perversion of Tennyson's *Princess* in a prologue and two acts
Savoy Theatre, 5 January 1884

What to say of *Princess Ida*? Every sort of opinion and evaluation of its qualities has been expressed, so the best I can do is add my personal tuppenceworth. The show contains some of Sullivan's most splendid Savoy music, it contains some deliciously characteristical Gilbertian lyrics, but they are set in an old-fashioned story, lacking the merry bouffe elements that were so admired and loved in a Savoy opera: the piece as a whole comes over, to me, rather like a group of shining jewels set in a slightly tatty old mount.

About sixty-five years ago, during my devoted-to-Tennyson phase, I read *The Princess*. I remember nothing of it; I much preferred *Oenone*. Now if Gilbert had turned his attention to *her*, but I guess Henri Meilhac and Ludovic Halévy had got there first. Then, about fifty years ago, I read Gilbert's text for his burlesque of the piece. I remember thinking it was more amusing, and better written, than the slightly stilted work of Planché and his ilk, but . . . well, as I've said before, there's not so much fun in a burlesque of something if you don't really care or know about the thing burlesqued. And blokes dressed up as girls to get into a girls' school was such an overused plot—one that had, in fact, been employed by Paul Ferrier, Jules Prével, and Louis Varney, just a handful of years earlier in their vastly successful opérette *Les Mousquetaires au couvent*, itself a version of the 1835 *Le Habit ne fait pas le moine*, which was undoubtedly a version of something even older.

So, we have a princess and a prince, betrothed at the ages of one and two. Now they are twenty-one and twenty-two, and 'tis time that they were wed. But the princess has founded an educational establishment disdaining all that is male—even chessmen. So . . . of course, all ends happily matrimonially after three (yes, three) acts of virtual "turns." But they were, mostly, turns by fun characters. Grossmith was King Gama, the Princess's father, equipped with two particularly good patter songs (although little else), Barrington was King Hildebrand, the father of the pining prince, equipped (to his expressed annoyance) with but one solo (in *The Princess*, the role had been decorated with a version of "Largo al factotum"!) . . . comical characters both. The soubrette was Lady Psyche, "professor of humanities" with a Savoy-Darwinian ditty about "The Lady and the Ape"; the mildly heavy lady was Lady Blanche—who supplied the principal (only?) subplot with her attempts to wrest control of the Academy from Ida ("Come Mighty Must"); and the men were six . . . three per team. Team Hildebrand (*due tenori e uno tenore-baritono*) was headed by the fine Welsh tenor known as Henry Bracy (Hilarion) as the budding bridegroom; with two friends, Cyril and Florian, as his backups; while the head of Team Gama (*bassi*) was Arac, represented by Richard Temple, supported, in turn, by his brothers Guron and Scynthius. Both teams got plenty of opportunities; the first act (or prologue), after all, was an entirely all-male affair, a soprano being heard only when, in the next act, the confrontation at Castle Adamant is reached, and the nitty-gritty along with it. For *Princess Ida* is, in reality, about only one person: Ida, and her "I shan't, I won't, I can't . . . oh, all right then." There is no Gilbertian twist, no Equity draughtsman to "fix" the twenty-year-old marriage contract. Everybody is exactly who they say they are. Not a single baby has found its way into the wrong bassinette.

But Ida has two of Sullivan's comic opera masterpieces to sing: a kind of burlesque "Casta diva," a hymn to Minerva (did you know they worshipped the pagan gods in those parts?) by way of an *aria d'entrate*; and her final scena, in which, seeing her way of life falling in ruin, she bewails, "I Built upon a Rock." Both pieces owed nothing to what Emily Peters-Petrelli had recognized as the soubrette-style music of *Patience* or of *Iolanthe*; this was superb light opera music. But the second-named solo came hard behind spoken lines in which the Princess uttered an appalling pun, straight from the days of Planché. It was and is an uncomfortable mix.

So, who was to play Ida? Nobody from the established company. Leonora Braham would be Psyche with her "Ape" song; Rosina Brandram, now the resident leading contralto, would be Blanche. The rest of the ladies' parts were little more than EdithKate'n'Isabels, although a pretty useless little role, as Lady Blanche's daughter, was fabricated for Jessie Bond. But a glorious soprano was needed for Ida's glorious music. Who? Emma Howson could have done it. Damme! Where was Helene Crosmond when you needed her? Oh. Making her Covent Garden debut as Aida. And, guess what, the gentlemen of the Savoy got it wrong, wrong, wrong once more. It was Blanche Roosevelt time all over again.

Lillian Russell (née Helen Louisa Leonard, Mrs. Braham) from Clinton, Iowa, was apparently a one-time pupil of Erminia Rudersdorff (and what an Ida *she* would have made!). Aided by a good soprano voice and extremely good looks, Miss Russell had risen from comic opera chorusing to Tony Pastor's burlesque house, and thence to John McCaull's classy musical-theater company, with which she had starred, at the age of nineteen, opposite none other than Selina Dolaro, in a version of Edmond Audran's *Le Grand Mogol*. The Dudes of New York must have been in their element: Broadway's new "Queen of the Dudes" and London's well-established one in the same show! She appeared with considerable success as *Patience* and as Aline in America, and also became involved with Teddy Solomon, the dashing (and bigamous) composer of *Billee Taylor*. In 1884, the couple traveled to Britain to showcase the composer's new work *Virginia and Paul*. The show wasn't liked, but Lillian was, and she was quickly signed up to appear for Alexander Henderson. But then Carte stepped in, Henderson bowed out, and Lillian Russell was—at an, alleged, huge fifty pounds a week—engaged for Ida.

Why? In heaven's name and by common sense's law, why? Carte already *had* a Patience on his books: the original Patience no less. And, having recognized that Miss Braham would be overweighted as Ida, he was going to hire her American shadow, Mrs. Braham (Harry Braham was Miss Russell's legal, pre-Teddy husband), instead. Yes, she was very pretty, like Blanche Roosevelt. But she could not, any more than La Roosevelt, cut the music Sullivan had composed for the part. Did men *never* learn?

Lillian never did play Ida. The story goes . . . well, both Lillian and Teddy had shown themselves, in the past, to be pretty heedless about things like contracts and rehearsals, and it is said that Lillian's unreliability—never a wise thing on a tight-run ship like the *HMS Savoy*—led, simply, to her being sacked. I wonder if, as in similar cases in my experience, that was merely an excuse. I wonder if the management realized that they'd hired another Roosevelt and needed out. Lillian sued, and lost. She said she had been offered the role for Broadway and refused it. Yeah; quite so. She said she'd been offered *The Beggar Student*. Marion Hood played it. Lillian went back to America, discovered (?) that she was a bigamous wife, split from Teddy (who went to jail), and carried on with a more suitable star career in more suitable star roles into the twentieth century.

The Savoy was into rehearsals and Ida-less. With more time, they might have availed themselves of one of the fine young British sopranos around town, but they took the clearest way out. Leonora Braham was simply promoted from Psyche to Ida, and a former chorine, Kate Chard, who had since risen in status in Australia, was hired to play Psyche. And the show got on.

There was no doubt that it was not a typical Savoy show, and the public and press recognized that. Some found it an advance; some found it a flop; some groaned at the blank verse, which was left over from the burlesque, others bemoaned the lack of comedy . . . so, *Princess Ida* turned out, at best, a half success. It was toured in Britain—proving

46. Sybil Grey as Sacharissa: "Cut off real live arms and legs?"

that capable Idas could be found—and it was given a rather half-hearted showing in America, by John Stetson, with Ryley as Gama, Brocolini as Hildebrand, and one more miscast Ida, the young actress Cora Tanner. She was swiftly replaced by the experienced Mary Beebe before the whole thing collapsed.

But if *Princess Ida* proved the least saleable of the G&S works to date, it produced some superb bits, and not only in the Ida solos and the comic songs. Henry Bracy, as the hero of the affair, set the story on its way with a tuneful wee ballad "Ida Was a Twelvemonth Old," joined his friends in the lightsome description of their weaponry ("Expressive Glances Shall Be Our Lances"), gave a perfectly straight, lovelorn song ("Whom Thou Hast Chained Must Wear His Chain"), and took part in one of Sullivan's most delicious pieces of concerted music, "The World Is but a Broken Toy." The role of Hilarion was altogether better furnished with music than either of the kings, and the experienced Bracy served it well, just as he had so effectively served Varney's music in the London production of *Les Mousquetaires au couvent*.

Henry Bracy (Hilarion)

Samuel Thomas Dunn, known for the stage as Henry Bracy, was born at Cwindu, Maesteg, Wales, on 8 January 1846, the son of an accountant in the Welsh iron fields. He escaped from having to follow in his father's footsteps, thanks to the early discovery of his tenor voice and a commensurate taste for comedy. After fulfilling some concert engagements in the midlands, he got his first job in opéra-bouffe, when he faked a knowledge of French to win a place in the chorus for Hortense Schneider's season at the St. James Theatre. He went through acting-with-songs engagements at Plymouth, and with Captain Disney Roebuck's touring company, but then moved firmly and finally into the musical theater when he joined Henry Leslie's company to play Trémolini in what became a long-touring version of *La Princesse de Trébizonde*. When the company extended its repertoire, he played Falsacappa in *Les Brigands*, Fritz in *La Grande-Duchesse*, and Cocorico in *Geneviève de Brabant*. And he went, from there, to make his first significant appearance in the West End in the Opera Comique production of *The Wonderful Duck* (*Le Canard à trois becs*).

In 1873, Henry acquired a wife, soprano and actress Clara (née Hodges) Thompson, a half-sister to the famous Lydia Thompson, and

47. Team Hildebrand (UK): Messrs. C. Ryley, Bracy, and Lely.

soon after, he and his wife were contracted to play a series of leading roles in Australia. In the years that followed, much of their time would be spent in the southern hemisphere, although they made several substantial trips "home," and others to America. Henry began his Australian career playing in *Lischen and Fritzchen* and in singing roles in several plays (*Guy Mannering*, *The Merchant of Venice*, *The Wedding March*) before being engaged by operatic producer W. S. Lyster. With Lyster, he performed in some of the first Offenbach and Lecocq performances in Australia (Menelaos in *La Belle Hélène*; Defendant in *Trial by Jury*; Piquillo in *La Périchole*; Boléro in *Giroflé-Girofla*; Ange Pitou in *La Fille de Madame Angot*, etc.), and appeared as Bras-de-Fer in the producer's famous operatic pantomime *Fortunatus*. His other Australian roles included Poirot in

La Jolie parfumeuse (1876), Eisenstein in *Die Fledermaus* (1877), Giletti to the Madame l'Archiduc of Catherine Lewis (1877), San Carlo in *La Petite Mariée*, and his well-worn old part in *La Princesse de Trébizonde*. In 1878, Henry launched his own Bracy-Leopold company with former colleague George Leopold, producing, directing, and touring such pieces as *The Bohemian Girl*, *La Fille de Madame Angot*, the pantomime *Egbert the Great*, and introducing *Les Cloches de Corneville* (Grénicheux) to Australia for the first time.

At the end of their first five-year stay, the Bracys returned to Britain and, in the years that followed, Henry created leading roles in the English versions of *Les Mousquetaires au couvent* (Gontran), *La Mascotte* (Fritellini), *The Grand Mogol* (Mignapour), *Belle Lurette* (Marly), and *Babette* (Duc de la Roche Galante), as well as introducing the role of Hilarion in *Princess Ida* and the tenor parts in two of the most successful English musicals of the time, *Les Manteaux noirs* (Don Luis) and *Erminie* (Eugene Marcel). He also appeared in the West End in *The Lady of the Locket*, as the Chevalier de Lauvenay in *The Lily of Léoville* (1886), and as Grénicheux (*Les Cloches de Corneville*), Hector (*Madame Favart*), Valentin (*Olivette*), Symon (*Der Bettelstudent*), Don Florio (*The Naval Cadets*), Offenbach's *Barbe-bleue*, and Peter in Cellier's *The Sultan of Mocha*, while simultaneously working as a stage director, latterly at the Avenue Theatre.

In 1889, the Bracys returned to Australia. Henry formed his own English and Comic Opera Company, directing and starring in *The Old Guard*, *The Sultan of Mocha*, *The Beggar Student*, *Nemesis*, Lecocq's *Pepita* (*La Princesse des Canaries*), *The Bohemian Girl*, *Charity Begins at Home*, etcetera. The venture ended, however, in a resounding bankruptcy, and, renouncing the cares of management, Bracy settled in, first as principal tenor in the flagship Williamson and Garner Royal Comic Opera Company (*Dorothy*, *La Cigale*, Wilfred in *Marjorie*, *Iolanthe*, *The Mikado*, *Trial by Jury*, *The Vicar of Bray*, *The Mountebanks*, etc.), and then as house director for the same company. In this capacity, over the most prosperous decade of J. C. Williamson's musical comedy activities, Henry was responsible for staging the Australian productions of such pieces as *The Geisha*, *Florodora*, *The Rose of Persia*, *The Mountebanks*, *Mam'zelle Nitouche*, *Dorothy*, *La Poupée*, and regular revivals of the Gilbert and Sullivan repertoire. At the same time, he still appeared on stage in such roles as Gaston in *La Belle Thérèse* (1895), Marmaduke in *Miss Decima* (1896), Simon in *The Beggar Student* (1897), Calino in *Nemesis* (1897), Peter in *The Sultan of Mocha*, Thaddeus in *The Bohemian Girl*, etcetera. In 1903,

48. Florence Bemister and the girls of Castle Adamant: "Man Is Nature's Sole Mistake."

Bracy was briefly made general manager of J. C. Williamson's production company, and he continued a close association with the theater until his death in Sydney, Australia, on 31 January 1917.

Rosina Brandram (Lady Blanche)

If Bracy was never likely to become a staple member of the Carte company, *Princess Ida* marked the "arrival" of one of the most solid staples of all: Rosina Brandram. She wasn't a newcomer; she had played with Carte for some seven years already: chorister, understudy, the middle slice of EdithKate'n'Isabel, a deputy Iolanthe. Now, with the indisposition of Alice Barnett, she for the first time took over the position of leading contralto. Paul, Everard, Cross, Barnett . . . it had been a position in the company that had changed incumbent too frequently: it would not change again. Rosina Brandram would create the contralto part in every Gilbert and Sullivan opera from now till the end, and she would be the *komische Alte* of the Savoy for nearly twenty years. A summary of her career pretty well comes down to a list of the Opera Comique and Savoy productions from 1877 to 1903. But it was with *Princess Ida* that she first "ruled the roast."

Rosina Moult was born at 80 Burrows Mews, St. Saviour, on 2 July 1845, the premarital daughter of William Moult, a cabman/proprietor, and his wife Sarah (née Gosling), who was at that stage officially a Mrs. Walke. Since Gänzl is, give or take an umlaut, German for Gosling, I briefly cherished a hope that we might be internationally related, but sadly we are not.

Mr. Walke died in 1850, and William and Sarah married, but William himself died when Rosina was twelve and, at nineteen, she was married to an auctioneer's clerk who suffered from the name of Champneys Charles Butcher. "Man is nature's sole mistake." The marriage fell apart, sometime in the 1870s, and Rosina went on the comic-opera stage. So, we can see that her Carte-manufactured biography claiming "a young gentlewoman's education," . . . "studied singing in Italy with Sig Nava" are . . . "most unlikely, most unlikely."

And thus it began: the most voluminous Savoyard career of all, from the chorus of *The Sorcerer* up to its turning point with *Princess Ida* and Lady Blanche, and with Katisha (*Mikado*, "Hearts Do Not Break"; "There Is Beauty in the Bellow of the Blast"), Dame Hannah (*Ruddigore*), Dame Carruthers (*The Yeomen of the Guard*, "When Our Gallant Norman Foes"), the Duchess of Plaza Toro (*The Gondoliers*, "On the Day When I Was Wedded"), Widow Jackson (*Captain Billy*), Mrs. Merton (*The Vicar of Bray*), Lady Vernon (*Haddon Hall*), Miss Sims (*Jane Annie*), Lady Sophy (*Utopia (Limited)*), the Marquise (*Mirette*), Inez de Roxas (*The Chieftain*), Baroness von Krakenfeld (*The Grand Duke*), Joan (*The Beauty Stone*), Dancing Sunbeam (*The Rose of Persia*), Wee Ping (*The Willow Pattern*), the Countess of Newtown (*Emerald Isle*), Queen Elizabeth (*Merrie England*, "O Peaceful England"), and Nell Reddish (*A Princess of Kensington*) to follow.

When the comic opera company left the Savoy, Miss Brandram went with it and appeared with William Greet on tour in *Merrie England* and at the Savoy in the Christmas show *Little Hans Andersen* (1903). But when Greet moved into musical comedy there was neither place nor part for her and, in the last performances of her career, she appeared, instead, as Ermerance in George Edwardes's very successful version of *Véronique*.

One last warning: If you listen to modern recordings of *Princess Ida* you will not be hearing the opera as it was played at the Savoy. One particularly important number has, unbelievably, been erased, and, with it, the whole credo and importance to the play of Lady Blanche. "Come, Mighty Must," purposefully situated just after the Princess's "Casta Diva" aria, sets up the internal divisions at Castle Adamant that, without it, are reduced to nothing. And it's not a mooing dirge: it's a piercing song of jealousy.

Mary Beebe (Ida)

Now, let's have a little look at some of the folk who played the show in America. Ida first, obviously. I'm ignoring the ridiculously bad casting

49. Mary Beebe: The Boston "Ideal" of a Josephine.

of Cora Tanner, and going instead with the chevroned lady who was hurried in to replace her.

Mary Beebe (b. Columbus, Ohio, 27 February 1859; d. Brookline, Massachusetts, 8 October 1902) was the first daughter (after four sons) of New Yorker James Henry Beebe, the state law librarian of Columbus, and his wife Elizabeth (née Knapp). Mary began appearing in Boston concerts in about 1877 (Napier Lothian's Sundays, Tremont Temple), and the tale has been oft told of how she was hired at short notice to play Josephine in Miss Ober's famed "ideal" production of *Pinafore* (14 April 1879). Miss Beebe had to resign her post at the Clarenden Baptist Church to do so, the Baptists refusing to have anything to do with anyone connected with the wicked stage. She triumphed in her theatrical debut, and thenceforth became meat for the gossip columnists, who chronicled her every doing or not-really-doing. She appeared as Lydia in *Fatinitza*, as Mabel in *The Pirates of Penzance*, and others such; she sang with H. C. Barnabee's Concert Party; and then announced her retirement, prior to her marriage with one Mr. Richard G. Haskell. They were married on 11 December, and early in the new year Mary moved out, came back, and moved out again . . . the marriage was clearly doomed. Mary sought solace elsewhere, Haskell divorced her, and the virtuous Ideal Opera Company (whose other leading soprano was the wife of an influential member of the troupe) ousted her.

Between 1883 and 1886, Miss Beebe appeared in various venues with the Chicago Church Choir troupe (*Iolanthe*), sang *Princess Ida* at the Fifth Avenue Theatre and with the Hess-Acme company, played with Henry Laurent in *Le Petit Duc*, in *Patience* at Haverley's, in Baltimore in repertoire (*The Merry War*, *Giroflé-Girofla*, *The Bohemian Girl*, *Fatinitza*, *The Pirates of Penzance*), and in John Stetson's *Mikado* company. She then remarried (23 June 1886), to Mr. Ethan Horace Cutler (b. Amherst, Massachusetts, 18 March 1848; d. 3 December 1923), left the stage for real this time, and largely vanished from the gossip columns. Well, in 1901–2, she did sue Cutler for divorce, but it turned out she had a brain tumor, and before the year was out, she was dead. Today she is just a name: the Boston Ideals' first Josephine.

Wallace McCreery (Hilarion)

Wallace McCreery or Macreery or . . . whatever; it was pretty surely a stage name (the frequent alternative spelling is usually a giveaway). A

50. Team Hildebrand (US): Messrs. Lang, McCreery, and Rising.

real McCreery was at that time a fashionable politician (along with a Mr. Wallace). I have no birthdate for Mr. McC, no census sightings, no official records, just a death date: 11 May 1905; place: the middle of the Hudson River.

His life was foredoomed to end in disaster, for Mr. McCreery was, from early in his ruined career, a confirmed alcoholic. For a decade, he went from one company to another, often being sacked; why did managers continue to hire him? Because when on song, he was good. But too often he wasn't, and the press didn't hesitate to mock him for "singing in whis-key." When he had a fall from a balcony in San Francisco, he was unhurt: it was reported in the papers that "alcoholic limpness saved him."

McCreery, by any other name, started his singing life under yet another name: "Signor V. Talberti." I wonder if his birth name was Talbert. As Talberti, he was announced for Strakosch's company in 1877, but I see him over the next couple of years only in the odd concert: at the Dime Sacred Concerts at the Cooper Institute; at the YMCA in Bridgeton, New Jersey, with Arabella Root; at D. L. Downing's concert at the Grand Opera House; and at Booth's Theatre supporting what was left of Ilma di Murska. And then he got his big break. As *Pinafore* mania struck, he was cast as Rackstraw in the Standard Theatre's production of the all-consuming comic opera, and—no longer "Talberti"—he scored splendidly. The Standard company went a-touring, and McCreery went with them, alongside Signor Brocolini (John Clark) and Lisette Ellani (Ellen Hatch), playing *HMS Pinafore* and *Trial by Jury*. A series of fine jobs in fine shows followed: with Emilie Melville in *The Royal Middy*; as Gaston in *Donna Juanita*; Valentine in *Olivette*; Pietro in *Boccaccio*; at the Casino Theater itself in *The Queen's Lace Handkerchief*; in *The Snake Charmer*; in *Hand and Heart*; on tour with the Duff Company, which included *Lakmé* in its repertoire . . . and somewhere in there, the rot set in. Cast as Hilarion in the New York production of *Princess Ida*, he was hissed from the stage for being drunk and incapable.

McCreery crossed the continent, and took a job at San Francisco's Tivoli, under another pseudonym: "Walter Temple." No one was fooled, and he was frequently "off," but he stayed in California for more than two years. Thereafter, I see him intermittently for a few years: with W. H. Hamilton's New York Church Choir Company, in *Ship Ahoy*; in *The Khedive*; playing Corcoran, these days, in *HMS Pinafore*, in Atlanta, Georgia, in a small company (1894); and then, nothing, until that day in May when he boarded the Weehawken Ferry and jumped into the Hudson River.

Charles F. Lang (Florian, later Hilarion)

Our other two tenors were saner. Both had fairly good careers in the comic opera theater, and both were born to German fathers, in the state of Ohio.

Charles Lang (b. Canton, Ohio, October 1847; d. Saint Augustine, Florida, 5 March 1914) was the son of Jacob or Jacques Lang and his wife Magdalena or Madeleine. The reason that they had alternative names is that they came from Schirrhofen, Alsace, so when they weren't being French they were being German, until they became American. The couple were married in Canton in 1840, and I see, in the 1850 census, that Jacob is a teacher and that in the past decade they have managed to produce half a dozen children, four boys and two girls. Then

Magdalena died (1853). Jacob swiftly remarried, a younger wife, Caroline Bechel[?], and, by the 1860 census, all but one of the children are gone from the Lang home, replaced by Caroline, her mother, and a new daughter. Where are they? Well, Charles is living with the nuns, in their Cleveland orphanage. Is this a case of a "wicked stepmother"? A year later, he actually was an orphan, because Jacob had died. Jacob's 1855 will left everything to Caroline, with nary a mention of the children.

Charles's fairly approximate obituary skates over the next years, merely saying that his voice "attracted attention" when he was young, and that he went "abroad" to study "when under twenty." Before 1868? But there he is in Cleveland, in an amateur performance of *Fra Diavolo*, with another striving local, Juliette Somerville, on 15 April 1872, and again billed as "the new American tenor," in 1874. Usually, when a young American went to Italy in pursuit of operatic glory, she or occasionally he was given centimeters in the local press. There was usually a "farewell concert" and the subject's progress (even if there were none) was thereafter charted in exaggerated detail. But I see nothing at all. The obituary claims for him a debut at La Scala, performances in "prominent companies" in Europe, and a concert for Queen Victoria . . . to all of which I, having combed the concert and opera notices of that period, say bunkum. Oh, I'm pretty sure he went overseas, maybe even to the Milan Conservatoire (perhaps the nuns paid?), because when he returned and played his "first appearance since . . ." it was announced as such. The occasion was a concert at the Cleveland Opera House (1 June 1877), and the press commented that his voice "possesses a peculiar sweetness and evenness of tone that is more notable than any great power, and his articulation is especially clear and distinct." In other words, Charles had a small, light *tenorino* voice. He wasn't going to sing anything heftier than *Fra Diavolo*, and he, wisely, didn't try to.

Mr. C. F. Lang's first job, soon after, was with Catherine Lewis, touring in Titus Tracy's Comic Opera Company (*Les Cloches de Corneville*). The French tenor music suited this German tenor admirably, but Miss Lewis was pregnant, and the tour folded. However, several other light and comic opera jobs followed in succession: *The Bohemian Girl* with the Rubens Opera Company; an *HMS Pinafore* with Annie Pixley; *The Contrabandista* and *The First Life Guards at Brighton* at Philadelphia, and others of the ilk. He spent some time with Alice Oates's comic opera company, played in Dudley Buck's *Deseret*, and in 1881 appeared as Valentin in *Olivette* at the Park Theatre. His notices had been fairly satisfactory till now, but not this time: "There is but little merit in Charles Lang's performance of the soldier-lover . . . his diminutive tenor voice appears at times in danger of cracking as he attempts more than it is capable of." A reviewer in Washington, DC, didn't agree and found that "the new tenor had a fine sympathetic voice and is a very clever actor."

Over the next years, Lang spent much time with Charles E. Ford's good touring troupe (*Patience, Billee Taylor, The Sorcerer, Iolanthe, La Mascotte, Manola*) and with Madeleine Lucette (*Les Mousquetaires au couvent, Patience, Madame Boniface, Niniche*), played at Uhrig's Cave (*Claude Duval*), and took part in the attempt to float Alfred Robyn's musical *Manette*, as well as playing the two roles in *Princess Ida*. But, after that, it was back to the touring circuits with Lillian Conway (*La Fille de Madame Angot*), Adelaide Randall (*Fra Diavolo, Le Serment, La Princesse de Trébizonde, Giroflé-Girofla, Billee Taylor, HMS Pinafore* as Corcoran), or for Hans Conried (*Der Zigeunerbaron, Der Hofnarr*) until their ship ran—literally—aground at Norfolk, Virginia.

I don't think that incident was the cause of Lang's ending his performing career, but he went back to Ohio, to his littlest sister, Rosa Clara Klorer, and took a job in her husband's Berger Manufacturing Company. Rosa—who became a decidedly prominent local figure in Catholic, charitable, and hospital affairs as well as an adept at business—shared her home with Charles ("manufacturer") and elder brother Edward ("labourer") in North Cleveland Avenue, Canton, in 1900. In his mid-sixties, Charles developed motor ataxia, and he died in Florida, where he had gone for his health, aged sixty-six.

William S. Rising (Cyril)

Our third tenor was probably the best performer of the three. But, after a grand start to his career, he rather faded away into less resounding projects. Seemingly, he was one of those people who had a lot of fingers, and found an awful lot of plumpuddings into which to plunge them, usually with at least some success: singer, actor, comedian, producer, playwright, lyricist, investor, film scenarist, and much more.

William Starling Reising (b. Lancaster, Ohio, 11 August 1852; d. New York City, 5 October 1930) was the son of Bavarian-born Philip Reising (later Rising). Philip arrived in America in 1845, joined the army in 1846 to fight in the Mexican-American War, married an Irish lass, Susan Starling, in 1848, began a family, and went into the dry goods business in Lancaster, making a specialty of the new-fangled ready-to-wear clothing. In quick time, he lost his wife, took over the next-door business, remarried (Caroline née McBride), rebred, and was on a determined "rocket to the moon." He would end up president of Ohio's Fairfield County Bank.

Will was another ambitious tenor who went to Italy to study. His teacher was Tito Palmieri, the tenor husband of prima donna Mary Ann Croft, who was indeed based in Milan, and he seems to have studied from 1878—after a "farewell" concert at New York City's Chickering Hall (6 May)—until early 1882, when he turned up in England. England welcomed "the American tenor" enthusiastically, and his 1882 appearances—as Fritellini to the La Mascotte of Violet Cameron, Pietro to her Boccaccio, and Hans van Slous in *Rip van Winkle*—immediately propelled him to a place among London's favorite comic opera tenors.

Rising's next engagements, however, were less strong—a feeble production of *Prince Methusalem*, the dogged *Estrella*, a couple of indifferent operettas—and, after two years, he returned to America, under contract to the Casino Theatre to play in *The Beggar Student*. The Casino production was cast to the hilt—Fred Leslie, Rose Leighton, William T. Carleton, Mathilde Cottrelly, Bertha Ricci—and Will played Janitsky, teamed with Madame Cottrelly. He took time out to repeat his role in *Estrella* at the Standard, but the theater burned down after three nights, and John Chatterson got the tenor part in the Casino's *Merry War*, while Rising was cast in *Princess Ida* and the local fairy-tale piece *Madame Piper* (1884). At the same time, Rising began to dabble in management, and, in tandem with Signor Brocolini, organized comic opera performances in Montreal. Later the same year, he appeared for Augustus Pitou in a boneless musical comedy *Off to Egypt, or An Arab Abduction* (Arch Street, Philadelphia, 17 November). The music was said to be by George LeJeune, but Will nevertheless interpolated Paolo Tosti's "Goodbye" for the few weeks the piece was played. He was recalled to the Casino to play Nitschano in *Apajune, the Water Sprite*, and then cast in the title-role of the Philadelphia musical *The Little Tycoon* (4 January 1886, Temple Theatre). This piece proved highly popular on the touring circuits, and avidly promoted by its author, played ninety-one performances in New York. But it would be a wee while, oddly, before "one of the most popular tenors and one of the best fellows in town" would be seen there again.

It appears that, at some point, Will had married, because, in 1888, the trade press announced the birth of a "twelve-pound son." The baby would die at the age of four. I have searched for mother and child in New York's documentation without success.

Rising had no luck with his next projects. He went to St. Louis to play HMS *Pinafore* on the lake (with Miss Loie Fuller, for heaven's sake, cast as Josephine), and in the Pompeian Amphitheatre, and announced his plans to produce two new American comic operas at Atlantic City. He also got involved with Miss Vernona Jarbeau (Mrs. Jeff D. Bernstein) and her husband, and invested fifteen hundred dollars in their production of *Starlight*. *Starlight* was to be the lady's vehicle for many years, but Will had to go to court to get any sort of accounting or a return on his investment.

Rising took the theater at Howard's Pier, Atlantic City, for a summer season and there produced, with the similarly inclined William Hamilton, the first of his new musicals. *Florette* (Thomas P. Westendorf/J. N. Fort, 19 July 1888) was set in Virginia, in colonial times (please note, those who give the date of "the first recognizably American musical" half a century later!). Rising, Hamilton, and Miss Fuller played the leads for the short term of its existence. The promised "new Planquette opera" didn't appear, but on 19 December, Will and his Columbia Opera Company tried again, at the Academy of Music, Philadelphia, with a piece called *America* (Ernest Peilor/William Augustus Smith). Philadelphia was offended: "A melange of music rot and literary drivel . . . the plot is inexplicable, the situations absurd, and the lines put in the actors' mouths ridiculous. A large but bored audience watched it." Will retreated to John Mackay's company, and then got involved with another amateurish musical. The two ladies who wrote, and effectively produced, *Dovetta* clearly had cash, for they inveigled not only Will but also Emily Soldene to play their piece—briefly.

In the 1890s, I see Will touring a foreign comedy, *Tangled Up* (adapted by Rising, starring Rising), yet again with Loie Fuller, and a repertoire of small pieces including *Charity Begins at Home*. I see "Will Rising's Entertainers" traveling a Percy Gaunt operetta, *Love on Wheels*, and presenting a program of the "Illustrated Songs" that he favored. In 1897 the press wrote, "[He] sings high-class descriptive and classical songs in a very capable manner for a salary of $125 a week. His clear tenor voice is always in demand and he is never out of an engagement."

Rising took over the comedy lead in *Miss Philadelphia*, sent out tours of *The Strange Adventures of Miss Brown*, played in vaudeville with a Miss Lilian Kemble, staged summer seasons at Koerner's Park, St. Louis, produced and played in a drama *At Valley Forge*, and mounted "the Rising Stock Co.," starring Miss L. Kemble. The press said they were married; maybe. Maybe she's the "Jennie Rising" from Wisconsin (age twenty-two) who, "married since 1898," was living with him, in Salt Lake City, according to the 1900 census. Well, if they were wed, it didn't last. Will writes a firm "divorced" in the 1920s census; of course, he may mean from his first wife.

In the early twentieth century, Will—ever chasing something new—became active in the motion picture world. I see him referred to as chief scenario writer for the Edison Film Company. He would act in some films, too, and, as his links with the theater loosened, I see him, in 1911, directing a production of *HMS Pinafore* at Asbury Park (and filming "the Asbury Park Baby Parade"), as well as "in Bermuda producing films for the Yankee Film Co." The advertising departments of the various film companies had him described as "formerly attaché to the American ambassador in Paris" and "of the Bostonians," when he turned out patriotic one-reelers during the war. The private life of Mr. Rising was the subject of a piece in *The Moving Picture World* of July 1915. Read it, but don't believe it. Will Rising collapsed and died in the street in 1930. He left behind him a colorful tale. And just a few little mysteries.

Mazellah Ainsley Scott (Arac)

The members of team Gama have been harder to track down. Mazellah Ainsley Scott (b. Nashua, New Hampshire, 26 July 1840), was born the son of George J. Scott, ship's carpenter, and his wife Elizabeth (née Danforth), and brought up in Charlestown, New Hampshire. Ainsley was on the stage before his teens were out. I see him playing in New Orleans by 1858, and in New York by 1861. In 1862, labeled "musician," he married Isabella McCrillis from Augusta, Maine, in Lowell, Massachusetts. And he had already found his niche: in minstrel shows, where he played comedy and burlesque, and sang ballads in "his fine deep bass voice." Scott rose quickly in the minstrel world, playing with the San Francisco Minstrels, the Morris brothers, Pell and Trowbridge's

51. Team Gama (US): Messrs. Earley, Scott, and Cloney.

troupe, and Billy Emerson's California Minstrels ("he is not only a good basso singer but a capital actor"; "excellent . . . clear in his enunciation, self-possessed in deportment")—his minstrel career is detailed in several of the careful American books on minstrelsy—and on the way (1867) wed a Miss Anna Farrell in Louisville.

In 1874, Scott visited Australia with the Emerson troupe, and he remained there, with his current wife, who also performed, playing in various troupes under his own management until, in 1875, he went bankrupt. I spot him, in 1879, taking out a Tasmanian hawker's license, and in 1880, playing Sir Joseph Porter in *HMS Pinafore* in Hobart. While in Australia, he fathered a son, George Clarence Ainsley Scott (28 May 1875), and a Blanche Nevada Scott, of whom the mother was registered as Nellie Moreton—which was not the name of either/any of his wives. The boy died at the age of one, yet when Scott arrived back in California he was said to have landed with a wife and a child. Presumably Blanche. But he, nevertheless, briefly married one Ida Ball, and was arrested for bigamy. He resisted arrest, "fired two pistol shots," and ended up before the judge. One way and another, Scott's private life seems to have been extremely irregular. But, professionally, he carried on. He sent out Ainsley Scott's Jubilee Singers and the Kentucky Jubilee Singers, and then suddenly he surfaced in New York playing Arac in *Princess Ida*.

Scott soon returned to the minstrel stage, to tour Ainsley Scott's Concert Troupe (1888), Ainsley Scott's Medicine Company (1890), and, with an alleged wife called "Isabelle Sidonie," as Scott and Sidonie. In 1894 he can be spotted ("actor") living at New York's 270 West 38th Street. And in 1901, he got married yet again. Eugenie Fisher was in her twenties, and he was listed as "three times a widower." Scott toured, doing illustrated readings from *Parsifal* and lecturing on Wagner (1904), married in 1906 one Undine Andrews, and, in 1907, can be seen giving "dramatic recitations," billed as "82 years old—the oldest actor in America." He was sixty-seven. I wonder what became of him. And his Bluebeardy contingent of wives.

Edward J. Cloney (Scynthius)

I drew an absolute blank on Mr. Earl[e]y. But Edward J. Cloney (b. c 1857; d. 1891) was to lead me into even more complex family details than had Mr. Scott of the multiple wives. It wasn't his fault, though. I can't find a birth record for him. Only a homonym (I presume) who was a plumber. He simply comes up before my eyes for the first time in 1878, as the bass singer in the quartet at Saint Francis de Sales Church in Boston, then in 1879, singing in concert at the YMCA in Boston Highlands, in 1880 in a memorial service in Boston, and in 1881, again, in Boston. But I do not see him in any public documents until 1888, when he turns up on a very scrappy marriage certificate from Jersey City, which says, merely, that he is thirty years old. His wife is listed as nineteen, which is a lie by at least three years. I rather suspect "Cloney" may have been a pseudonym.

I see our man on the stage for the first time, in 1884, playing in a production of *The Beggar Student* at the Spanish Fort, New Orleans. Adah Richmond is featured, our friend "Ralph Wreckstraw," Henry Laurent is Janicki, and W. A. Gillow is Enterich. Spanish Fort usually staged seasons with a stock cast, but this one must have soon finished, because next thing Cloney was up in New York playing in *Princess Ida*! Sometime around now, he also worked with the Selina Dolaro company, and at some point he was stage manager for John Stetson. I spot him being damned for a weak portrayal of the Mikado, and then playing in *Ruddigore* with J. W. Herbert, Brocolini, and Agnes Stone. On July 4, 1886, he became a father; and on 5 October 1888, he married the mother of his child, Miss Josephine Folch. My last sighting of Edward is in 1890, mentioned as the assistant manager of the Casino, Parkersburg, West Virginia. My next sighting of his wife, she is listed as a "widow." Miss Folch was to go on to become a well-known comedienne under the name of Josie Intropodi.

Princess Ida Today

What to say about *Princess Ida* today? Well, a selections recording with a well-selected (which means by me!) cast and, of course, including "Come, Mighty Must," would be welcome. A production with a slightly rewritten book (by me) that gets rid of the wretched Melissa . . . ah, no. I mustn't touch. If WSG didn't see it fit to fiddle . . . but, of course, WSG isn't responsible for the disappearance of Blanche's number. It was sung in all nineteenth-century productions. Some Dummkopf (not Ernest) of the twentieth century saw right to remove it. He'd probably have removed the Queen of the Night's Vengeance aria from *Die Zauberflöte* too. But *Princess Ida* lives on. She has even become fashionable with folk and groups needing a variation from *HMS Pinafore*, *The Pirates of Penzance*, and *The Mikado*. From what I see on YouTube, some of them are making it live with a vigor and a zest that might have surprised the Savoy triumvirate. Go for it! But first catch your Ida.

9

The Mikado, or *The Town of Titipu*

Japanese opera in two acts
Savoy Theatre, 14 March 1885

The Mikado, the piece that followed *Princess Ida* (and a revival of *The Sorcerer*) on to the Savoy stage, was a wholly fresh, original work, with no elements recycled from the librettist's earlier works or, indeed, from anywhere else. Of course, musical-theater pieces set in oriental places—a veritable Ruritania of the nineteenth century—had been manifold in Britain and, from *Ba-ta-clan* to *Fleur de thé*, in Europe. In the modern age, Alfred Thompson and Hervé's *Aladdin II* (1870)—with Johnnie Toole as its villainous star, Ko-kil-ko—had been one of the first British attempts at "opéra-bouffe." However, that piece leaned, in its text, firmly toward old English burlesque: "How do you wish to die? I should suggest fire in preference to the axe; it is more sensational. I will order it myself. Make the most of your minutes . . . stakes for two, well done!" And that style had now been rendered rather old-fashioned—not the least by Mr. W. S. Gilbert.

However, the fad for "all one sees that's Japanese" in mid-Victorian England was not exactly of a Ruritanian nature. It was very much the work of one Mynheer Tannaker Buhicrosan, who had first been seen in Britain as early as 1869, presenting the shows of his "Royal Tycoon Performers." With commercial motives in view, Buhicrosan had more recently set up a veritable trade fair circuit, where things Japanese could be marveled at and, of course, bought. Japan being viewed as an "ancient civilization," the fashion for things oriental fitted in snugly with the fashion for aestheticism. And where there is one hit comic opera . . . why, there may very well be a second. Topical humor didn't go down only in comic songs in the music halls.

There is a tale purveyed that Mr. Gilbert was inspired to write a Japanese piece after an oriental sword fell from his wall. All I can say is that it was jolly hard to get good help in the 1880s, and I hope the housekeeper was sacked. The fact that he actually owned a Japanese sword is sufficient to show us that he was a follower of Mynheer Buhicrosan's fashion.

The outline of *The Mikado* was, in comparison to the bald simplicity of that of *Princess Ida*, delightfully twisty-and-turny—but wholly logical! No magic was needed to get the play's plot out of its tight corners, just a nice bit of contractual jiggery pokery and a venal Japanese registrar of marriages. The script also just happened to include extraordinarily fine roles for the principal members of the Savoy company; there would be no Barringtonic whinges about being underserved this time!

Nanki-Poo, the (handsome, tenorious) son of the (elderly, ugly) Mikado of Japan, has fled his father's halls, rather than wed his designed (elderly, ugly) bride, Katisha. Disguised as a trombone player, but, revealingly, carrying a guitar, he comes to the town of Titipu, where he has fallen in love with (teenage and gorgeous) Yum-Yum, the schoolgirl ward of Ko-Ko, the town's Lord High Executioner. Well, of course, Englishmen knew that every Japanese town has an executioner (see *Aladdin II*). But Ko-Ko (a) has designed Yum-Yum for himself and (b) is a rotten executioner. In fact, he's not an executioner at all, because, by a legal twist, the first person to be executed, should he commence his position's duties, is . . . Ko-Ko. Alas! The Mikado has got wind of this seeming state of sinecure-ism and is heading, with all his train, for Titipu. Ko-Ko must hurriedly execute *someone* or he'll be chopped chicken. And he gets a volunteer! Nanki-Poo, distraught at losing his bride, agrees to be terminally decapitated, if he can first have a month of wedded bliss with Yum-Yum. Papers are signed, but Yum-Yum reads the small print, Ko-Ko can't do it, so tenor and soprano arrange simply to disappear, and pretend to be dead. The Mikado is satisfied with the deed as described and documented, but Katisha has read the certificate of execution. Ko-Ko has chopped off the head of the heir to the throne! He is in a worse pickle than ever, as Nanki-Poo stoutly refuses to come alive again while Katisha is unwed. So, Ko-Ko has no choice but to marry her.

The endearing role of Ko-Ko, with its memorable solos "I've Got a Little List" and the mock-pathetic "Tit Willow," and a rib-tickling duet in praise of the elderly and ugly ("There Is Beauty in the Bellow of the Blast"), was a gift for Grossmith; while the stentorian Mikado ("My Object All Sublime") "with a senile grin and a waddling walk" was custom-made for

Richard Temple. Rosina Brandram was the melodramatic Katisha, soaring above the first-act finale like a vengeful Valkyrie and burlesquing a parlor singer in her handkerchief aria "Hearts Do Not Break," while Lely and Miss Braham were the young people with the nursery names (left over from *Thespis*?), both with stand-out solos: his "A Wandering Minstrel, I" and her "The Sun Whose Rays." And Barrington? Well, Barrington was woven into the plot as the pompous Pooh-Bah, Lord High Everything Else of Titipu, the purchasable "vicar," in short, the sort of venal local dignitary we all know too well. And very well he was woven.

There was, of course, no place in this entirely humorous musical for soaring melodies of the "O, Goddess Wise" type, nor, indeed, for ensembles of the delicate fragility of "The World Is But a Broken Toy." But the ensembles of *The Mikado* came in all sorts of splendid sizes and shapes: the twittering trio of the three schoolgirls ("Three Little Maids"); the burlesque kissing duet for the juveniles; the madrigal "Brightly Dawns Our Wedding Day" and the glee "See How the Fates Their Gifts Allot"; the superlative narrative trio relating the fake execution ("The Criminal Cried"); and that jaunty, catchy bit of tralala "The Flowers That Bloom in the Spring."

The vast success immediately scored by *The Mikado* didn't stop a few post-opening-night rearrangements, but all settled quickly into place, and the show was on its way to an outstanding London run of nearly two uneventful years.

As you can see, the cast was largely made up of Savoy regulars, but there was one unfamiliar name on the bill, and one that had heretofore appeared only in the tiny print. This last was the lass who is remembered, alongside Misses Braham and Bond, as "the third little maid."

Sybil Grey (Peep-Bo)

Sybil Grey was born Ellen Sophia Taylor, on 3 January 1860, in London's Conduit Street West, the second daughter of a linen draper, Henry Taylor, and his Exeter-born wife, Susannah. Sybil Grey was the name of an aristocrat, a racehorse, and a novelistic and dramatic heroine (*Marmion*), thus, just the sort of nom de théâtre for a young lass.

Sybil began as a chorister and understudy during the original London production of *The Pirates of Penzance* at the Opera Comique, where I see her, for a short time, depping as Kate. During the run of *Patience*, she seems to have sung only in the chorus, but when *Iolanthe*

52. Three Little Maids: Misses Grey, Braham, and Bond.

was produced, she was given the small part of Fleta and later moved up, infinitesimally, to play Leila. When *Princess Ida* was given, she took the tiny part of Sacharissa. When *The Sorcerer* and *Trial by Jury* were revived in October 1884, she was the First Bridesmaid, all as a part of a thoroughly discreet Cartesian "EdithKate'n'Isabel" career that would come to a peak in the role of Peep-Bo.

But there was much more, and much more of consequence to come. Miss Grey had another decade and more to spend on the stage post-Peep-Bo, and she would take part in more than one hit show. Suffice it to say that, the main part of her years with Carte done, Miss Grey moved in the right direction: to the new top-dog manager of the London musical stage, George Edwardes. She was hired for the Gaiety Theatre, to play in the richly cast burlesque of *Frankenstein*. As Vanilla, she was but one of four decorative lasses who led the chorus of "bandits, villagers, soldiers and shepherdesses." In the following *Miss Esmeralda*, likewise, she featured as a gipsy of whom "pretty looks and an arch bearing" were all that was required.

A little nostalgic return to the Savoy Theatre over, Sybil moved on to another monument of the British theater: the Theatre Royal, Drury Lane. It was Christmas pantomime time, and the show was *The Babes in the Wood* starring the great Harry Payne, Dan Leno as dame, and Harriet Vernon as Robin Hood. Sybil and the statuesque Maggie Duggan headed the merry men. Sybil and best-friend Rosina Brandram appeared in a musical version of *Newport* ("The Song of the Looking Glass") in a vanity production at Devonshire House, while, all the time, Sybil continued on at Drury Lane ("flitting about gracefully" as Deborah Wood in *The Royal Oak*, the Royal Housemaid in *Jack and the Beanstalk*, the King of Diamonds in *Beauty and the Beast*). But Mr. Edwardes had other plans for her. He placed her, as a takeover, in the long-running, surprise hit "triple bill" production, and there she remained through a run of many, many months, playing, at various times, different roles in the three playlets that comprised the entertainment, notably the title-role in *Nan, the Good-for-Nothing*.

When the triple bill was finally withdrawn, she got herself noticed as Sally in W. J. Hill's old comedy vehicle *Crazed*, played as a forepiece to *The Guardsman*. The press commented on "a clever and experienced actress who, one imagines, would do well at one of our 'improved' music halls." But Sybil wasn't going there; George Edwardes had other uses for her. He imported her into the cast of his new hit musical comedy, *The Gaiety Girl*, and then into a second hit London musical, *An Artist's Model*, where she would later take over Lottie Venne's prominent role of Madame Amélie. The third little maid had become a veritable leading lady.

Next, our Miss Grey was engaged at the Vaudeville Theatre, where the English adaptation of the famous farce *L'Hôtel du Libre Échange* (*A Night Out*) was being produced. Again, it seems to have been a case of understudy and/or takeover, but, by August 1896, she was being billed for the leading role of Mme. Pinglet. When Edwardes produced the comedy *Jalouse* (*The Dovecot*) at the Duke of York's Theatre (February 1898), Sybil was cast as the scheming servant girl Durnford through the one-hundred-plus nights of the run. The cast also included Miss Leonora Braham.

Sybil went on to join Horace Lingard's Strand Comedy Company, playing Mrs. Smith in another French comedy, *Why Smith Left Home*, and then toured for Edwardes in *A Night Out*. But at the turn of the century and the arrival of the age of forty, she seems to have changed priorities. In the 1901 census, she can be seen (with Rosina) listed as thirty-four years old and working as an "actress and masseuse." She seems to have done more massaging than acting in the following years. While Rosina plunged on with her celebrated career, I see Sybil announced to play in *Three Little Maids* (she was not one of the little maids, however, but Miss Deare, the postmistress), and in 1907 touring for Edwardes one more time as Poo-See in *See-See*.

Ellen Sophia Taylor lived latterly in Lordship Lane, Dulwich, and died at the age of seventy-nine, in the nursing home at Ivy Bank, Queen's Road, Taymount Rise, in Forest Hill, on 20 August 1939. What she did in those last thirty years, I have no idea; but she'd had twenty enjoyable, if not exactly starry, ones in the theater. A reunion photo of the original three little maids, in the 1930s, shows that while two had shrunk, Sybil was now a rather large little maid.

Frederick Bovill (The Pickler Who Pish Tush-ed)

I have worked hard to sort out our remaining *Mikado* man. A year or two ago, Savoyland challenged me to solve the mystery of the appearance, disappearance, and identity of Frederic[k] Bovill, which was not something, quite honestly, that had ever been high on my list of priorities. Mr. Bovill's career can be (and has been) summarized in a few lines. He comes from nowhere, is featured as Pish Tush in *The Mikado*, and plays it through the run at the Savoy. He goes on the road with the J. W. Turner and Henry Walsham Opera troupes, playing baritone roles such as Don José, Arnheim, Devilshoof, Luna, and Danny Mann for eight months ("too much vibrato"; "lacking in incisiveness"), then disappears for a while, resurfacing only to take tiny parts in the Carte productions of *Ivanhoe* and *La Basoche*. And that is effectively it.

Not many clues in there. Was he, I wondered, an amateur with something of a voice, fulfilling a desire to go on the stage? A friend of a friend of someone? Another "Mr. Hollingshead"? There must be a reason for Mr. Bovill—who couldn't even sing the role adequately and had to hand over his part in the madrigal to one with a better range—being cast in *The Mikado*, apparently with no previous experience.

And his name: Could it be real? I checked out all the Fred Bovills of Britain: a grocer in Kingston, the Rector of Eggington, Mr. F. W. Bovill of Harrow and New, a classics scholar from Dorking, a fish sauce and pickle maker. Date-wise, only one of those Freds seemed to fit. And yes, I'm afraid it's the pickler. I see that, during the years 1885–91, when our Fred was what might be described as "flourishing," the pickler and his wife produced three children. Each birth certificate confirms him as a "merchant." One son was christened Claude Hardwicke Knight

53. Bovill the Pickler.

Bovill . . . what a name! Hang on! I *know* Mr. C. H. Bovill; he was a minor librettist and lyricist to the British musical theater of the twentieth century! Coincidence? Red herring? Anyway, here's a photo of Pish Tush. And one of the pickler. What do you think? Yes? I incline that way. Frederick Anderson Bovill: b. St. John's Wood, 6 August 1860; d. Essex, 16 November 1933.

54. Bovill as Pish Tush. The same man?

The Mikado across the Waters

If everything went pretty silk-smoothly in the production and reception of The Mikado in England, it was not to be so across the water. Once again, there were foolish attempts to be first in with the merchandise. Something under the title The Mikado was produced in Chicago, with a respectable cast (and a disreputable producer) and hurried to New York's Union Square Theatre. But John Stetson had already confirmed his possession of the Mikado rights for America; he leaped, and the production was shut down, after one performance, amid a shower of writs. Emma Mabella Baker, who played Katisha on the occasion, would, nevertheless, advertise, for years, that she had been "America's first Katisha."

The tatty provincial versions of the piece that were flung on to the stage, after the surprise American publication of the score and script, were not really going to bother Carte and Stetson, but when they heard that the very respectable J. C. Duff was—perfectly legally—preparing a New York production, they leaped. Silently. A "provincial tour" company was put into rehearsal in London, and headed for Liverpool. But, when they reached Liverpool, the troupe headed not for the theater but for the docks, the good ship *Aurania*, and New York's Fifth Avenue Theatre. They opened one day before Duff could be ready and scored the predictable success.

With the Savoy's A company engaged in London, the New York company was, necessarily, a number-two company: but a pretty ritzy number two! And not quite all from England. The leading lady was the proven young local Geraldine Ulmar who had, so it was said, retired, preparatory to marriage. Various tales have been told about her "re-emergence from retirement," and the cancellation of the engagement or marriage to one Robert L. Ide, South End stockbroker. Anyhow, instead of taking the part with a Stetson company (or was she let into the big secret?), she was slotted in to the prerehearsed British troupe. And thus became (because we don't count Alice Harrison, the farce-comedy actress from the approximate "unofficial" Union Square troupe) America's first real Yum-Yum.

Geraldine Ulmar (Yum-Yum)

The daughter of a Boston South End jeweler, John B. Ulmar, and his wife, Susan, pretty, dark-eyed Annie Geraldine Ulmar (b. Charlestown,

Massachusetts, 23 June 1862; d. Merstham, England, 13 August 1932) started a concert career as a young teenager. I see her, first, on 6 August 1878, at Charlestown's Monument Hall, appearing in "Mr. George H. Ulmar's concert"; George was her baritone brother. She is quoted as having studied with "Madame Condelle, Madame de Angelis and Charles Adams." The following year, she became a member of the Boston Ideal Opera Company, and apparently made her first appearance with what was, then, regarded as the country's best light opera company, as Josephine in HMS Pinafore at New Bedford, Massachusetts. Thereafter, "Dolly" Ulmar appeared throughout the country, during some five years, in roles as diverse as Bettina in La Mascotte, Beatrice in Boccaccio, Germaine in Les Cloches de Corneville, the title-role(s) in Giroflé-Girofla, Constance in The Sorcerer, Arline in The Bohemian Girl, Marie in The Musketeers, Mabel in The Pirates of Penzance, Bathilde in Olivette, Giralda in Giralda, and Susanna in The Marriage of Figaro. In between her engagements with the Bostonians, she played Josephine with "The Peerless Pinafore Company" in Chicago (1880); sang with Flora E. Barry's comic opera company (1880, Josephine in Pinafore; Rita in The Contrabandista, etc.), with the Boston Opera Company, and with the Grayson Opera Company (1881); and appeared at the Boston Museum as Patience (1882) and at the Boston Globe in The Weathercock (1883) e tutti quanti—before she announced her retirement to marriage. Well, someone announced it. She said she "retired" because Miss Ober, the manager of the Bostonians, had done so. However, the connubial plans seemingly (and fortunately, but that's another story) didn't work out. Instead, she became the original Yum-Yum in the official Broadway production of The Mikado.

After her large success as Yum-Yum, Dolly went on to appear in New York in the title-role of the second go at Princess Ida and as Rose Maybud in Carte's Ruddigore (1887) and—when Leonora Braham left the London cast of the latter show, to go to Australia/get married/give birth—Miss Ulmar was moved, by Carte, to Britain, to take over as leading lady at the Savoy. She remained there for the subsequent revival of HMS Pinafore and to create the roles of Elsie Maynard in The Yeomen of the Guard (1888, "'Tis Done, I Am a Bride"; "I Have a Song to Sing, O") and Gianetta in The Gondoliers (1889).

Although Dolly then left the Carte company, she spent the rest of her career in Britain. In 1890, she starred as Marton in the highly successful London version of Audran's La Cigale et la fourmi. In 1892, she introduced the leading female part of Teresa in Gilbert and Cellier's

The Mountebanks, and she took over the title-role in Haydn Parry's light romantic opera *Cigarette*, when it was recast for a first-class London run. She also made a surprise shift to lighter things, when she appeared for a while as the juvenile heroine of the burlesque *Little Christopher Columbus* (1894). In 1896, she starred as O Mimosa San in George Edwardes's first tour of *The Geisha*, but she was not seen again in the West End until she was persuaded out of retirement in 1904 for a disastrously amateurish piece called *Ladyland*.

In later life ("a mountain of pale blue hair and a staggering cascade of bosom"), Geraldine became a singing teacher at the Wigmore Hall, numbering among her pupils such coming stars as José Collins, Binnie Hale, and Evelyn Laye, but she was forced from her work by blindness before her death at the age of seventy. Married, between 1891 and 1903, to Ivan Caryll, she later wed Jack Thompson, a less-high-profile performer and composer.

Josephine Findlay (International Yum-Yum)

When the Carte company set sail secretly from Liverpool, they had not yet received the news as to whether Miss Ulmar had accepted the role of Yum-Yum. So "in case Miss Ulmar could not be secured," they brought along a Yum-Yum of their own: Miss "Josephine Findlay."

Three generations of G&S scholars have pored over the identity of Miss Findlay, the latest being Michael Walters, George Low, and, now, K. Gänzl. Each has added his stone to the monument and, by teamwork, we may finally get there!

Josephine began with the Carte organization, it seems, in 1882. Which is a pest: if she'd made it 1881, we'd have had a chance of finding her with the touring company in the census. She quickly rose to playing the principal soprano roles on tour, and, as such, when the *Mikado* was rerouted to America, made the trip as a Maybe Yum-Yum. However, by the time the *Aurania* arrived, Miss Ulmar was confirmed, and Miss Findlay could catch a soon ship back. She did not return to the provinces, however: she was hired as understudy to Leonora Braham at the Savoy and played both Yum-Yum and Rose Maybud in *Ruddigore*, and in the supporting operettas, as required. When Miss Ulmar took Miss Braham's place, Josephine was deployed to the Carte company playing on the Continent.

In 1888, Josephine was cast in the soubrette role in the comic opera *Carina* at the Opera Comique. *Carina* had been touted as something special, but it wasn't. The management made desperate moves to save it, and one of those moves was to "name cast" it up. Josephine was replaced by Leonora Braham—but still the ship sank.

Miss Findlay had a good career thereafter. She played panto at Newcastle (*Puss in Boots*) and York (*Bluebeard*); took her original role in the tour of the dogged *Carina*; played on tour for Carte as Gianetta in *The Gondoliers*; and returned to London to play the vamp role of Señorita Inez in *Miss Decima* (*Miss Helyett*). Her 1891 pantomime was at Edinburgh ("A better Robinson Crusoe could not be found. A sprightly actress and a neat dancer . . . vocal accomplishments of a high order"), before she scooted off to the Continent again, playing Carmen in *Carmen-up-to-Data*. She sang at the Palace Theatre in the "oriental choral ballet" *The Sleeper Awakened*; toured with George Edwardes's Gaiety company as Isabella in *Don Juan*; spent Christmas 1894 as Cinderella at Camberwell; went on the road in *King Kodak*; and took part, with John Coates, as the ingenue of a provincial piece named *Love and War*.

Then Miss Findlay found a long-term role: she was cast as the smart, society lady Mrs. Ralli Carr, a role created by her sometime Savoy understudy, Aida Jenoure, in the tour company of the hugely successful *Gentleman Joe*. With time out for pantomime, she was still playing the part into the new century ("comely and vivacious . . . and sings well"). Then she seems, after twenty years on the stage, just to have stopped. I can't find her, anyway. Her fine career—what might it have been, had she been New York's Yum-Yum?—was seemingly at an end.

What became of "Miss Findlay"? Well, it's hard to track someone down when you don't know what her real name was. But . . . Mr. Walters found an old scrapbook in the Carte archives, with a clipping of an interview, titled "A Forgotten Prima Donna," with an aged ex-Cartesian lady named Miss Dale. The lady had traveled the Continent with the Carte company and there sung the role of Patience. Surely "Miss Dale" has to be "Josephine Findlay"! She says that in her (unmarried) retirement she tried running a boarding house in Hove, but, at the time of the (undated) interview, she is eightyish and living at Whiteley Village, Walton-on-Thames. Hmm, there are a few clues there! How about Jane Ann Dale, born Leak, Yorkshire, admitting to the age of forty-seven in the 1911 census when she is running a lodging house at 35 Lansdowne Place, Hove? Could be . . . Or what about Miss Annie M. Dale and

Miss Marion Eliza Dale (b. 2 April 1853; d. 9 March 1941), spinster sisters from Bloomsbury, sometime of 63 Circle Road, Whiteley Village, or Miss (?) Sarah Dale down the road . . . Oh, dear, I hope this isn't another puzzle like the "Zare Thalberg" mystery that infiltrated the world's reference books, for years, with an utterly false identification of the star! We'll get there.

George Thorne (Ko-Ko)

Ko-Ko was played by George Tyrell Thorne (b. Blackfriars, 6 January 1856; d. Edelsborough, Bedfordshire, 24 July 1922). George was the youngest brother of the well-known actor, producer, and theatrical pedagogue

55. George Thorne as Ko-Ko.

Sarah Thorne, of the Theatre Royal, Margate, and he began his theatrical career and life under her aegis. After a little youthful world wandering, George joined the Carte companies, at the age of twenty-five, already as a principal comedian, and played the "Grossmith" roles of the Savoy canon for nearly eighteen years, in all corners of Great Britain, as well as in America and South Africa. His curriculum vitae theatralis is, like those of other long-serving Cartesians, simply a list of the line of roles, as known. His particularity (I was going to say "credit," but I ween it not so) is to have introduced the melodramatic moritural ending to *The Yeomen of the Guard*. But, that apart, Thorne gave satisfaction to G&S audiences everywhere for the last two decades of the nineteenth century.

Fred Federici (The Mikado)

The Mikado himself was played by good old Fred Federici (né Anatole Frederic Demidoff Baker; b. Florence, Italy, 22 April 1850; d. Melbourne, 3 March 1888), in the original "King Gama" style. The life story of Federici is much less well known than his death story. He died, after a heart attack, at the Princess Theatre, Melbourne, and has been called "the theater ghost" by the Australian press, who periodically purvey imaginative tales about the circumstances of his death. Little was known about his life and career until I put my hunting hat on a wee while ago and dug up the truth about this apparently internationally social baritone.

Cutting a long story very short: Anatole Frederick Demidoff Baker was the son of Mr. Erick Thomas Baker (b. Deal, 25 December 1810; d. Bentinck Terrace, London, 26 September 1882), himself the son of Admiral Sir Thomas Baker KCB, and his wife Georgina Barbara (née Crossman). Georgina was the daughter of a British clergyman, George Brickdale Crossman, "late of St John's Withycombe," who died in 1854, and is buried in the English cemetery in Florence—where our Fred was born. The unusual domestic arrangements of the Crossmans, in Bellosguardo, have come under the investigation of students of the Robert Brownings, owing to some friendly connection between the two families. Erick was a bit of an aristocratic wastrel. He had gone glaring bankrupt at the age of twenty-four. Was he one of those who fled the English legal system and/or English disapproval to sunny Florence? Well, he was in England in 1843–44 ("eldest son and heir-at-law"), when his landed father was declared a lunatic. The Bakers and the Crossmans were hardly your average family.

56. Fred Federici as The Mikado.

Fred turned up in London for the concert season of 1872, and he soon rose to a respectable rank, appearing in the London Monday pops, and in oratorio around the country. He then joined an opera troupe promoted by Michael Gunn, playing the King in *Maritana*, Rodolfo in *La Sonnambula*, Valentine in *Faust*, Arnheim in *The Bohemian Girl*, and the Baron in *Lurline*. The other baritone roles were taken by Tom Aynsley Cook and Richard Temple. In October 1877, he was engaged by Arthur Sullivan for the Royal Aquarium concerts, then visited Manchester to play in Cellier's *The Sultan of Mocha* and *Belladonna*; he taught singing, and performed at the Covent Garden proms, the Langham Hall, the Marble Club Tuesday pops, the Exeter Hall national concerts, the Brighton Dome, and the Saturday pops in a promising but strangely stop-start career. He would later say he joined the army to escape his creditors. Others say he changed his name and sang in music halls. I have a feeling that, basically, he may have been suffering, already, from the heart ailment that would kill him at the age of thirty-seven.

In 1879, Fred joined up with the D'Oyly Carte organization to play the role of Bill Bobstay, and shortly afterward, while the troupe was in Huddersfield (28 October 1879), he married twenty-one-year-old chorister Jane Eleanor Finili ("Lena Monmouth"). For more than half a dozen years, the couple toured, together, stalwartly in Carte's provincial companies. Fred played Bill or Corcoran in *Pinafore* and—as the new shows succeeded in the repertoire—he added Samuel and the Pirate King in *The Pirates of Penzance*, Colonel Calverley in *Patience*, Strephon in *Iolanthe*, Florian in *Princess Ida*, the Counsel, and the Mikado. He played the Mikado for Carte in America and in Europe, and returned to America to appear as Sir Roderick in *Ruddigore*.

In 1887, the couple were contracted by Williamson, Garner and Musgrove for Australia. Fred was seen as the Pirate King, Colonel Calverley, Strephon, Dick Deadeye, the Mikado, Florian, the Marquis de Pontvert in *Erminie*, Harry Sherwood, and Squire Bantam in *Dorothy*. Lena took small parts such as Lady Betty (*Dorothy*) or Celia in *Iolanthe*. In March 1888, the company produced *Faust*, and Federici was cast, now, no longer as Valentine but as Mephistopheles. On the first night, while leaving the stage on his final exit, he suffered a heart attack, and died in the theater green room, not on stage, as has become part of his myth.

Fred Billington, another very long-serving Cartesian, was Pooh-Bah, and a young dolly-boy by the name of Courtice Pounds was Nanki-Poo. Courtice Pounds is a musical-theater monument; somebody should write a whole book on him and his remarkable family of singing sisters. Maybe they have. To condense his remarkable career into a few lines is really rather rude. But I guess I have to—without letting the wives, mistresses, sisters, cousins, and aunts distract me—so here are the bare facts.

Courtice Pounds (Nanki-Poo)

Charles Curtice Pounds (b. Pimlico, London, 30 May 1861; d. Surbiton, 21 December 1927) was the son of a sometime vocalist, Mary Ann Jane Curtice, and her builder husband. He did his first singing as a boy soprano, and was a choir soloist at St. Stephens, South Kensington at the age of eleven. He subsequently studied at the Royal Academy of Music and—after a brief turn in the building trade—won his first professional singing job, at the age of nineteen, in the chorus of *Patience*. He rose briskly through the Savoy ranks, acting as understudy to Durward Lely and Rutland Barrington, playing in forepieces at the Savoy, and moving

57. Courtice Pounds as Nanki-Poo.

up to leading-manship with the Carte touring companies and as New York's first regular Nanki-Poo (*The Mikado*). During his American stay, from 1885 to 1887, he followed up as Hilarion (*Princess Ida*) and Richard (*Ruddigore*) and also took the tenor roles in the Broadway productions of Paul Lacome's *Jeanne, Jeannette et Jeanneton* (aka *The Marquis*, Prince de Soubise), and Lecocq's *La Petite Mademoiselle* (aka *Madelon*, Jolivet).

Pounds returned to Britain in 1888 and replaced Durward Lely as principal tenor of the Savoy company, creating the roles of Colonel Fairfax in *The Yeomen of the Guard* (1888, "Is Life a Boon?"), Marco in *The Gondoliers* (1889, "Take a Pair of Sparkling Eyes"), Indru in *The Nautch Girl* (1890), Sandford in the revised *The Vicar of Bray*, and John

Manners in *Haddon Hall*, before leaving Carte's company, in 1892, to appear in the London version of *Ma mie Rosette* (Vincent).

In 1893, Pounds staged three one-act operettas, with a company of his own, on the pier at Brighton, then, after appearing fairly briefly as Ange Pitou in a revival of *La Fille de Madame Angot*, in the disastrous *Miami* (1893) with Violet Cameron, and as the heroic Mark Mainstay in the short-lived *Wapping Old Stairs*, he returned to the Savoy to play Vasquez in *The Chieftain* (1894). He subsequently went to Australia, accompanied by a lady who was not his wife, for a six-month season (Louis Pomerol in *La Belle Thérèse*, Marco, Fairfax). On his return, now noticeably plumper, he was cast with great success in the juvenile comedy/tenor role of Lancelot in *La Poupée* (1896). *The Royal Star* and *The Coquette* for the same management were less successful, and a London revival season of *Dorothy* (playing the role made popular by Ben Davies) was briefer than a subsequent tour.

Pounds then moved away from the musical theater to spend a period playing supporting roles (with the occasional song) in Beerbohm Tree's company (*Twelfth Night*; Touchstone in *As You Like It*; *The Last of the Dandies*; *The Merry Wives of Windsor*, etc.). He returned to the musical theater briefly in 1901, playing Box (*Cox and Box*) in a triple bill at the Coronet, and, more substantially, in 1903, as the extravagant King in a revival of *Chilpéric*. Over the following decade, he appeared in a long series of varying singing character roles in a long series of popular musicals—from *The Duchess of Dantzic* (1903) to *My Lady Frayle* (1916), often stealing the show from the nominal stars with his mixture of fun and fine singing. He also appeared, between times, in the music halls in musical sketches such as *Fritz*, *A Very Modern Othello*, and *Charles his Friend*.

The biggest success of the second half of Pounds's remarkable career came in 1916, when he created the principal comic role of Ali Baba in *Chu Chin Chow* ("Anytime's Kissing Time"; "When a Pullet Is Plump"), a part that he played throughout the whole of the show's record-breaking run. Oscar Asche provided him with a similar role in the show's successor, *Cairo*, but the final great starring success of his career awaited him at the age of fifty-three, when he was cast as Schubert in London's *Lilac Time* (*Das Dreimäderlhaus*). He made his last appearance on the musical stage in his sixties, in the Spanish musical *The First Kiss* (1924).

Other American Cast Members

Most G&S fans know something of Miss Ulmar and Pounds, and the Federici mythology, if not the fact, but here are some lines on a few members of that "provincial" company that they perhaps don't know so well, pictured as they appeared on the stage of the 5th Avenue Theatre.

Kate Forster, who took the part of Pitti-Sing on the American stage, was a fine and useful mezzo, who played with the Carte companies for two decades. Of course, "Forster" was a stage name. She was born (depending on your Polish) Jankowski, Jancowski, or Jankowitz. Her father, William, arrived in England, from Poland, around 1840, and he set himself up in Sheffield as a bunion specialist: a podiatrist of sorts, I suppose. He married Elizabeth Hardwick, daughter of a Chesterfield maltster. In the course of time, William gave up treating feet in favor of merchandising in Berlin wool, and they moved to The Cliff in Scarborough. There, in 1857, was born a daughter, Kate Jancowski; her baptism is recorded, but not her birthdate.

Skip ahead to 1873, and teenage Kate got married. The bridegroom was, by name, James Graham Wigney, son of a "gentleman" from Huddersfield. Gentleman? Mr. Wigney Sr. ran the Imperial Hotel. Mr. Wigney

58. *The Mikado* at the Standard Theatre, New York.

Jr. was, it seems, to prove an ephemeral husband. He lived till 1921, but by then had long, long since given up describing himself ("banker's clerk," "sculptor," "artist in watercolour") to the census-takers as anything but "single." And Kate went on without him, to become "Miss Forster" (mezzo-soprano, then contralto) of the D'Oyly Carte companies, through twenty years, as a much-appreciated principal player. She died in Norwich on 5 February 1915.

Elsie Cameron (Katisha) and George Byron Browne (Pish Tush) were a Cartesian couple—for a while, anyhow. The two met while appearing in D'Oyly Carte's touring company of *Patience*. George was playing Colonel Calverley; Elsie was cast as Lady Angela. This was just after the 1881 census, in which they can be seen, separately, making their only known appearances in any census: George in Torquay with the Carte company, and Elsie up north, touring with Alfred Hemming's company in *Crutch and Toothpick* and the burlesques *Cruel Carmen* and *Corsican Brothers Babes in the Wood*. Oh, she tells the census-taker that she is nineteen years old, which may very well be true. She tells him her name is "Elsie Cameron," which is not true. George admitted to being twenty-eight, and declared that he was born in America. Maybe he was; maybe he wasn't. I've no idea, any more than I have any idea whether the name under which he worked, for twenty years, was anything but a stage name.

Of George, in fact, I know nothing, prior to his becoming the Pirate King with Carte when already in his later twenties. Of Elsie, I know a tad more, some proven, some not. In 1890, Elsie gave a large interview to the Australian paper *Table Talk*, in which she said that she was born in Leeds on Christmas Day 1862, and that her father was a superintendent on the railways. She said she was heard as a child by Sims Reeves (oh! not him again), and then had lessons from Dr. Spark (highly probable) after which, at the age of sixteen, Reeves (!) got her into the Royal Academy of Music. She stayed, she said, for two years, and mentions an odd list of fellow pupils including Miss Etherington ("Marie Tempest"), Marion Hood, Ben Davies, Orlando Harley, Hilda Wilson, and Ellen Orridge. Well, Ellen Orridge was a star pupil at the RAM in 1876–77, at which time the Academy also housed Mary Davies, James Sauvage, and Leonora Braham! I don't think the unfortunate Orlando de Forrest Harley arrived from Norwalk, Ohio, till several years later, and I think the Miss Etherington date is out too. Anyhow, I see no sign of Elsie in any of the Academy's concerts, under whatever name.

It seems as if Elsie's correct name was Elizabeth Fowler. Why do I insist on Fowler? Because when "Elsie" wed Browne in Dublin in 1882 (and she really did) she was listed as "Elsie Elizabeth Fowler." When their daughter was baptized, the mother was listed as "Elizabeth Browne." I wonder if that Irish wedding certificate has parents' names on it?

Well, the next bit of Elsie's story—guess what!—has her going off to Milan to study with Lamperti for six months. So be it. After which, she came home and got a job with daddy's friend Wilson Barrett, who was running the Leeds Grand, and he got her that job in the Hem-

59. Elsie Cameron as Katisha: "A left shoulder-blade that is a miracle of loveliness."

ming-Walton troupe. But hang on; did she forget something? Who is the Miss Elsie Cameron (already) singing in the Hull pantomime, *Little Red Riding Hood*, at Christmas 1880 (oh, it is she, all right). Then she joined the Waltons, got censused, and got into the *Patience* troupe, which at Eastertime, 1882, played Dublin, where Miss Fowler and Mr. Browne were married. Baby (Mary Nonie Gladys) was born on 14 March 1883, but died at the age of eighteen months.

The couple accomplished a fine Cartesian work schedule over the next years, peaking with their voyage to New York for *The Mikado*. Mr. and Mrs. G. B. Browne were advertised as cast for Pooh-Bah and Katisha . . . so, what happened? When the show opened in New York, Elsie was Katisha and Fred Billington was Pooh-Bah; George was, or took over as, Pish Tush. Why? And then he departed . . . for personal reasons? Professional reasons? After all, he had been for six years a praised baritone lead player in Carte companies; there has to be a story here. All I know is that George went steadily down from that point. Oh, he worked, but in less and less reputable companies. In 1898, he is trouping with the fifth-grade Marie Bell "opera company." I don't suppose he and Elsie were ever divorced, but right there in New York their marriage seems to have fallen apart. I think I know who was to blame, but it's a guess!

So, while George went off into the one-night stands, Elsie went home and played in London and on tour for Carte until 1890, when she crossed to Australia. She was now "Mrs. Harold Russell," or so she and the papers said. I think that was Harold Russell the actor rather than Harold Russell the singer, but it doesn't really matter because Mr. Russell went home to England after a couple of years, and the soi-disante Mrs. Russell didn't.

Elsie, instead, became "Mrs. Cowell" and, until 1896, continued to perform lead contralto roles in comic opera on the Australian stage. She was referred to as "massive" in 1895, which, at thirty-four, doesn't sound very healthy. Mr. James R. Cowell was a well-known Victorian (as in Melbournian) sportsman. He was heavily into cricket, hunting, and racing, so, undoubtedly, a bit rich—and with, clearly, special tastes in ladies. So he became the new, rather older, Mr. Cameron. Elsie and he zoomed off to San Francisco, where that impeccable authority, Emily Soldene, reported helpfully on Elsie's soirées. In 1907, Mr. Cowell was found on the beach at Boulogne, his throat cut; I wonder where "Mrs. Cowell" was. So, I can supply no tops and tails in this tale. But we've started, and if I don't find the answers, I'm sure someone else will!

Well, that covers the cast in this splendid picture. Excepting one. See that Peep-Bo snuggling up to Pish-Tush on the right: She was known as "Geraldine St. Maur." I mean, really! Miss St. Maur was a long-serving EdithKate'n'mostly-Isabel with Carte for many years, playing in the United Kingdom, United States, and Europe. None of the wisest scholars in the G&S world have the faintest idea who she was. I've tried, but although I've divested dozens of Cartesians of their stage names, Miss St. Maur has defeated me. After "Alice May," she is, to me, the most annoyingly total mystery in the nineteenth-century Savoy cast lists.

The Mikado Lives On

The Mikado, the longest running of the Savoy Operas on its maiden production, has one more particularity among the Gilbert and Sullivan shows. It had a fine success in Europe, and in other languages than English. Which is why I grew up with the German sheet music of *Der Mikado* on our green room piano, and why my Viennese father became a G&S fan . . . and I, thus, became a G&S fan . . . and am writing this book. It's a bit like the knight and the horseshoe nail . . . in reverse!

10

Ruddigore, or The Witch's Curse

Supernatural opera in two acts
Savoy Theatre, 22 January 1887

Following a megahit with another hit is, as I have animadverted before, one heck of a job. Messrs. Gilbert and Sullivan had managed it, notably, with the *Pinafore-Pirates* enchaînement; could they possibly do it again? Fashion was in their favor, but expectation was against them; perhaps slightly unfairly, *Ruddigore* was expected to equal or top *The Mikado* in success, something that no G&S musical would ever do. So, in the end, that particular battle was unlikely ever to be but half won. If, after some struggling beginnings, *Ruddigore* didn't secede, it didn't, truthfully, succeed either.

In a parody of *Il Trovatore,* the opening "story-so-far" solo revealed: "Each Lord of Ruddigore, despite his best endeavor, shall do one crime, or more, once, every day, for ever . . ." To escape the family curse, Sir Ruthven Murgatroyd of Ruddigore has feigned death, and reinvented himself as a blameless toiler on the land, under the clod-worthy name of Robin Oakapple. Things come unstuck when his foster-brother, Richard Dauntless, comes home from sea and, having set sweet eyes on Robin's girlfriend, Rose Maybud, dutifully (aye, that damned Duty again!) reveals his milk-brother's identity to the incumbent Lord of Ruddigore, Sir Despard. Despard is delighted to be relieved of his horrid obligation, and Robin finds himself bad Sir Ruthven once more.

Then: a set piece. The narrative of the piece was built around a secondhand piece of Gilbert: the delightful scene in *Ages Ago* in which a gallery of ancestral portraits descends, en masse, from their frames to wreak their ancestral influences on the newest generation. The deceased Lords of Ruddigore duly descend to make sure that their heir is living up to his doom. After all, the fricasseed sorceress who had cast the family curse hadn't actually specified the degree of dastardliness that was required. But the new "bad bart" finds a typically legal twist with which to tie up a typically connubial ending.

How, now, to fit the Savoy company of favorite performers into such a show, more felicitously than had been done in *Princess Ida*? The part of Robin-Ruthven was tailored to measure for Grossmith, and that of Sir Despard for Barrington. The baritonic chief ghost was turned into a grand role, with a magnificent aria bouffe ("The Ghosts' High Noon") for Temple. The sailor was, of course, a tenor (Lely); Miss Maybud, who lives her life by the strict rules of a book of etiquette, was the soubrette soprano of the piece, as portrayed by Miss Braham. Miss Brandram, with one good scene and a rather twee ballad, and Miss Bond (whose roles were increasing notably in size), in a slightly unsubtle caricature of operatic madness, provided partners for Temple and Barrington. The

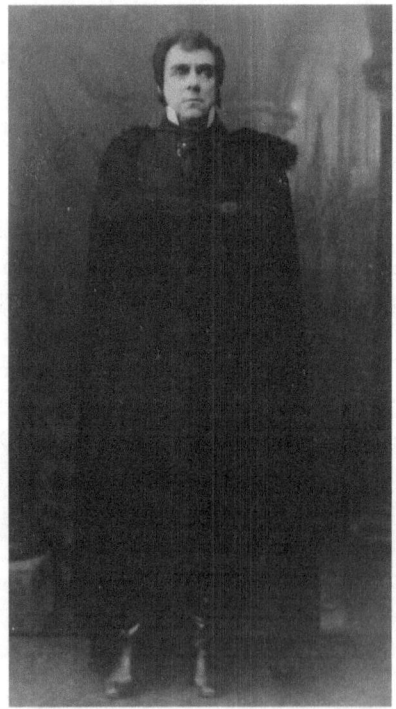

60. Richard Temple as Sir Roderic: "When the night wind howls . . ."

ladies' chorus personated a troupe of ditsy *Der Freischütz* bridesmaids who seize every opportunity to carol out their theme song.

The score of *Ruddigore* contained some grand pieces. A sailor-song for Lely ("I Shipped D'Ye See in a Revenue Sloop") got things off to a brisk start; Grossmith had his usual ration of word-filled numbers; Rose's pretty ditties ("If Somebody There Chanced to Be") were as pretty as ever; and Temple's song was a real winner (though some first-night dullards took it for operatic rather than mock-operatic). There were also some top-notch ensembles, notably the first-act "In Sailing O'er Life's Ocean Wide" and a nifty patter trio ("My Eyes Are Fully Open"), in the second. But, on the first night, the new show was not a success. All went well through act one and the gallery scene, and then things fell seemingly apart. The press leaped: "Never has there been a greater consensus of critical opinion than there has been over the demerits of the second act of *Ruddygore*," they cried. What didn't they like? Yes, Dame Hannah's song was probably the least effective of its kind, and the very concept of Margaret and Despard (which had been worrisome since the start, a planned duet for them having been cut without being set) was pretty ineffective; their "dancing quaker" business—portraying devout characters with an unexpected terpsichorean twist—was quite simply old hat. It had been a feature of Jack Ryley's well-known music-hall act many years ago.

Panic hit at the Savoy, and alterations and trims were promptly instigated—promptly, but curiously. Grossmith's second act solo, "For Thirty-five Years I've Been Sober and Wary," was replaced by another of the same kind ("Henceforth All the Crimes that I Find in *The Times*"), but otherwise it was just surgical nips and tucks. A change of title from *Ruddygore* to *Ruddigore*. The real sore spots were not touched. One wonders why. Surely Barrington (who would exit the Savoy after this show, anyhow) didn't wield that much power. Or Miss Bond . . . Or did the creators just think that the critical quibblers were wrong. Who knows?

In spite of those widespread criticisms, *Ruddigore* held up for a good nine months at the Savoy Theatre. It was sent on tour, and it was given a six-week showing in New York. But, thereafter, it was shelved for over thirty years before the D'Oyly Carte company revived it—with the replacement Grossmith song cut!—in 1920.

The principal casts for both the London and Broadway productions of *Ruddigore* are almost entirely made up of old friends, who have been profiled in earlier chapters. So, I shall help myself to the opportunity, here, to indulge my hobby of working out the "who" and "what" of some of the smaller players.

61. George Grossmith as Robin Oakapple: "A pure and blameless peasant."

Rudolph Lewis (Old Adam)

Rudolph Lewis was born at 20 Fan Street, Cripplegate, on 2 March 1846; and, yes, that was his real name. His father was Joshua Lewis, furrier, who later took up the bonnet and straw-hat business run by his Hertfordshire wife, Elizabeth (née Costin). While his sister duly went into the bonnet business, Rudolph became a wood engraver, married Miss Frances Dalton, fathered two children, and took singing lessons from Giovanni Febo Alfeo Gilardoni. His first public appearance as a bass singer seems to have been in 1882, in a concert performance of *Faust*, given by the Signor's pupils. He "made the success of the evening" as Mephistopheles. It was, apparently, in 1884 that he and his rich bass voice joined the Carte company, where he played several little parts (Go-To, Old Adam, Bob Beckett, Fourth Yeoman, Ottavio, etc.) and sang in the chorus up until 1893. During that time, he played the occasional Benefit and concert date, singing Mr. Molehill in *Won by a Trick*; joining Richard

Temple and Josephine Findlay at the Gaiety Theatre for Meyer Lutz's Benefit (1885); and playing Sparafucile to Temple's *Rigoletto* alongside Rose Hersee and Durward Lely (1886).

Lewis left the Carte company to join the Carl Rosa Opera (1893), where the kind of roles he was due came his way: Ramfis in *Aida* with Ella Russell and Barton McGuckin; one of the Anabaptists in *The Prophet*; one of the Knights in *Tannhäuser*. But then it was back to the touring theater—the Vizier in *Morocco Bound* (1894–95); Moran in *Robbery Under Arms* (1895); John Brown in *The Shop Girl* (1896); *Skipped by the Light of the Moon* (1897); John Mayfield in *Kitty* (1897); Donald in *Little Miss Nobody* (1899); and a London engagement at the Adelphi Theatre in *Two Little Vagabonds* (1900, Dido Bunce).

At the end of that engagement, having crammed in enough shows and enough roles to compensate his tardy beginning, Lewis rejoined the Carte company (Executioner in *The Rose of Persia*; Second Footman in *The Vicar of Bray*; Sergeant Pincher in *The Emerald Isle*; the tinker in *Merrie England*; Jem Johnson in *A Princess of Kensington* with its "Four Jolly Sailormen"). He continued, with many others of the company, into *The Earl and the Girl* (Rossiter) and *Little Hans Andersen* (The Witch), and was still to be seen touring in *Little Hans Andersen* as late as 1909. In 1905 he played in London's *The Talk of the Town* (Juddy Wuddy Ah), and he also joined with the other three original-cast sailors from *A Princess of Kensington* to give "Four Jolly Sailormen" at the Palace Music Hall. He was seen as "First Footman" in *The Catch of the Season* out of town, and, in 1914, knocking the age of seventy, I see him yet on the road in George Edwardes's tour of *The Marriage Market*. He died in London on 21 November 1917.

At some stage, Lewis lost his wife and, in 1888, he married a second time. However, he and Alice Maud (née Wharton) don't seem to have stayed together. His daughter, Frances Louisa Elizabeth Lewis (b. Argyle Street, Clerkenwell, 29 July 1881) was registered as a homeless pauper in 1911. Rudolph had left her in the care of his eldest sister, Amy Eliza, at the age of eight, but Amy had died in 1903, and Frances had gone from one servant's place to another, and repeatedly to the workhouse ("father: Rudolph Lewis, 19 Bath House, Newington Causeway"). I leave her in yet another workhouse infirmary in 1912, "destitute." At the same time, son Rudolph was working in an iron foundry. Rudolf Lewis may have been a fine basso, but he was apparently a lousy father.

The Ruddigorean Picture Gallery

I forget, now, who suggested I try to identify the gents in the Picture Gallery, in the same way that I had done with the Jury and the Bridesmaids of *Trial by Jury*. I thought I'd be lucky to score one out of the seven, but I actually did a little better than that.

HAROLD CHARLES (SIR JASPER MURGATROYD)

This identification may be, just *may* be wrong. I lack the one final *poussière* of proof. But I'm pretty sure I'm right, even though there are a couple of odd joins in my tale. Between 1886 and 1901—with possible, probable gaps—a gentleman by the name of "Harold Charles" was engaged as a baritone with the Carte company at the Savoy Theatre. And, at odd periods during that time, an aspiring baritone concert singer, by the name of H. C. Portway, appeared in London and the provinces. I posit that they were one and the same baritone.

Harold Charles Portway (b. The Croft, Halstead, Essex, 1869; d. 139 King's Avenue, Clapham, 10 July 1918) was the son of a well-off ironmonger, Charles Portway, and his wife Anne Winifred (née Attfield). In 1881, he can be seen attending Faversham Grammar School. In 1891, he is back in Halstead, boarding, solo, with an elderly lady, and professing to be an "ironmonger's assistant." In between times, according to me, he had spent four years as a chorister and etcetera at the Savoy. Had he given up? In March 1894, he can be seen returning from America. He's still a singer . . . he's been singing in St. Paul's church choir in Los Angeles! It seems that, in 1897, he ("pupil of Modini-Wood") then tried to reinvent himself. Mr. H. C. Portway, baritone from Milan and the Royal Academy of Music (!), took an advertisement featuring glowing reviews from the Gloucestershire press. Alas, the notices were from an amateur tryout of a local opera, *The Lady of Bayonne*, at Cheltenham (9 February).

Harold had a go. In 1897, he appeared singing Schumann songs in a concert in which Rutland Barrington was also on the bill; he staged a concert of his own, performing *In a Persian Garden* with Emily Squire, Adelaide Lambe, and Gregory Hast; and he returned to the Savoy to play a small part in *His Majesty*. In 1898, Mr. Portway appeared in concert once more, promoting an evening of Browning-lyric-ed songs at St. George's Hall; in 1899 he took a part in C. J. Abud's tour of *A*

Pantomime Rehearsal (Tomkins); and in 1900–1901 he was again back at the Savoy. I see him just once more, in 1905, playing "a waiter" in a tour of *The Orchid*. In the 1911 census, in two rooms in Streatham, he insisted he was living "on his own means." When he died in 1918, he had fifty-five pounds to his name. He can hardly have been living very lavishly.

ARTHUR TUER (SIR DESMOND MURGATROYD)

Arthur Tuer was a Lancashire man, born on 30 July 1854 at Waterloo, near Liverpool, son of Thomas Tuer, MRCS, licensed apothecary and general practitioner, and his wife Eliza. In 1881, he was living in Everton, working as a wine merchant, married, and with two sons. By 1885, he was singing tenor in the chorus at the Savoy. In 1887, he was cast as "Sir Desmond." But he left the Savoy to go to the Cork School of Music as a "professor of solfeggio and voice cultivation." He also acted as musical director for the Corkish amateur productions. He died at the age of forty-one, on 2 February 1896, of double pneumonia, leaving a widow and seven children. His obituary boasted that he had been "the original Rolf Murgatroyd in *Ruddigore*."

PERCY BURBANK (SIR CONRAD MURGATROYD)

Mr. Burbank was a member of the Carte choruses for more than a decade, emerging only occasionally from anonymity. He is listed in the touring company of HMS *Pinafore* in 1880, in *The Gondoliers* at Windsor Castle, and in concert at the Aquarium in 1891. So who is the "Percy Burbank" singing in the local amateur-dramatics production of *The Doctor of Alcantara* in Duluth, Minnesota, in 1882? And who is the one living in Mortlake in 1888?

HARRIS TREVOR (SIR LIONEL MURGATROYD)

"Harris Trevor" was another singer who stayed a decade and more with the Carte companies. Prior to his joining up, I see him delivering "The Vagabond" and "Nancy Lee" on a bill with Mackney at the Poplar concert hall (1877), as baritone with the Southend Variety Concert Party (1878), and at the Brighton Aquarium supporting ventriloquist Lt. Walter Cole (1879), before he disappears into the Carte chorus until 1894. In

1895, he pops up in the chorus at the Lyric Theatre and in a concert with Clara Samuell and Norman Salmond for Napoleon Vert. My last sighting of him is in a newspaper ad in 1900, with the tag line: "please communicate." I wonder if he did.

JAMES WILBRAHAM (SIR GILBERT MURGATROYD)

Mr. Wilbraham was born in Dublin on 14 November 1853 and, like many of his fellow long-stay Cartesian choristers, he sported a stage name. But he had the kindness to tell us so. Mr. St. John James Cottingham was the eldest son of Christopher Cottingham, "public writer and lawyer," and his wife, Margaret Clare (née Welch), and he had originally been destined to be a schoolmaster. However, he sang tenor on the side: I see him at the Crystal Palace in 1879, in concert at Northampton, and singing *Judas Maccabeus* at Ampthill. By 1883, he was playing in the *Iolanthe* cricket team, so he had clearly joined the chorus. He also married Miss Jessica Elizabeth Webb, "singer." A Cartesian singer? In the decade 1883–92, Wilbraham played both on the road—where, for a period, he took the lead tenor roles—and at the Savoy (Associate in *Trial by Jury*, etc.), where he covered and played the main tenor parts, while appearing in the forepieces and/or small roles and as chorus.

I see Wilbraham occasionally elsewhere, such as in a charity matinee of *The Bohemian Girl* (1888), playing Florestein to the Devilshoof of Richard Temple; or at the Crystal Palace ("Refrain thy voice from weeping"), but I don't sight him in the Carte lists after 1894 and, soon after fathering child nine, he did the macho midlife thing, and walked out on his wife and family. I see him in 1900 musically directing a *Cloches de Corneville* company, and in the 1901 census, while Jessie is working as a cook in Peckham Rye, he is shacked up with a twenty-three-year-old named "Rae" (Rachel Abrahams) who claims to be Mrs. Wilbraham. Habits die hard: he produced two more children by her. Rae must have sensed she was backing a loser, because in 1909 she hoofed it, with her babies and her brother, to Christchurch, New Zealand, married a carpenter, and lived half a century more.

Now the twist in the tale. Rae's son by St. John, Sidney Leonard, retained the surname "Wilbraham," and he duly wed and fathered. As soon as I saw the word "Christchurch," my Kiwi brain clicked back half a century. The director of my first-ever TV show was named Wilbraham: Phil Wilbraham. Yes, it's true. I made my first appearance on any screen under the direction of James Wilbraham's grandson! Yes, I have a little link to the Murgatroyds of Ruddigore!

I can't find St. John James or Jessie in the 1911 census. They have to be there: James Wilbraham is credited with the music for a Manchester pantomime in 1913. I find just their deaths: his in Bath in 1921, hers in Southwark 22 February 1929.

SIDNEY PRICE (SIR RUPERT MURGATROYD)

Originally a touring chorister, Price was brought to the Savoy, where he understudied Rutland Barrington in *The Mikado* and *Ruddigore*. I see him in *Beauty and the Beast* in Liverpool (with Alice Burville and E. J. Lonnen) in 1883–84, and the next year in *Aladdin*. Is he the "Sidney Price" who appeared with Richard Mansfield at the Globe in 1889?

Well, that's six of 'em. Admittedly, not all solved (yet), but it gives you some idea of what the front line of the male chorus (the equivalent of the EdithKate'n'Isabels of the ladies' team, if less frockily featured) at the Savoy was like: pretty solid.

Ruddigore's "Failure"

After its original productions, *Ruddigore* was, like Sleeping Beauty, put into suspended animation for three decades. It was seemingly destined to be the Cinderella of the Savoy canon. But, since its reinstatement in that canon, it has won some favor, and although it will surely never reach the popularity of an *HMS Pinafore* or a *Mikado*, it still finds the odd stage. A century later, Ryley's "dancing quakers" are all forgot, so *Ruddigore*'s "sore spots" have been soothed somewhat. Me, I simply wonder what might have been had the Savoy team had the courage to take a sickle to the roles of Despard and Margaret. And I wonder if it were the perceived "failure" of *Ruddigore* that prompted Messrs. Gilbert and Sullivan to make their next little deviation from their accustomed way.

11

The Yeomen of the Guard, or The Merryman and His Maid

Opera in two acts
Savoy Theatre, 3 October 1888

While Carte kept his theater bustling with reprises of past hits, the press waxed imaginative on the subject of what Messrs. Gilbert and Sullivan would next come up with in the way of a novelty: an Egyptian opera; a piece about Buffalo Bill's Wild West Show; another "lozenge" musical; a Scandinavian piece about the Darlecarlians and the Falun miners? Well, one has to fill newspaper columns somehow. Although I can't help regretting, just a little, that Gilbert and Sullivan didn't give us their "Willie Get Your Gun." C. V. Stanford took up the Swedish miners.

What they did give us was rather more "safe." After the half-fig/half-raisin results of *Ruddigore*, they simply abandoned the English opéra-bouffe style of plot with its burlesque humor and laughable twists, which they had led to its present exalted position, and instead turned out a piece that was a straightforward and sentimental comic opera. "Comic" opera not as in "comic-haha," of course, but comic opera as in its original meaning, opéra-comique: a musical piece with spoken dialogue. The show was to be called, the press announced, *The Tower of London*, and it would be set in the time of Henry VIII.

Flash back to 1875, *Trial by Jury* time; place: the Prince's Theatre, Manchester. The theater had notched up a decided success, the previous year, with an original comic opera titled *The Sultan of Mocha* and, this year, they were gunning for a repeat. The new piece was titled *The Tower of London*. By the machinations of a bad Baron, Captain Harold Trelawney has been imprisoned in the Tower, and is doomed to be executed. He is, of course, after three acts of song, dance, and not-very-comical comedy from incidental characters, saved, in the last reel, by his sweetheart Barbara, daughter of the Governor. So? It's a fairly utilitarian plot. Coincidence? I think not, because the music of *The Tower of London* was the work of Mr. Alfred Cellier, close colleague of the triumvirate and brother to the Savoy's musical director. The libretto, however, was uncredited, and what survives in the British Library doubtless resembles the final text only loosely—hopefully: "What a wonderful place is the tower, where they let people in every hour, it's the prettiest garden that ever was seen, with a sweet little block on the green." After opening night, principal comedian, J. G. Taylor (once of *Thespis*), got to work on his part and . . . well, Gilbert may have taken the idea and the setting from Cellier's piece, but, I suspect, nothing much more! Some of Cellier's music did survive, but elsewhere: it was reworked into the score for the successful *Doris* at the Lyric Theatre, the plot of which just happened, usefully, to end up at the Tower of London.

A more obvious source, in the eyes of British theatergoers, was one of the most popular operas of the century, *Maritana* (1845), itself based on Adolphe d'Ennery and Dumanoir's vastly successful French play *Don César de Bazan*. However, once again, Gilbert took only a couple of plot elements/situations from *Don César de Bazan*, and his libretto to what would, eventually, be titled *The Yeomen of the Guard* includes neither of the pivotal characters of the play and opera—the boy, Lazarille, and the villainous Don José—among its dramatis personae. And, of course, the tale in Gilbert's hands would have an entirely different flavor to that of the melodramatic French and English versions of *Don César*, just as Sullivan's score would sing a wholly different song to that of the operatic scores of Wallace and Massenet.

By the machinations of a nasty relation-who-will-inherit (unseen), Colonel Fairfax has been imprisoned in the Tower of London and is doomed to be executed. In order to foil said nasty relative's financial hopes, Fairfax determines to marry before his death, and Elsie Maynard, a strolling player, agrees to wed him, cash down, if he promises to die tomorrow. So, she is wed, blindfold, and . . . he doesn't die! He escapes, and while those involved describe the manner of his death in enthusiastic tones, he stays around the Tower precincts, disguised as the son of a Sergeant of the Guards, and falls in love with his own wife.

What took this hardly "new and original" tale into a different league was the characters with which Gilbert peopled it. This time—alongside the standard juves and the basic baritone—Grossmith, Barrington (even though it didn't end up being Barrington), and Miss Bond were particularly well suited by their parts. Barrington was to be Fairfax's lugubrious jailer, Wilfred, again paired with Miss Bond, this time in a role in which she didn't even have to act, because, as Gilbert allegedly told her, "It is you." She was the Sergeant's daughter, Phoebe, who with her father (Temple) engineers Fairfax's escape. But it was Grossmith who pulled the plum role: jester Jack Point, Elsie's partner in their double-act entertainment "The Merryman and His Maid," and shyly in love with her. Forty years ago, I wrote, "In Point, Gilbert created a character of sincerity and humanity. Loveable as had been Ko-Ko, Little Buttercup and the rest, none of them could have been taken seriously for a second. When Major General Stanley and his daughters weep, when Frederic and Mabel part to 'pine alone,' or when Bunthorne loses all of his brides, fancy is stimulated but real sympathy is never aroused . . ." I don't think I could say it better, now, so I shall simply say it again. In Jack Point, Gilbert created a first-class character in whom one could believe, but

62. George Grossmith as Jack Point: "I've jibe and joke, and quip and crank."

who nevertheless melded perfectly into this comic-opera world. It was different, nay somewhat daring, but it worked.

The reaction to *The Yeomen of the Guard* was, predictably, two-pronged. Those folk who had loved the bouffe comicalities of *The Pirates of Penzance* and *The Mikado* found the piece rather sober, while those to whom the music was all-important found that Sullivan had excelled himself. And he had. Given words to set that did not indulge (too often) in extreme whimsicality, in a story that was almost sentimental, he was in his element. The ballads for the tenor ("Is Life a Boon"; "Free from His Fetters Grim") and Elsie's scena "'Tis Done, I Am a Bride" were a lyrical treat; the ensembles—notably, the quartet "Strange Adventure"—likewise; Phoebe had a pretty opening ballad, and even the nameless First and Second Yeomen had bits of delightfully tuneful solo music.

But there was plenty of fun, as well: Jack Point had two prize numbers ("A Private Buffoon," "I've Jibe and Joke") describing his calling; Dame Carruthers, the Tower housekeeper, boomed out the history of the edifice in not exactly humorless tones ("the screw may twist and the rack may turn, and men may bleed and men may burn"); Phoebe distracted Wilfred from the dungeon keys at his belt by teasing him with a delicious "Were I Thy Bride"; and Wilfred and Jack's rehearsal of their mendacious version of circumstances of the escaped prisoner's death ("Hereupon We're Both Agreed") was a comedy highlight to equal its equivalent in *The Mikado*. However, there was no doubt as to the top tune of the evening: Jack and Elsie delivered, as their "act as known", the singing farce of *The Merryman and his Maid* and the simple, charming "I Have a Song to Sing, O!" was a full-blown hit.

Those critics who joyfully acclaimed *The Yeomen of the Guard* as Sullivan's finest score to date certainly had justification, but in their joy they were most unnecessarily hard on the book and lyrics that had given birth to that music. If they missed Gilbert's "exuberant drollery," surely they could appreciate the skill on show in a script with none of the padding or dead moments that they had criticized in *Ruddigore*, a script in which every character from Kate to the Second Yeoman had their moments? Even Bridget Maynard (unseen), Elsie's mother, who is responsible for the only cringeworthy lines in the piece, when Elsie uses her in old-melodrama style—"I-wouldën-ha'-dun-it, milud, 'cept for me poor sick mum"—to justify her acceptance of her marriage. You're singing for pennies in the street, girl, and you would turn down one hundred crowns for one day's marriage? Do you think you are La Périchole?

Anyway, if the critics camped each in their own camp ("it caused quite a flutter in the critics' dovecote" remembered a scribe, six months into the run), the public showed no doubt. Wisely trimmed of a teensy bit of excess fat (one song for Temple), *The Yeomen of the Guard* proved a huge success, and stayed at the Savoy for some fourteen months as it established itself in theaters, and on pianos, round the world, and in the heart of the classic comic opera canon.

Since *Ruddigore*, there had been a few changes of personnel at the Savoy. Some old favorites were missing from the cast of *The Yeomen of the Guard*: no Barrington, no Lely, no Miss Braham—Pooh-Bah, Nanki-Poo, Yum-Yum—but, in two cases, those favorites had been simply replaced by other favorites, from the other side of the pond. Instead of Britain's Yum-Yum and Nanki-Poo, we had New York's equivalents, Geraldine Ulmar and Courtice Pounds. And the Barrington role was taken by a gentleman who had been a fine Cartesian player as long ago as the days of *La Périchole* and *The Duke's Daughter*.

W. H. Denny (Wilfred Shadbolt)

William Henry Dugmore (b. Balsall Heath, Birmingham, 22 October 1853) was born to the theater. His father, Irishman Henry [Thomas] Dugmore, known as "Mr. H. Leigh," and his mother Elizabeth (née Brown; "Mrs. H. Leigh") had been, in fine careers, longtime members of the Birmingham Theatre Royal company. "Mrs. H. Leigh" we have already met; she joined the Gaiety Theatre as "first old lady" soon after its opening, and played, yes, the part of Diana in *Thespis*. She would remain at the Gaiety for over a decade, and lived to the age of ninety.

Their son, Mr. W. H. Leigh, began in the adult theater at seventeen and appeared in London for the first time with Samuel Phelps's company, playing small roles in Shakespeare and in classic plays. He was seen at the Gaiety in comedy, operetta (*Chanson de Fortunio*), and burlesque (Nick Vedder in *Young Rip van Winkle*; Marquis in *Little Don Caesar de Bazan*), and toured with the D'Oyly Carte company of 1876, playing Trénitz in *La Fille de Madame Angot*, Barthel in *The Duke's Daughter*, and Tarapote in *La Périchole*. He also married (4 March 1876) the very lovely nineteen-year-old Alice Julia Burville, who would play Josephine at the Opera Comique, the Petite Duchesse in the Philharmonic *Le Petit Duc*, and, later, Lady Angela and Arabella in Carte's American

63. W. H. Denny (Shadbolt) and Jessie Bond (Phoebe): "Were I thy bride . . ."

productions. The marriage did not last, and Alice went on to marry composer John Crook.

Mr. W. H. Leigh was seen in drama, comedy, and in burlesque (*The Miller and His Men*, 1883; Aurungzebe in *Lallah Rookh*, 1884; Dr. Chanery in *Scalded Back*; Captain Crosstree in *Black-Eyed Sue-usan*, 1885, under the name of Denny) around London, toured America (1886, again as "Leigh") with Lydia Thompson (Generalissimo in *Piff Paff*, etc.), and appeared in New York and London in both drama and comedy. Then, in 1888, now definitively W. H. Denny, he joined D'Oyly Carte's company at the Savoy Theatre to create *The Yeomen of the Guard* in the room of Rutland Barrington. When the chastened and poorer Barrington returned to Carte, Denny nevertheless remained with the company to create further memorable Savoy Theatre comic roles in *The Gondoliers* (Grand Inquisitor, "I Stole the Prince"), *The Nautch Girl* (Bumbo, the idol), *Haddon Hall* (The McCrankie), and *Utopia (Limited)* (Scaphio), and to play Bedford Rowe in the revived *The Vicar of Bray*.

Denny moved on from the Savoy, after some four years in residence, to feature in the London edition of *Poor Jonathan* (1893, Herr Steinbach), and to work with Arthur Roberts as General Jenkinson in *A Modern Don Quixote* and Sir Philip Saxmundham in the burlesque *Claude Du-Val*. He appeared with Lillian Russell in Jakobowski's Broadway-bound comic opera *The Queen of Brilliants* at the Lyceum (1894, Lucca Rabbiato), and toured for Morell and Mouillot in *Don Juan* (Rodrigo), and then rejoined Roberts to play the fine role of the comical nouveau riche Pilkington Jones in *Gentleman Joe* (1895); the star's policeman rival-in-love in *Dandy Dan the Lifeguardsman* (1897); and Bob Chaffers in the loose-limbed *HMS Irresponsible* (1900–1901). In between those engagements, Denny also took the chief senior comic role of Major Fossdyke in the West End run of *The Gay Parisienne* (1897, "The Battersea Butterfly Hunters"), and featured briefly as the Court Clown in the extravaganza *Her Royal Highness* (1898).

In 1902, Denny appeared in the British touring musical *The Gay Cadets* before working out the latter end of his multicolored career in Shakespeare in Australasia (Malvolio, Bottom), in both drama and musical comedy in America—Mr. Hazell in *The Earl and the Girl* (1906); Loofah in *The Tourists* (1906); Baron Lecocq in *The Beauty Spot* (1909); and Herr Starke in *The Gay Hussars* (1909)—and, finally, back in Britain, in the music halls. W. H. Denny died at Herne Bay on 31 August 1915.

His son, Reginald Denny (né Reginald Leigh Dugmore; b. Richmond, 20 November 1891; d. Los Angeles, 16 June 1967), after early appearances in touring productions of such perennials as *The Merry Widow* and *The Quaker Girl*, and, in America, as Gaston in *Alma, Where Do You Live?* (1916), became a well-known stage and screen actor (Algy Longworth in the *Bulldog Drummond* series, etc.). He was seen in the 1927 film of *On Your Toes* (Elliott Beresford).

Rose Hervey (Kate), a Useful Niece

Another "Kate"; this one with no Edith'n'Isabel attached, because the supporting roles in *The Yeomen of the Guard* were not female but male.

64. Kate (Rose Hervey) is the lass who spills the beans.

The little solos, lines, and verses that had been wont to be allotted to daughters, schoolgirls, and fairies fell to performers such as James Wilbraham and Antonio Medcalf as, naturally, yeomen.

But this Kate, niece to Dame Carruthers, had a place in the plot: it is she, by Elsie's chevet, who overhears the heroine give away the fact she is a married wife. And she had a lovely part to sing: the top line in the quartet "Strange Adventure."

The part of Kate was taken by Rose Hervey. Miss Hervey spent a dozen years as a Cartesian, much of it as a chorister, small-part player, and understudy, but latterly in lead soprano roles on tour. There was a reason for her fidelity. Her real name was Rosa Elizabeth Sullivan, and she was cousin to Mr. (now Sir) Arthur Sullivan. She played little outside the Cartesian establishment, although I spot her at the Crystal Palace, at Easter 1883, with her sister, Kate, playing in an extravaganza called *Mazeppa or the Wild Horses of Tartary*. She was born on 27 June 1857, in Chelsea, married Scotsman William Alexander Lindsay in 1892, and then retired from the stage. Rose bore three children, but died of the fourth, at Glenart, Waterloo Park, Liverpool on 7 October 1899. I see, in the 1901 census, Mr. Lindsay listed as a "general produce broker," and "widower," with his two daughters, two servants, and his brother-in-law, Bert Findon, who was to be (one of) Arthur Sullivan's biographer(s).

Antonio Medcalf (Second Yeoman)

The second Yeoman has not one but two solo verses to sing: the very attractive "This the Autumn of Our Life" (originally intended for Temple) and a bit in the jaunty couplets in the act 1 finale. The First Yeoman has just the latter, but he is a tenor, so is "first." The tenor was Mr. Wilbraham, our ghost from *Ruddigore*, whose incontinence I have ruthlessly exposed. So, I think the baritone deserves at least as many column inches.

Antonio Alfred Medcalf—it was his real name—was born in Felixstowe on 9 August 1866, the son of William Alfred Medcalf and his wife Rosina Maria (née Coppini). Yes, the Antonio comes from his mother's side. Rosina was born in Norton Folgate to an Italian father, of whom she knew nothing, and of whom her mother, seemingly, knew not much more. Shortly after Rosina's birth, her mother married an Italian looking-glass maker by the name of Antonio Bianchi, had sons Antonio and Alfredo, and her illegitimate daughter became Rosina Bianchi (1846–1921) until she wed Mr. Medcalf. Rosina's sons were named Antonio Alfred (that's our Antonio) and Albert Victor.

The Medcalf family settled in Woodford Essex, and there father William changed his profession. No longer a furniture dealer, he was now an "operatic vocalist." I spy him singing, for a while, at local concerts and even in a little opera program, but he soon reverted to being an "estate agent." It looks as if, at some stage, he may have been a professional chorister.

Antonio was educated at Salcombe College, Loughton, musically by one Walter Latter, and, in 1886, I see him singing in the school operetta *The Flower Queen*. Later the same year, he joined the Carte establishment. During the next years, while he sang at the Savoy Theatre, he continued to study: I see him at Edward Wharton's pupils' concert in 1890 and at the Guildhall School (Don José in *Maritana*, "a full and powerful baritone voice") as well as taking part in a concert at Chelmsford for Mr. Latter. In 1891, he was to be seen in Essex concerts, until he was hired for the Carl Rosa *Carmen* company, headed by Marie Roze. He sang Escamillo to Mme. Roze's Carmen, Belamy in *Fadette*, and Don José in *Maritana* with Edna Gray, Lily Moody, and Wilbur Gunn/Durward Lely.

When the company's tour was over, Antonio returned to Woodford, family and friends, local concerts, and, in 1893, married a local girl, Alice Lichfield. In 1893, he took part, also, in an embarrassing piece named *Peterkin*, before launching his own Antonio Medcalf Opera Company. In his production of *The Bohemian Girl*, father William played Thaddeus, brother Victor conducted, and frequent colleagues Jessie Browning, of the Carte companies, and a Mrs. Eugenia Morgan sang the ladies' roles. Antonio would put out several little opera groups over the years, giving concert performances in small venues, as well as appearing with tiny opera troupes such as "The Brescian Family's Opera Company" in such pieces as *The Bohemian Girl*, *Maritana*, and *La Fille du régiment*.

In 1898, I spot Antonio at Tudor's Circus in Ipswich, then for several summer seasons at Hornsea, at Fields' Oriental Café, Bridlington, where Victor was bandmaster, and at Dover's Promenade Pier, always with the Carl Rosa credit attached to his name. But it was not a vanity. More than twenty years on, Antonio returned to the Carl Rosa company. It was no longer the kind of company that employed a Marie Roze, merely a touring English opera troupe of a fair standard. His roles, this time, included Laertes in *Mignon*, and Wagner in *Faust*.

Meanwhile, Antonio's family life had developed. Alice had given birth to Norah, Doris Maria, Jeannette, Antonio Jack, Alfred Liston, and Sylvia Marjorie, and they had all moved together from Woodford to Melcombe Regis, where Antonio ran a tobacconist's and sweet shop. In later life, the girls would join Mr. Medcalf "of Weymouth" in concert; a much nicer ending to his life and career than that of his tenor colleague. Antonio died at 15 Compton Road, Islington on 19 March 1921, of "severe pontine haemorrhage" at the age of fifty-four.

W. R. Shirley (Leonard Meryll)

A newcomer played the small but highly plotworthy role of Leonard Meryll. W. R. Shirley (possibly b. 9 January 1870) evidently wasn't born under that name. Before I "knew" his date of birth, I investigated all British W. R. Shirleys within a reasonable span of time. They had all died or were otherwise disposed of when he was still alive and singing. So, the obvious answer, as so often, was "stage name." I didn't give up easily. I established from one tiny mention that the "W" was probably for "William"; no result. Walter? No. Clearly it was the "Shirley" that was the problem. Was he related to the two Shirley girls who had sung with Carte? Apparently not. I put his identity aside, and delved instead into the career.

Shirley's first theatrical engagement, under that name at least, was apparently with the Carte organization, on tour, as Robin Oakapple, after which he played with the company at the Savoy (Leonard in *The Yeomen of the Guard*; Marco in *The Gondoliers*) between 1887 and 1891.

65. W. R. Shirley: The dauntless Leonard Meryll.

He then joined the company at the Criterion Theatre, replacing George Giddens in the hit F. C. Burnand adaptation *Betsy*. While at the "Cri," he also played in Gilbert and Grossmith's *Haste to the Wedding*. He fulfilled engagements under Charles Hawtrey's management as Bob Briscoe in *The Sportsman* and Ned Moreland in *Tom, Dick and Harry*, before traveling to America (1894–96) as juvenile lead for Charles Frohman (*The New Boy*; *The Gay Parisians*, i.e., *L'Hôtel du Libre Échange*).

On his return to Britain, Shirley toured for George Edwardes in *The Circus Girl* (1897–98), then for a spell in the drama *The Great Ruby*, played a short season in a botched version of Antoine Banès's *Le Bonhomme de neige*, then went back on the road, playing opposite Ada Blanche in *La Demoiselle du téléphone*. He was back in London in 1901 to play Sonny in *The Thirty Thieves*.

George Musgrove of Australia picked up *The Thirty Thieves* for export, and he picked up Mr. Shirley, too. William would spend 1902–3 in the antipodes, playing *The Thirty Thieves*, *A Chinese Honeymoon*, *The Fortune Teller*, *The Serenade*, and *Fra Diavolo*. In the last-named opera, he played not the title-role but the comic one of Lord Allcash. In the decade since *The New Boy*, Mr. Shirley the jeune premier actor-vocalist had become Mr. Shirley the somewhat bulkier comedian. He returned to Britain but, before long, he was off again, to America, to play for Edwardes and Frohman in *The School Girl*.

A long career as a classy singing character man seemed in prospect, but, oddly, that is the last time I see Mr. W. R. Shirley on the stage. Yes, he went back to Britain. And, on the passenger manifest, theoretically revealed his year of birth (age: thirty-four). He was alive and on the guest list at a Cartesian party in 1907. And in 1913, the faithful Australian papers said "happy birthday" to him, on 9 January; so, it seems he was born on 9 January 1870? And here, W. R. Shirley vanishes from the stage and from my ken. Odd. Sigh. It has to be an oddity to "know" someone's date of birth, yet not know his name!

Wallace Brownlow (Sir Richard Cholmondeley), Womanizer and Drunkard

I've left the worst to last. I don't like Wallace Brownlow. But apparently he had a pretty fair baritone voice and, from photographic evidence, a suave if slightly predatory appearance.

Brownlow was born on 21 November 1861, the son of Edward Brownlow, "Yeoman of the Queen's bodyguard, Chelsea pensioner, drill master at the Potter's Fields Grammar school." He seems to have joined the Carte touring establishment by at least 1884, because in that year he married (22 March 1884) Cartesian soprano Sarah [Siddie] Symons (b. Launceston, Cornwall, c. 1857; d. Southampton, December 1911). "Siddie," after a trial as Princess Ida, no less, did well. She played Yum-Yum and Rose Maybud on the road between 1886 and 1888, was principal girl in Glasgow's 1888 *Mother Goose*, and took the title-role of *Dorothy*, on the road, in Cellier's inexhaustible comic opera (1889–90). But her marriage was already in tatters, as Brownlow carried on a career of serial infidelity while, at the same time, his professional career took him up to the Savoy Theatre and the English Opera House.

Brownlow's future looked, professionally, bright. After his time at the Savoy, where he created not only Cholmondley but the "private drum" Luiz in *The Gondoliers*, he moved to Carte's English Opera House, where Sullivan's *Ivanhoe* was being produced. He stayed there until the venture folded. In 1892, he was seen in London as William in an Osmond Carr burlesque by title *Blue-Eyed Susan*. William's beee-aut-i-ful Susan was played by Australian soprano Nellie Stewart. And, next thing, Mr. Brownlow was on a boat to Australia; no, I'm not really suggesting Nellie was the latest member of the Brownlow parade of fallen women . . . well, who knows? Read Miss Stewart's autobiography, which, I feel, rivals Jessie Bond's for disingenuity.

Brownlow played in (and played around in) Australia for some years. He ran a pub; he drank. He tried his luck as a barihunk in America (*Love's Lottery*, etc), and ended up in alcoholic penury in California. Ultimately brought back to Australia, a drink-sodden pauper, Brownlow committed suicide, in September 1919, near the Melbourne hotel from which he had just been evicted. Siddie was already gone. She had been in the South Stoneham workhouse for years, and had died in the local insane asylum in 1911. It is not the happiest Cartesian marriage story, but then, so many weren't: "I love ya, honey, but the season's over."

Yeomen Cis-Atlantic

The days of the crazy rush for the latest G&S&C show in America were over. Arrangements were made with the Casino Theatre, New

York's premier comic-opera house, for a *Yeomen* production there. It opened just weeks after the London premiere, and did very nicely. But it was cast largely from the Casino's forces, and few of the recognized American "Cartesians" were there. Except for the best of them all: Jack Ryley was cast as Jack Point. But there were some fine names among the cast: Fred Solomon—brother of composer Edward and a veritable musical comedy star since his Ben Barnacle in *Billee Taylor*—was Shadbolt; the globe-trotting tenor Henry Hallam (whose history would take a chapter to itself) was Fairfax; ex-Soldene man George Olmi (né James H. Baxter) was Meryll . . . oh, dear, I had better not get into details on these fellows: they were performers who happened to be in a G&S opera (or several) rather than genuine Cartesians, and if I start in on them, we'll be into two volumes.

Yeomen Thereafter

The Yeomen of the Guard has survived for 150 years in splendid health. Marred only, for a while, by the silly melodramatic ending introduced by a touring company. By some it is loved best of all of the Savoy canon. I was among that number in my teens. But in my teens, in provincial New Zealand, my father's productions were the only G&S available to me. Otherwise, it was reading and records. And on record, *The Yeomen of the Guard* is superb. I've never actually seen it on a stage, only in the moat of the Tower of London, with Tommy Steele as an ideally cast Jack Point, but I suspect it is superb there too—when it is played without that silly fake ending. "Strange Adventure . . ." Great stuff.

12

The Gondoliers, or The King of Barataria

Comic opera in two acts
Savoy Theatre, 7 December 1889

While the Yeomen stood their guard over the fortunes of the Savoy Theatre, a bit of wondering, and this time not over subject matter, was going on. Would Messrs. Gilbert and Sullivan continue in the vein of quite-light-opera into which they had ventured with their latest success, or would they return to the more exuberantly comical style of, in particular, *The Mikado*.

Those who pondered such things must have had their minds settled when the title of the forthcoming piece was known. *The Gondoliers, or the King of Barataria*. Barataria: Where the deuce is *that*, sir? Somewhere down by Ruritania? Or Louisiana, or Trinidad, or Quixoteland? But, hey! kings and queens, and gondolas, the favorite opéra-bouffe setting of Venice, with all those canals, and doges, and councils of ten, and Catarina Cornaro; this is definitely going to be another grand chunk of craziness. Remember what fun Hector Crémieux, Halévy, and Offenbach had with *Le Pont des soupirs*? Ooh, Grossmith as a dirty doge? And the high jinks of *Eine Nacht in Venedig* . . .

Well, as we know, it wasn't like that at all. I'm still not sure where Barataria isn't, but apparently it is "an island fair, that lies in a southern sea." Not too southern, surely, because the whole chorus "at the risk of their lives" make their way there "where the roses blow all the winter while" in act 2. And the Grand Inquisitor of Barataria . . . oh! are we going to have Mr. Denny in blackface? But, wait a minute, he's Grand Inquisitor of Spain! Well, truthfully, the piece didn't have much to do with Venice, except that the famous lagoon provided a picturesque setting, pretty caroling contadine and muscled, musical gondolieri (even though their trade is "quite honorary"), and there was not a doge in sight—just his palace, as a backdrop to act 1.

We also know that *The Gondoliers* was in no way comparable, in style or content, with the French pieces. In its fancies, it turned back from the straight-taled mode of *The Yeomen of the Guard*, and returned to that wonderful world where "things are seldom what they seem." Twists and turns ad libitum and yes! a good old *Pinafore* baby swap!

Things were not what they seemed right from the opening scene. I thought, at the age of ten, that act 1, scene 1, of *The Gondoliers* was the most delicious bit of tuneful trickery, and I still do. All the over-sixteen Venetian boys and girls are gathered in the Piazza San Marco, caroling and muscling to lovely, lightsome music. Particularly in evidence is a lass with a good upper register named Fiametta (ahha! here's our leading lady!). Arrive, poling along the canals in a double gondola, the dishy Palmieri brothers with a grand song ("We're Called Gondolieri"), and all the maidens are instantly lovesick. The brothers have come to choose a bride apiece and, so as not to show unkind particularity, they agree to marry whichever girl they catch in a game of blindman's buff. Fiametta and Vittoria fix the blindfolds, the game is played, and surprise! Two girls from the back row of the lineup win the prize. We've been fooled; Fiametta and Vittoria are only the understudies! Marco (tenor) pairs off with Gianetta (soprano) and Giuseppe (baritone) gets Tessa (mezzo)—and off they jolly go to be matrimonified.

Status quo established. Now the action begins. Up that same canal comes a slightly shabby ducal family. They have come all the way from Spain: the Duke of Plaza-Toro (*anglice*: Bullring); his forceful wife; their soprano (oyoy!) daughter, Casilda; and their entire ducal suite, who is called Luiz, and who carries a drum. They've come to see the Grand Inquisitor, because things are seldom what they seem. Casilda was married, as a child, to the baby King of Barataria, who was stolen in infancy (no, not by pirates) by the Inquisition during a particularly horrid revolution. Now that she's twenty-one (and sadly, not born in a leap year), daddy the Duke has brought her to Venice to be connubial. There is one problem. The baby-snatching Inquisitor confided the care of the royal child to a highly respectable gondolier, to bring up alongside his own son. Respectable but rather dipso. Yes, it gets tricky now. The gondolier could never remember which boy was which. Is Marco the king and Giuseppe the puntsman? Or vice versa? And they are—*what!*—married? Then one of them is a bigamist. The kingly one of them, whichever that may be, is long-since wed to Casilda Bullring! And as Barataria is in a state of revolution (maybe it *is* the one in Trinidad!), it is decreed that Marco and Giuseppe shall reign there in tandem until all is untangled.

The two ex-gondoliers try to rule their shared island on republican principles (giving Gilbert excellent opportunity to mock such principles), before everybody concerned arrives from Venice, and the king's identity is to be revealed. His foster-mother has been found! And, in a high-scoring double-twist, she declares that in the (previous) revolution, to protect the wee king, she substituted in his place her own little son. So, neither of the gondolieri is the king: one is il piccolo Palmieri and the other is Master Inez! Who, then, is the king? Well, Casilda has been singing lovelorn duets with her father's suite since act 1. So, it's no surprise (after so many) that it is Luiz!

66. Rosina Brandram as the Duchess of Plaza-Toro: "Baxtaberry, baxtaberry ba!"

If I've spent three times as long describing the plot of *The Gondoliers* as that of any other of the operas, it is because it is really one of the most ingenious of the lot. I know the geography is confusing, and whatever would Gilbert do without folk who entrust their babies to nannies or influential fairies, and I would like to know what became of Fiametta, but . . .

Sullivan, needless to say, did his usual glorious job, but just as *The Yeomen of the Guard* had come across, rightly or wrongly, as "Sullivan's show," *The Gondoliers* came across, rightly or wrongly, as "Gilbert's show." In an otherwise lively score, Casilda and Luiz were allotted the soulful oh-woe-is-me songs: they were pretty enough, but nothing to make you sit up. The more lightsome ones were the property of the two postulant kings and their Venetian brides. The tenor came out the best, with the enduring ballad "Take a Pair of Sparkling Eyes." But it was the Plaza-Toroi, the Duke and his Duchess, who got the winners. Their canal-sick entrance song, with its refrain "If ever, ever, ever we get back to Spain, we will never, never, never cross the sea again," was a cast-bronze hoot. The Duke's song about how "he led his regiment from behind, he found it less exciting" (my father's favorite G&S number) was to become a classic; the Duchess's song ("On the Day When I Was Wedded") was a hilarious account of "how to handle a man," and the couple's duet, about the usefulness of a pauperish title ("Small Titles and Orders") is as relevant today as it was then.

Frank Wyatt (Duke of Plaza-Toro)

In the Duke of Plaza-Toro, Gilbert and Sullivan wrote one of their very best "Grossmith" roles. Only, Grossmith was not there to play it. After a dozen years, he had done his lot and assured his place in theater history. So, who was to replace him? It was, if not a "star," a very effective musical-theater performer indeed, with the odd pretty fierce credit to his name.

Frank Wyatt (né Francis Nevill Gunning; b. Greenwich, 7 November 1852; d. London, 5 October 1926) was the son of a Devonshire barrister and, for a number of years, an artist and illustrator. He moved into the theater in his twenties and made his earliest appearances in small parts in comedy with Charles Wyndham under the stage name of "Francis Wyatt." He interleaved musical and nonmusical assignments, the former of which included Don Pedro in *La Périchole* and Gouget in the Zola burlesque *Another Drink* (1879) with Selina Dolaro at the Folly; *La Fille de Madame Angot* with Cornélie d'Anka at Holborn; the burlesques *La Sonnambula* (Notary) and *Don Juan Jr.* (1880, Baba) at the Royalty; a Drury Lane pantomime (1880); the little operetta *Rosalie* (1881); a tour with the Hanlon-Lees in *Le Voyage en Suisse* in America (1881, Henri d'Escargot); and the burlesques *Valentine and Orson*, *Ariel*, and *Blue Beard* at the Gaiety. Following his first, rather costly, musical engagement in a starring role—as Célestin to the *Nitouche* of American actress Lotta (he was also the management and lost 959 pounds, thirteen shillings, and sixpence in the affair)—and an appearance opposite Lydia Thompson at the Crystal Palace, Wyatt played in Shakespeare with Henry Irving at the Lyceum (Aguecheek), comedy with the Bancrofts at the Haymarket, and comic opera with Alexander Henderson and others (silly-ass Captain Coqueluche in *The Grand Mogul*; Don José in *Manteaux Noirs*).

67. Frank Wyatt as the Duke of Plaza-Toro: "He led his regiment from behind, he found it less exciting."

Then, in November 1885, Wyatt paired with Harry Paulton to create the role of the suave thief Ravannes to the author's low-comical one, Cadeau, in the megahit comic opera *Erminie*. The success that he won in that part—and the huge success of the show itself—led to a list of major musical roles over the following years: Alphonso in Paulton's burlesque *Masse-en-Yell-oh* (1886); Alfred Pasha in *Our Diva* (*Joséphine vendue par ses soeurs*); Karl in *Mynheer Jan* (1887); Hippomenes in *Atalanta* (1888); Pedrillo in *Pepita* (1888); Don Trocadero in the Carl Rosa Light Opera's *Paul Jones* (1889); and then, at the Savoy, the Duke of Plaza-Toro in *The Gondoliers* (1889) and Baboo Currie in *The Nautch Girl* (1890). He followed up as Arrostino Annegato in *The Mountebanks* (1892) and Woodpecker Tapping in *Haste to the Wedding* (1892) for W. S. Gilbert, and as Bouillon in *Ma Mie Rosette* (1892).

The partner of his wife (1886)—*Erminie* producer Violet Melnotte (née Emma Solomon)—in the building of the Trafalgar Square Theatre (now the Duke of York's Theatre), Wyatt appeared there in *Dora, or Diplunacy*; *Nitouche* (1893, this time opposite May Yohé with his wife as Corinne); and in several of the unsuccessful new musicals produced there (Octopus Sharp in *The Taboo*; Count Acacia in *Baron Golosh*). He also played the title-role in Robert Buchanan's *The Pied Piper* (1893), appeared at the Avenue in the little *The Mermaids* (1897, John Doricus), and made a last West End musical appearance in the unfortunate *The Gay Pretenders* (Earl of Oxford) in 1905.

Decima Moore (Casilda)

The other newcomer to the company's principal cast was a "second soprano": the one who got the heart-full bits of music, while Gianetta got the sparky ones.

Lilian Decima Moore (b. Brighton, 11 December 1871; d. London, 18 February 1964) was the third daughter ("all sopranos, high sopranos") of Edward H. Moore, public analytical chemist for Sussex. A scholarship student at the Blackheath Conservatory, she was "discovered" by Carte at the age of sixteen, and promptly cast in the role of Casilda. She did not remain a member of the Savoy team, however, but moved on to succeed Juliette Nesville in the title-role of *Miss Decima* (*Miss Helyett*) and Edith Chester as Violet Eaton-Belgrave in *A Pantomime Rehearsal*, before starring in the title-role of a London revival of *Dorothy* (1892). She was top-billed as Yvonette in the short-lived *The Wedding Eve*

The Gondoliers, or The King of Barataria

68. Decima Moore (Casilda) and Wallace Brownlow (Luiz): The King and Queen of Barataria.

(1892), returned to the Savoy to play the schoolgirl Bab in *Jane Annie* (1893), and was Clairette to the Lange of Amy Augarde in a revival of *La Fille de Madame Angot*.

Miss Moore then came under George Edwardes's crook, and moved into the world of musical comedy to create the ingénue role of Rose Brierly in *A Gaiety Girl*. In 1894, she went to Australia as the star of Edwardes's musical comedy company to play Rose, Bessie Brent in *The Shop Girl*, Kitty Hetherton in *In Town*, and Emma in *Gentleman Joe*. Back in Britain, however, she did not stay firmly in the Edwardes stable, but starred opposite Arthur Roberts in *The White Silk Dress* (1896), as Rose d'Été in the American musical comedy *Lost, Strayed or Stolen* (1897), and as Renée in George Musgrove's production of *The Scarlet Feather* (*La Petite Mademoiselle*). In between times, she toured as Winifred Grey in *A Runaway Girl* (1898). Covering the whole gamut of musical theater styles, she played Lucia in the burlesque *Great Caesar* (1899);

succeeded to the roles of Scent-of-Lilies in Sullivan's *The Rose of Persia* and Angela in *Florodora*; played in the Christmas musical *The Swineherd and the Princess* (1901, Swineherd); toured in *The Gay Cadets* (1902, Cara Luna); and created the ingénue to Sybil Arundale's *My Lady Molly* (1904, Alice Coverdale). Then, after fifteen years as a favorite singing ingénue, Decima effectively put her musical career to rest, turning to nonmusical theater for the remainder of her career.

At first married to Cecil Annesley Walker Leigh of the *Gaiety Girl* chorus, after a divorce, she became the wife of the future Brigadier General Sir Frederick Gordon Guggisberg. Her elder sisters, Eva Moore (1868–1955) and Jessie [née Emily] Moore (1857–1910), both played successfully in the musical theater. Jessie married the Savoy player [Lewis] Cairns James.

A Clutch of Gianettas

However, the particularity of the cast of *The Gondoliers* was in the leading soprano part of Gianetta, at first taken by Geraldine Ulmar. It was played, during the run of the show, by at least fifteen different ladies. Why? At the Savoy, long tenancies were the rule, and the only cast change, usually, was the sending on of an understudy at holiday time. Why did they have fifteen (some say sixteen) different Gianettas? Some, admittedly, just for a few days, but . . . why? Here is my list of Miss Ulmar's fourteen successors.

1. Carrie Donald (née Caroline Kerracher Rodger Donald; b. Edinburgh, 9 February 1870; d. North Berwick, April 1930) was a choir singer at St. Giles Cathedral, Edinburgh. She had played Gianetta on tour and was more than capable. Carrie went on to play for Carte in *Ivanhoe*, *La Basoche*, and *The Vicar of Bray*, before retiring to marriage as Mrs. Thomas Lamb.

2. Miss Alice Baldwin, if that were her name, played the role just a handful of times then utterly disappeared. Chorister? Understudy? Friend of the management? Amateur paying her way? Fake name? I have no idea.

3. [Wilhel] Mina Cleary (b. Allumette Island, Quebec, 17 August 1862; d. Brookline, Massachusetts, 27 June 1929) was an established performer. Daughter of an Irish hotel-

The Gondoliers, or *The King of Barataria*

69. Geraldine Ulmar: The first of the fifteen Gianettas.

keeper, Martin C. Cleary, and his wife, Maria Coghlan, she had played supporting roles with the Boston Ideal Opera Company between 1885 and 1888. Her sister married the company's bass, Eugene Cowles. She subsequently went to Paris to study and, on the way home, played some, seemingly "audition," performances at the Savoy. Miss Cleary returned to America and the Bostonians, before marrying physician John Masury and retiring.

4. Nita Carritte (née Lillian Henriette Temple Carritte, b. New Brunswick, Canada, c. 1864; d. New York, 1 August 1929) was the daughter of Dr. Thomas Carritte of Amherst, New Brunswick, and his Swiss wife, Susanna Louisa Givaudin. Brought up in Saint Paul, she studied, after her father's death, with Anna de Lagrange in Paris from where she (billed as "Nita Carita") was hired for Augustus Harris's 1890 Covent Garden opera season.

Maybethology says she played Micaela. However, although that underliked role went through several tenants during the season—Minnie Evans, Margaret McIntyre, Mdlle. Colombati, and Regina Pinkert—Nita, seemingly, did not go on. Mind you, neither did Harris's other new hiring, Mdlle. Luisa Tetrazzini. However, Miss Carritte did get to play Micaela, to friendly notices and the *Carmen* of Zélie de Lussan, when the opera was produced by the Carl Rosa company in October 1890. Her publicity says she also played *Faust* and *Mignon*, but contemporary notices credit, first, Georgina Burns and then Amy Sherwin. On 5 January 1891 she succeeded to the Savoy, and played Gianetta till 21 March, when the show was advertising its "last weeks." Four years later, she rejoined the Rosa company for some performances as Carmen ("lacked the verve and dash which the character demands"), but, on her return to America, appeared only in the flop musical *1999*, as well as in "concerts and drawing rooms . . . an immense favorite in society," and in repertoire at Castle Square, before marrying twenty-two-year-old musician Frederick Emil Gramm (on 28 December 1899) and retiring. The marriage seems to have ended in divorce. Her marital adventures were, however, less colorful than those of her brother, de Blavier Carritte, who was dragged to court for having "forcibly abducted his own wife."

5. [Alice] Maud Holland (b. Girlington, Bradford, 24 February 1867). Did she or didn't she? It seems that she did. During August 1890, while Carrie Donald was in possession of the role of Gianetta, Maud Holland, an established West End soprano, was billed for a few nights in the part. A pupil of the Royal Academy of Music, Maud had made her debut as a teenager, as cover to another ex-student, Miss Etherington (Marie Tempest) in *The Red Hussar*. Maud went on to play lead roles in *The Rose and the Ring*, in *Maid Marian* (*Robin Hood*), in an English version of *François les bas-bleus*; and on tour as Charlotte in *La Cigale* and as Teresa in *The Mountebanks*; before creating the principal girl's role in *Little Christopher Columbus*. She later succeeded May Yohé in the star part of that last-named

show, and appeared as Alésia in *La Poupée*, before fleeing across the Atlantic, following her divorce from the actor known as Lytton Grey (né Charles Ford Morgan). Maud did not make a notable career in America. I see her, only, advertising cough lollies, and rumored to be preparing for a F. C. Whitney tour of *Dolly Varden* (1904). Her second daughter married into the aristocracy as Lady Alvingham.

6. Nellie [Louise] Lawrence (b. Kemp Town, Brighton 1868; d. 52 Walsingham Road, Hove, 29 March 1912) seems to have been another ephemeral Gianetta. She is a little bit tricky to follow, as there were two other contemporary ladies of the same name in action. Our Nellie was born in Brighton in 1868, where she was brought up, with her sister, Jane, by their widowed mother. Her venture into the musical theatre was brief, but she seems to have been a useful Cartesian, stepping in for those in larger parts than hers in *The Pirates of Penzance*, *The Yeomen of the Guard*, *The Gondoliers* (where she was the original Fiametta), and *The Nautch Girl* (Cheetah), before once again going back to "living on her own means."

70. Nellie Lawrence (Fiametta): Only the understudy!

7. Esther Palliser (née Emma F Walters, b. Germantown, Pennsylvania, 28 July 1868) was, perhaps, the most vocally talented of D'Oyly Carte's American prime donne. This fact was not slow to be recognized, and, apart from her engagements with Carte, she restricted her operations to opera, oratorio, and concerts, largely in England, before her return to America, and her retirement, as a singing teacher in California.

Tall and willowy, Miss Palliser, daughter of music teacher B. Frank Walters (1840–1918) and his wife Kate (née Fronfield), first appeared on stage in America, as Gianetta in *The Gondoliers*, which role she repeated as her debut in England, on 9 December 1890. She appeared

71. Esther Palliser as a Gianetta looking out for low-flying lagoon birds.

for Carte in *Ivanhoe* and in *La Basoche* in 1891, before moving on to Covent Garden and Drury Lane to sing *Carmen*, *Faust*, *Cavalleria rusticana*, and *Lohengrin*. In 1893 she sang Brangaene at Covent Garden, and created C. V. Stanford's Mass in G with the Bach Choir. Miss Palliser moved to California in the mid-1910s, and taught music for a while ("specialist in English and French diction"; "Santa Barbara's favourite"), before vanishing from public view. My last sighting of Mrs. (!) Esther Palliser, vocalist, of 1500 Figueroa Street, is in 1923. However, her birthdate is not quite so well hidden as that of her death. She was not born in 1872 or 1873, as she claimed. She can be seen in the 1870 census of Philadelphia, aged two or three, living with her parents, aunt, and maternal grandparents.

8. Louise Pemberton (b. Chelsea, c. 1868) played four performances at the Savoy in September 1890. Was it an audition, a tryout? Who was she? She appears to have been a greengrocer's daughter from Chelsea who taught piano. Unless she changed her name thereafter, it seems to have been her only venture on the stage.

9. Norah Phyllis did change her name, only I'm not quite sure from what and to what. She was "Norah Phyllis" when she came on the scene in 1887–88, at All Saints' Rooms, Kensington ("Poor Wand'ring One," "I Know That My Redeemer Liveth") and at St. Colomb's Church, Notting Hill, under the aegis of teacher George Ernest Lake. On 20 March 1889, she made a "debut" in concert at the Crystal Palace. Later that year, she joined the Carte company on tour, playing Elsie Maynard, and on 16 December, just after appearing at the Chelmsford Corn Exchange in a Mr. E de Lisle's concert, she was hurried on at the Savoy to dep for Geraldine Ulmar as Gianetta. Mr. and Mrs. Carte took her to America, some weeks later, to bolster their *Gondoliers* company ("she is capable of playing any role"), and she ended up playing Casilda to the Gianetta of Miss Palliser. When the "American company" returned to England, she again played Casilda,

to the Gianetta of Lenore Snyder, before taking over the role at the Savoy. In December 1890, she sang at St. George's Chapel; on 1 July 1891 she performed with Richard Temple's Crystal Palace company in *The Mock Doctor*, then at the German Reed entertainment and on tour in *The Old Bureau* and *The Barley Mow*, under the name of Norah MacGuire (or Maguire). At some stage she also got married. Her husband was apparently a doctor (named Maguire?), stationed in Bombay, and thence she traveled. However, by 1897, she had returned to England, the stage, and, after appearing with the Torquay amateurs in *The Pirates of Penzance* and *Iolanthe*, she rejoined Carte to play Lazuli in *The Lucky Star* and Winifred in *The Vicar of Bray* in the country. She followed up as Nadine in the unfortunate *The Prince of Borneo*, as Lauretta in *L'Amour mouillé* for Tom Davis, and sang Blush-of-the-Morning in *The Rose of Persia* on the road and as a replacement for Agnes Fraser at the Savoy. My final sighting of her is as prima donna of several Carte repertoire companies, the last in 1905. In 1909, she can be seen playing Josephine with the Lichfield amateurs . . . Lichfield? Hmmm.

10. Emily [Jane] Squire (b. Ross on Wye, 2 May 1867; d. 3 Bourne Court, Bournemouth, 1 September 1948). I was most surprised to find the name of Emily Squire listed as having played Gianetta for a couple of weeks, in June 1890. Miss Squire had a long and fine career, but certainly not as a musical theatre player: oratorio, concerts, and the great provincial music festivals would be her natural habitat, for some two decades. Emily was the eldest daughter of the musical family of Cornish bank clerk (later manager) John Squire and his wife, Emma (née Fisher). She studied at the Royal College of Music, and later at the Royal Academy of Music (Parepa Rosa Scholarship, Sainton Dolby Prize, Llewellyn Thomas Gold Medal). She appeared in concert in Cardiff, Bath, Exeter, and in London at the Crystal Palace Saturday Concerts and the Handel Festival, supporting Lillian Nordica in *Israel in Egypt*. In 1889, she sang the quartets in *Elijah*

behind Nordica and behind Madame Albani; performed *The May Queen* and *The Woman of Samaria* in a Devonshire Festival; *The Prodigal Son* and *The Last Judgment* at Hadleigh; and Charles Parry's *Judith* at Exeter, where the program also included her brother, Willie, the 'cellist and songwriter W. H. Squire.

In 1890, I spot her in concert in Swansea, Glasgow, Leicester, and Hereford, and as Ursula in *The Golden Legend* at Newport. Then came the news: Miss Squire had been offered the role of Gianetta; but she was turning the part down. A fortnight later she appeared at the Savoy. She played a dozen or so performances, then zipped back to Swansea to become (on 18 September 1890), Mrs. Edward William Jennings, after which she returned to her natural habitat, the concert platform—performing in Edvard Grieg's *Olav Trygvason*, *The Fall of Babylon*, another *Prodigal Son*, and fulfilling four engagements at the Three Choirs Festival—where she led a fine career over the next twenty years.

11. Cissie Saumarez (née Mary Jane Bartrum; b. 9 Barton Street, Bath, 27 May 1870; d. London, 23 July 1930) was the second daughter of cabinetmaker Edwin Bartrum and his, wife Mary Jane (née Summers). She studied in London with an unknown signor, and went on the stage in 1890, covering and taking over the role of the little bride in *Dorothy*. She moved to the Savoy, where, initially, she appears to have been a general swing, playing, at some time, every one of the principal contadine in *The Gondoliers*. She went on to play Suttee in *The Nautch Girl*, but, by March 1892, she was on the road, featuring in the title-role of one of the interminable *Dorothy* tours. A selection of mostly unimpressive touring musicals (*Wapping Old Stairs*, *Sport*, *The American Belle*, *The Transit of Venus*) and pantomime princesses was relieved by a stint as Mrs. Ralli Carr in *Gentleman Joe*, and as Diana Vernon in a Durward Lely *Rob Roy*. She subsequently found a niche as singing lady (and sometimes man) in Shakespearian productions and became a long-

time adjunct of F. R. Benson's troupe. She later played in comedy under her married name, her husband, Mr. Arthur Herbert Whitby (1869–1922), being an acting member of the Shakespeare company.

12. [Frances] Amy [Lillias] Sherwin (b. Judbury, Tasmania, 23 March 1855; d. Bromley, 20 September 1935). Quite why Amy Sherwin played a week as Gianetta, I cannot imagine. She was at least a decade older than the other Gianettae and thoroughly established as a concert and operatic singer, in places from her native Australia—she sang in *Namaan* in Tasmania, in the shadow of her elder sister, in 1872, and in May 1878 made her operatic debut as Norina with a visiting opera troupe—to America (*La Traviata* with Strakosh; *HMS Pinafore*; Leopold Damrosch's Oratorio Society of New York; Brooklyn Philharmonic Society; *Damnation of Faust*; Cincinnati Festival), Italy, and Britain where, in 1883, she was engaged by Carl Rosa, for whom she first appeared as Maritana (7 May). In the seven years that followed she led a highly successful career in Europe and the colonies, only to come to rest at the Savoy, at the age of thirty-four, for this incomprehensible week of Gianetta. Amy continued to work as a vocalist into her fifties, before retiring to teaching. She had married the agent Hugo Heinrich Ludwig Görlitz (1854–1935) in New Zealand in 1878, and had by him a son, journalist Hugo Louis (1881–1978), and a daughter, Jeannette (Mrs. Jolley, 1884–1936).

13. Annie Elizabeth Sophia Schuberth (b. 7 Hugh Street, Pimlico 1869), daughter of a Jewish Russian-born accountant and musician, was not a novice when she played her little turn in *The Gondoliers* in July 1890. And she was no longer "Miss Schuberth," either. She had made her first stage appearance in a musical comedy, *The Beautiful Duchess*, at Templar Saxe's concert in 1887, and on 19 June 1889 she married the said gentleman, and quickly bore him a couple of sons: Derrick (8 December 1889) and Jack (10 December 1890). A pupil of Randegger (she tells us), she began her stage career on tour in the

title-roles of the French musicals *Pepita* and *Falka*, before joining Saxe (who was understudy to the leading lady) in the London cast of the Carl Rosa company's *Paul Jones*, taking over the role created by Kate Cutler. And then she made her short stopover at the Savoy.

Miss Schuberth went on to play Charlotte in *La Cigale* alongside Geraldine Ulmar; took over from Josephine Findlay in *Miss Decima*; toured some more in the star roles of *Pepita*, *Falka*, and *La Cigale*; and appeared as both Marion in *Poor Jonathan*; and as Lolika in *The Magic Opal*. She divorced Saxe (né Templer Edward Edeveian) for persistent adultery; they both remarried. Saxe whisked off to America, where he became a cinema actor, while Annie wed (on 3 December 1895) an ageing Bradford lawyer, Charles Law Atkinson (1841–1916). After playing a while in Willie Edouin's *Qwong Hi*, she let her theater career fizzle out while she had two more sons. However she reemerged from marriage, in 1906, to play in the Manchester panto, and can be seen in the northern music halls until 1913, giving "I Dreamt I Dwelt in Marble Halls" and a sketch *The Deputy, or a Private Rehearsal*. After that, I cannot tell.

14. Lenore Snyder (b. Indianapolis, IN, c. 1868; d. Camden, London, July 1911) was raised in Indiana, the daughter of Frederick W. Snyder (machinist) and his wife, Virginia (née Ballenger). The three of them can be seen, in 1880, living at Brightwood, Indiana. She apparently sang, first, in the local Presbyterian church, and in 1887, performed with the Indianapolis Lyra Society. As an amateur, she took part in a local opera called *Maganon*, and appeared as Mabel in *The Pirates of Penzance*, which latter led to a first professional engagement in 1889. She appeared for the Duff company in the title-role of *Paola* (played in Britain by Leonora Braham) and in the Chicago musical *King Cole II*, before being hired to deputize for Esther Palliser as Gianetta in New York's *Gondoliers*. Miss Snyder subsequently sang the role on tour in Britain and, briefly, at the Savoy. In August 1890, she returned to

72. Leonore Snyder as Gianetta in *The Gondoliers*.

America, where she played in *The Pirates of Penzance*, *The Red Hussar*, *Carmen*, *Dorothy*, *Iolanthe*, and others such, before being recalled to Britain, in place of Australia's Nellie Stewart, to create the lead role in *The Nautch Girl* and play in the revised *Vicar of Bray*. Back in America, she joined Harry Dixey for an attempt to float *Mr. Dobbs of New York*, and was featured in more productions of *Patience*, *Iolanthe*, *The Sorcerer*, and *The Mikado*. The press judged her "irreproachably correct . . . and tame." It was advertised that she was to go to Paris to study, and that she had married American basso William H. MacLaughlin. She returned to the stage in *The Wizard of the Nile*, but that seems to have been it: a professional career of impeccable credits, but seemingly less éclat. There was, alas, a reason for its ending. Lenore retreated to Paris, and, in 1897, was reported to be seriously ill. Mrs. Lenore [W.] MacLaughlin died of tuberculosis and was interred at London's Camden cemetery on 15 July 1911.

Well, that is the who. As to the why? We will never know. The Savoy would flounder its way through the unimpressive likes of Ellen Beach Yaw and Nancy McIntosh, and the novelty castings of Hungarian star Ilka Pálmay and noted opera singer Pauline Joran, to the stabler days of a Ruth Vincent, but never again would it devour fifteen (or sixteen, if Decima Moore or Agnes Wyatt really did take a turn!) prime donne—genuine and wannabe—in one leading role. Did they all fit the same costumes, I wonder? Why did it happen? And who the hell was Alice Baldwin?

All Good Things: The (Temporary) End of a Triumvirate

During the run of *The Gondoliers*, Gilbert, Sullivan, and Carte came to the disagreement that led to the end (albeit temporarily) of the collaboration that had so long, so happily filled the Opera Comique, the Savoy, and theaters all around the world with joyous—and intensely profitable—musical theater. The story of their quarrels, and the insignificant spark that set it off, has been told a million times in biographical books. This book is about the plays and the players, so I'll save my pages for them rather than debate the who-was-right and who-was-wrong of the affair. Collaborations wear out, even those crowned with unparalleled success. Familiarity can get too familiar. A change is as good as a holiday. The moon is made of green cheese. Things are seldom what they seem.

Carte had to look elsewhere for his next show. There had been two British comic operas, during those years that had been dominated by the Gilbert and Sullivan shows, which had vied with his productions for popularity. *Billee Taylor*—which had come out in the same season as *The Pirates of Penzance*, and had even been declared in some circles to be superior to the G&S show—was the first. The other was *Erminie*, which was not at all in the Gilbert and Sullivan style, but boasted one of the best comical libretti in years. And, as every producer knows, if you ain't got a book, you ain't got a show! Carte had produced *Billee Taylor* in America, as he had done with two other book-strong British-born pieces of the era, *Les Manteaux noirs* and *Rip van Winkle*, but *Billee Taylor* had been the real hit. So, what could be more natural than that he should turn to that show's composer, Teddy Solomon—already acclaimed in the press as "second only to Sullivan"—in his hour of need. Unfortunately, there was no use turning to Solomon's *Billee Taylor* collaborator, "Pot" Stephens. He had turned out to be a nonrepeater.

Well, this is not a Teddy Solomon book either, but if it were Carte who teamed him with the very un-Savoyish George Dance on *The Nautch Girl*, it just goes to show what a skilled producer Mr. Richard D'Oyly Carte was. Dance provided the theater with what was by far the best "Gilbertian" book of the post-*Gondoliers* era, before he went on to write the megahit of the next era, *A Chinese Honeymoon*, a piece in the modern musical-comedy vein. Yes, "musical comedy" was coming: "comic opera" was about to get a kink in its coronet.

So, the Savoy went on without Gilbert, and without Sullivan. Although some decidedly attractive works would find their way to the little house on the Strand, nothing was and never would be quite the same.

13

Utopia (Limited), or The Flowers of Progress

Comic opera in two acts
Savoy Theatre, 7 October 1893

Together again! The theater world could breathe a sigh of expectation—nay, of relief. Things theatrical would be, once more, back to normal. But which normal? Normal 1888, or normal 1893? Because there was quite a difference. In spite of Gilbert's *The Mountebanks* (music: Cellier) and Sullivan's *Haddon Hall* (words: Grundy) having knocked up London runs of over two hundred nights apiece, the big success of 1892 had been the loose-limbed musical farce *In Town*, concocted by Adrian Ross and starring comic opera star Florence St. John alongside comedian Arthur Roberts, a comic performer of an altogether different type from that seen at the Savoy. The year 1893 had, already, seen comic operas with scores by Arthur Goring Thomas, Isaac Albéniz, and the Savoy's Ernest Ford fail: the enormous hits of the day were the free-and-easy *Morocco Bound* and *The Lady Slavey*. Three days after the opening of *Utopia (Limited)*, the virtual variety show titled *Little Christopher Columbus* opened; it would outrun *Utopia* comprehensively. Four days further on, George Edwardes opened *The Gaiety Girl*. So, the theatrical world to which the triumvirate was returning as a team was not at all the same.

It was not a case of "comic opera out, musical comedy in," just as, at the opera, a couple of decades earlier, it had not just been "Mozart out, Verdi in": there was room for the two. But audiences and profits had to be shared. A comic opera of the Savoy kind had, as the end of the century approached, to work much, much harder to hold its place in the box office stakes.

This phenomenon was, naturally, not exclusively British; it was nobody's "fault." Across the Manche the same "changing of the guard" was taking place: opéra-bouffe had had its heyday, and even the splendid opéras-comiques of the *La Fille de Madame Angot* and *Les Cloches de Corneville* kind had given place to such as the saucy, book-orientated vaudeville-opérettes: *les temps*, they were a-changing.

So, it was to this theatrical temperature that Messrs. Gilbert and Sullivan were returning. The challenge was on. And was it won? Well, an eight-month-long London run, an American production and four touring companies cannot be considered a failure. But, after a decade, *Utopia (Limited)* would effectively disappear from the Carte repertoire as played. Why?

Sullivan penned some splendid music—especially in the way of ensembles, which were present here in their greatest number ever—even though the plot, characters, and lyrics rarely allowed him to get into his best, sweeping mode. The soprano/tenor duet had more of the feel of an off-cut from the soulful Casilda/Luiz music of *The Gondoliers* than of the joyous tones of Nanki-Poo and Yum-Yum. But there was a waltz song for contralto, there were a couple of lively stand-up pieces, a tenor solo ("A Tenor, All Singers Above") that could have been a merry music-hall number, and a three-ages-of-man piece ("First You're Born"), which, similarly, could have been popped into any role in any show.

Gilbert's "pointed dialogue" was appreciated, and the *Times* declared *Utopia (Limited)* "one of the best of the set . . . it is hard to remember any work of the same hands that is worthy to stand beside the new production." Dialogue fine, lyrics fine, music fine . . . plot? Well, there wasn't much of a plot. Mythical country reorganizes (like Marco and Giuseppe in Barataria, but at endless length) its institutions to copy those of Britain, giving Gilbert a chance for two acts of mockery, much of it regurgitated from earlier works, before everyone goes home, leaving Utopia, as a legacy, the worst of all evils: "government by party." He was right, of course, but that's fun? It's more like an illustrated lecture.

And, of course, where you have no plot, you cannot have those delicious plot twists that so well deserve the epithet "Gilbertian." There's no Inez or Buttercup with a final admission that turns all on its head; no legal nicety to turn logic upside down; no things that are seldom what they seem. There's just "brittle and sometimes petulant satire" of most things British.

The general tone of *Utopia (Limited)* was, even in its lighter moments, somewhat bilious. The satiric hits—all important and legitimate ones—were all more direct than usual, less subtle and less humorous. The dialogue was occasionally convoluted and long-winded and purposeful rather than merry. Gilbert's wit and wisdom had failed to adapt to the subject he had chosen and, although his great talent ensured that the libretto of Utopia (Limited) was a much better piece of writing than most contemporary musicals, it lacked the lightsome spirit of The Mikado and HMS Pinafore and the topsy-turvy comical element that had made them so likeable.

The characters of a piece can always add fun to a bald and unconvincing (lack of) narrative. Did Gilbert come up with merry people to populate his lecture? The answer is "mostly"—with one devastating exception. No longer was the "old team" of performers working at the Savoy. There was Rutland Barrington, back in harness, as Utopia's King Paramount, playing the kind (and size) of role he and his public expected. There was Rosina Brandram as the dame in the affair: one of Gilbert and Sullivan's jollier English dames, with her waltz-lecture on how to be an English lady. W. H. Denny had a really fine role as Scaphio, a "wise man" to the King, teamed with John Le Hay (Phantis), who had played in The Pirates of Penzance for Carte a decade earlier. Denny and Le Hay had the show-stealing roles, and an insanely funny entrance duo, but in five years, much of the basic personnel at the theater had changed.

Charles Kenningham (Captain Fitzbattleaxe)

The new tenor was Charles Kenningham (b. Castle Place, Hull, 18 November 1862; d. Prince Alfred Hospital, Sydney, Australia, 24 October 1925), a former St. Paul's chorister and tenor soloist at Canterbury Cathedral. The Kenningham family of Kingston upon Hull was one of those northern English families of the nineteenth century that simply abounded with music. Generation after generation of, otherwise, comparatively humble workers took part in choral and orchestral music, at a level that had made the northern choirs outstanding examples of their kind, and several solo performers of a professional level emerged from the Kenningham ranks. The musical Kenninghams of Hull go back to before Queen Victoria's reign—their story is detailed in G. H. Smith's book Hull Organs and Organists—but the nineteenth century brought forth three men who each made a full life and career in music.

Joseph Kenningham (baptized Drypool, 9 May 1831; d. London, 24 May 1923), originally a bass soloist with the Hull Harmonic Society, in

May 1856 became a lay clerk of Salisbury Cathedral. He led a full career as a church vocalist, ultimately at St. Mark's, Battersea. His cousin, John Kenningham (b. Sutton, 1810; d. Hull, 1881), a dock company foreman, and his wife, Elizabeth Ann (née Finningley), produced a large brood, from which two sons became professional singers. Their son, Alfred, also graduated from the ranks of the Hull Harmonic, and from various posts as a choirboy, acted as organist and choirmaster to the Mariner's Church of Hull, and choirmaster of the Fish Street Congregational Church, and sang principal tenor in local churches and performances until, in 1872, he was appointed to the church of St. Andrew's, Wells Street. He was active beyond the reign of Victoria and into the twentieth century, as a vicar choral of St. Paul's and in various other London church posts. His elder brother, George (b. Drypool, November 1841; d. Huntington, New York, 1920), a bookkeeper by day, was a baritone singer with the Hull society in the 1870s. Charles was the youngest of the brood.

Charles had taken to the stage in the role of de Bracy in Sullivan's opera *Ivanhoe*, which he followed up by spending some half a dozen years with the Carte organization, interrupted only by an engagement to play in Gilbert and Carr's *His Excellency* at the Lyric Theatre. During his time at the Savoy he created roles in *Haddon Hall*, *Jane Annie*, *Utopia (Limited)*, *The Chieftain*, *The Grand Duke*, and *His Majesty*, as well as appearing in the revivals of *The Gondoliers*, *The Yeomen of The Guard*, *The Mikado*, and the Savoy version of *La Grande-Duchesse*. In 1898, Charles left the company to travel to Australia, seemingly without his wife and daughters, and there he played the leading tenor roles in J. C. Williamson's companies for the next seven years. He latterly retired to teach music in Bundaberg and Maryborough. In 1919, he underwent two operations, but recovered and lived till 1925. The wife at his funeral doesn't seem to be the same one he had in Hull.

Nancy McIntosh (Princess Zara)

The story of Nancy McIntosh has to be dealt with somewhere. I'm going to be brief. Miss McIntosh (b. Cleveland, Ohio, 25 October 1866; d. London, 20 February 1954)—daughter of Mr. W. A. McIntosh, who had been in some way connected with the Johnstown flood—came to London, like endless other high, light, pretty American soprani, to "study." She "studied" largely with Georg Henschel, but it was evident that she would not cut the brisket in the classical music world. Enter Mr. Gilbert, who seems to have suffered some sort of a chaste (?) *coup de foudre*. Well, what happened next is the stuff of a lot of mythology, but I think we can credit Miss McIntosh for a fair share in both the curiosities of *Utopia (Limited)* and the final demise of the Gilbert and Sullivan partnership.

The part of Princess Zara is far too extensive, prolix, and pompous. It is also musically set in an unpleasantly thin, high register, presumably because that was Miss McIntosh's register. Well, we know it was. We are told that Sullivan agreed to her casting. Maybe he'd had a nice dinner and a jollifying session with one of his mistresses; maybe he was being agreeable to the seemingly smitten Gilbert. Neither was a good reason for destroying a potentially moneymaking stage show. Sullivan, we may note, never put any of his ladies (who were, in any case, certainly not actresses) into the Savoy company. The cry was out even before opening night. Miss McIntosh's big solo was cut; she couldn't cope with it. After an appeal to/from Gilbert, she was allowed to sing it on the first night. That was the last time it was heard. Come back, Helene Crosmond . . . alas, the out-of-work Miss Crosmond had shot herself, in a cab in the Strand, several years previously.

Miss McIntosh became a part of the Gilbert family. Unofficially "adopted," she moved in with Mr. and Mrs. Gilbert and, quite simply, stayed there, until death did them part. Gilbert pushed her, for a while, into roles in several productions over which he had influence. She was sacked after a week from *Fallen Fairies*, the last of them. I am sure Nancy was a lovely girl, but she was utterly not a comic opera prima donna. She was pretty, ladylike, and without an ounce of personality or sex appeal. And *Utopia (Limited)* and the Savoy suffered therefrom.

When *Utopia* was sent to America, another lady had to be found to play "Princess Nan." The choice was somewhat better. And, this time— as we see from surviving documents—it was Sullivan who was behind it.

Isabel Reddick (Princess Zara)

Isabel Rayner was born at 127 St. John's Road, Goswell Road, on 14 March 1865. She was the daughter of a Ramsgate-born baker named Edward Rayner (1828–1869), and his wife, Mary Ann (née Hutchison); the couple can be seen baking at the St. John's Road address in the 1861 census. Edward died, at the age of thirty-eight, and mother "remarried" a Mr. Bell. The marriage record seems to have been mislaid by officialdom. Anyway, by the time Mary Ann went to court, listed as a "confectioner of St. John's Rd.," in September 1870, to bear witness against a lassie who had tried to pass her a dud half crown, mother was "Mrs. Bell." And, by 1871, they were gone from St. John's Street Road. Mama would later give up baking in favor of running a boarding house.

My first sighting of the Misses Rayner (two) is in January 1885, when they appeared in Orsett alongside some musical Scruby children. Then, in 1886 (7 December), Isabel turns up at Kensington Town Hall at a concert given by a pianistic Edith Bell. Lindsay Sloper played, and Edith Marriott and Percy Palmer were on the short list of singers. I spot her again, on 16 May 1889, at Stroud, singing "The Years at the Spring" alongside Eleanor Rees and Thomas Brandon, and then at Henry Leslie's promenade concerts on a bill with no less a star than Edward Lloyd. In 1892, she appeared at Mr. Graham Price's concert at St. James's Hall Banqueting Room on 29 June, with Belle Cole and Hirwen Jones, and on 16 November in a charity performance of a mainly amateur *The Statue of Albermarle* at the Trafalgar Square Theatre ("deservedly encored for her sweetly expressive treatment of a song"), where the professionals included Claire Solomon and Sylvia Grey. Rutland Barrington gave a W. S. Gilbert scena to follow. During 1893, she turns up for Wilhelm Ganz at the Society of Female Artists, at a flash bazaar at Whitehall in fine company, and at the home of the social Mrs. Ronald Taylor, pianist, composer, and cookery writer, amid aristocratic amateurs, including Edmond Depret and "Marie de Lido." And then Miss Rayner became Miss Reddick, and went on the stage.

Isabel had a brief, but successful, career with the Carte organization, which was followed by a highly promising engagement with George Edwardes (*An Artist's Model*). I presume that she went on the Edwardes trip to Africa, because, on 23 July 1896, Isabel wed Scotsman William Dalrymple there. Mr. Dalrymple was into gold, in a fairly big way, I understand. Whether he was already on his way to becoming Sir William Dalrymple KBE, deliciously rich, social, globe-trotting, and glamorously living, or whether that came later, I am not sure, but there will be a South African book somewhere that tells all.

Isabel, thus, became Lady Dalrymple of Johannesburg, and globe-trotted wealthily with her husband, producing four or five children on the way (all scrupulously recorded, as the children of the "aristocracy" are) into the happily ever after. Splendid! And a long way from Orsett and the Scruby children, and the bakery and confectionary in Islington. Isabel died on 30 December 1938; William survived her by some three years.

Kate Talby (Lady Sophy)

There are lots of names that are connected with *Utopia (Limited)*. Names, even, that would later become starry. Others who would have whole books, booklets, or theses written about them. I'm a bit fuzzled about what and who to "do" next. So, like Richard Dauntless, following the dictates of my 'art, I'll make a crazy wee selection among the other *Utopians* from London and New York.

73. Kate Talby (Lady Sophy) with her charges:
Aileen Burke and Millicent Pyne.

Winkling out the identities of "Kate Talby" (and her chorister husband "Percy Charles") took several days out of my life. But I finally unveiled them. Kate Louisa Finlayson (b. Trigon Terrace, Kennington, March 1861; d. Baker Street, Marylebone, 28 December 1935) was the daughter of Alfred Finlayson, architect, and his wife, Sarah-Jane (née Howse). And on 16 June 1884 at St. James's, Lambeth, Miss Finlayson married Mr. Charles Vennell (aka "Percy Charles"; b. Kent Road, Newington, 1855; d. Lambeth, 1914), son of Charles Vennell, iron merchant, and his wife, Sarah (née Adams).

I first see Kate as an actress in March 1882, playing with Alfred Hemming and the Walton family in touring comedy. Thereafter she turns up in William Sidney's *Queen's Evidence*; in pants for the Preston panto of *Gulliver's Travels*; in Frederick Neebe's southern tour; in John Shine's *Three Hats*; in more panto, at Birmingham, as a very tall singing fairy, Elfinella, in *Cinderella*; in a touring *The Forty Thieves*—and then she joined the Carte organization. Chez Carte, as a character contralto, Kate was to become a fixture. During her dozen years with the "family," she played not only the Gilbert and Sullivan repertoire but also the contralto roles in such as *Billee Taylor*, *The Vicar of Bray*, *The Chieftain*, and *Mirette*. I think, maybe, had Rosina Brandram not been around, Kate would have been *the* Savoy contralto. From Carte, she moved with notable success to musical comedy, appearing as the heavy ladies of *The French Maid*, *The Circus Girl*, and *The Runaway Girl*, among others, and even returned to the dramatic stage to play in such as *Sappho* with Olga Nethersole.

Aileen Burke (Nekaya)

The best theatrical future, however, was reserved for the little lass who played one of the fifteen-year-old princesses on the American trip. Aileen Daisy Burke (b. Calcutta, 14 February 1873; d. London, August 1939) was born in India—not in London, four years later, as she would later claim in her *Who's Who in the Theatre* entry. Her father was a London commercial traveler by the name of Alfred David Burke (this she did admit!), and her mother was Emily Isabel[la] (née Outhwaite). The couple were married in India (I wonder what Mr. Burke was traveling in), and had their first five children there, before returning to Britain and Battersea. There, they had a bunch more children (making ten in total), before father decided he'd had enough and did that midlife thing of walking out on his family. In the meanwhile, Aileen had begun to study music and attended the Royal Academy. In 1893, she was commended in the contest for the Parepa Rosa Scholarship behind three ladies I don't know. And a few months later, she was on the road playing the Princess Nekaya in a D'Oyly Carte company. She traveled to America to repeat her role and, following that season, remained in America for more than two years, appearing with Louise Beaudet's company, at the Star Theatre as principal girl, opposite Irene Verona, in *Sinbad*, and as the little Duchess of Parthenay to *The Little Duke* of Lillian Russell ("a dainty little singer with black hair and eyes"). And then Miss Burke vanished.

Mdlle. Aileen d'Orme, pupil of Marchesi, Sbriglia, *e tutti quanti*, arrived in London in early 1897, and, on 31 March, "fresh from the Paris conservatoire . . . making her stage debut," opened at the Shaftesbury Theatre in "the Armenian opera," *The Yashmak*. I think Mdlle. d'Orme's true identity was recognized ("a newcomer, apparently, with a charming voice and appearance"), but I can't see that anyone outed her. But the Web still features quotes such as "Miss Aileen D'Orme was born in London of French and Irish parentage and completed her musical education in Paris . . ."

Aileen sang "Hush, Little Girl, Don't Cry" and Napoleon Lambelet's "La Vie" in *The Yashmak*, and then moved on to feature in London's productions of *The Wizard of the Nile* (Abydos), *The Royal Star* (Lucy Jebb), and *The Coquette* (Nella). She was then engaged at Daly's Theatre, where she played the Juliette Nesville role of the French maid, Mina, in the revival of *A Gaiety Girl* (1899), took over the part of Yung Shi in *San Toy* from Florence Collingbourne, then succeeded Maggie May as Princess Mehelaneh in *The Country Girl*.

I'm not wholly sure what happened next. I think it was a man. Anyway, she disappeared from Daly's Theatre and, a few years later, was married to one George Earle Baker, who was said to be "connected with mining speculations at Great Cobar in Western Australia." She tells us that she "retired on her marriage" (in 1908) and did not appear again until 1914. That appearance was in concert, and it was followed, in 1916, by the role that would make her a name: the plump and pleasing Alcolom, opposite the Ali Baba of Courtice Pounds, in the wartime spectacular *Chu Chin Chow*. She duetted "Any Time's Kissing Time" with Pounds and, later, gave the beautiful "I Long for the Sun" for five years. Her domestic arrangements, however, simultaneously, went downhill.

Mr. Baker's speculation went sour, he went bankrupt, and he also began messing around. When Aileen divorced him, it was not the Great Cobar fortune that featured in the headlines, it was *Chu Chin Chow*! In her post–*Chu Chin Chow* years, Aileen went on a concert tour with Clara Butt. Mrs. Aileen d'Orme Baker, "dramatic soprano," can be heard on WEAF, New York, in 1924, and, as late as 1930, she was still singing on British radio. She also made a number of recordings. She died in 1939, seemingly in Hinde Street, London. The British registers say that she was fifty-five; she was sixty-six.

Robert Scott Fishe (Goldbury)

Among the "Flowers of Progress" whom Zara forced upon her island (was it, I wonder Barataria, and Luiz was now King Paramount?) was one Mr. Goldbury, a company promoter. The character (well, he isn't really one) exists solely to sing his description of the "limited company"—"Some Seven Men Form an Association"—which, I gather, was quite liked in its time. All of the Flowers of Progress had a wee solo in the first act

74. The Flowers of Progress jam session.

finale, Gilbert's *plaque tournante*, from which, I imagine, the whole piece had emanated. Goldbury—was it meant to be a "Richard Temple" part, in that it was given a second, rather dreary solo?—was played in London by R. Scott Fishe.

Robert Fishe was born in Kentish Town, on 12 February 1871, the son of an ironmonger's assistant, also named Robert Fishe, and his wife, Jenny, and began singing as a boy. A review from the town of Thame, in 1882, reports, "Master Fishe in his character song 'The Englishman,' quite took the house by storm, being loudly and persistently encored . . ." After a trip to South America, with the famously shipwrecked Edwin Cleary troupe, he was engaged at the Savoy, to replace Richard Green in *The Vicar of Bray*, but he did not stay, instead taking a supporting role as Ségur in the Savoy-weight cast (Pounds, Wyatt, Miss Bond, Cairns James) of William Boosey's attempt to float a heavily botched version of Lacome's opérette *Ma Mie Rosette*. Although Fishe was but twenty-two, the first signs of the tuberculosis that would end his life were showing, and he spent several months thereafter in Switzerland taking the cure. On his return, he rejoined the Savoy and created roles in *Jane Annie*, *Utopia (Limited)*, two versions of *Mirette*, and played the brigand monarch in *The Chieftain*.

After a Cartesian tour, he appeared in the title-role in *The Mikado* and created the part of the Prince of Monte Carlo in *The Grand Duke* at the Savoy, but his illness had not abated. When he joined the Carte company that was headed for South Africa, to play Richard Temple's roles, he was forced to return to England. Carte employed him at the Savoy in a barely existent role in *La Grande-Duchesse*. His condition, however, worsened, and, told that he would not recover, the twenty-seven-year-old singer shot himself, at his home at 31 Thorneybush Road, Chiswick, on 31 August 1898.

In America, the role of Goldbury was played (or, rather, sung) by a young man named John Coates, for the history of whom we have rather to turn to the operatic reference books of the time.

James William Hooper (Scaphio)

There are so many Cartesians who are new to us, at this stage of the collaboration, that I can't cram them all in: Jessie Rose, Lawrence Gridley, Herbert Ralland, Enes Blackmore, Frank Danby, poor Bowden

Haswell . . . some such as H. Scott Russell, C. H. Workman, and Walter Passmore who would go on to fine careers . . . however, I'm going to sign this chapter off with a player who worked only once for the organization, but in a splendid role: as New York's Scaphio.

J. W. Hooper (b. Headington, Oxfordshire, 25 April 1865; d. after 1939) was a real, working actor. A juvenile, a comedian, then an older character man, in plays, musicals, pantomimes, and, eventually, films, he followed one job with another, for forty years.

Hooper was born in Oxfordshire to a Canterbury "cook and confectioner," James William Hooper, and his wife, Scotswoman Christina Frances (née Irvine), and brought up in Cheetham. He first ventured into the theater in 1887, in Liverpool, in a fifth-rate company called "the Troubadour Burlesque Company" playing *A Fish Out of Water*, *Arcadia*, *Amy Robsart*, and *Aladdin*. His "bass singing" was one of the saving graces of the performance. Hooper next appeared in a marginally less embarrassing Scotch spectacle *The Gathering of the Clans* (1889), but got into his stride in 1891, playing, on the road, first in *Muldoon's Picnic*, then for Fred Wright in *Dashing Prince Hal* and *Jack and the Beanstalk* (Demon Hategood). In 1892–93, he went on the road as Friar Tuck in Reginald de Koven's *Maid Marian* (*Robin Hood*) and, in 1894, joined Carte's organization, for the American trip with *Utopia (Limited)*, in the role of Scaphio.

Hooper followed up his undoubted success with a series of engagements in musical pieces of all kinds: the *Dorothy* copycat; *Dorcas* (1895, Jawkins); the comic opera *His Excellency* (1895, Mats Munck); the merry musical comedy *The Gay Parisienne* (1896, Major Fossdyke); the virtual variety show *A Trip to Chinatown*, in which he played the lead comic role of Ben Gay, off and on, for four years; the musical drama *Stirring Times* (1897, Absalom Levi the Jew); and the once-French musical comedy *The Telephone Girl* (1897, Sylvester Bartram). He played Abanazar in a Dublin *Aladdin* (1897), in which production one George Grey (later to be famed as George Graves) was Widow Twankey.

After a quick turn at the Foresters Music Hall, Mile End, Hooper toured as Casca in *Great Caesar*, appeared as Mr. Turpin in a vanity production of *His Satanic Majesty* at Southend, and played for Milton Bode in pantomime (Stickiton Al Kipper in *Beauty and the Beast*). In 1901, he returned to playing Ben Gay, for another tour, and in 1902 played Joshua Cagney in a tour of the Drury Lane melodrama *The Great Millionaire*. Latterly he gave the provinces his version of the star comedy roles of such as *The Girl from Kay's* (Hoggenheimer) and *The Quaker Girl*. As late as 1923, Hooper could be seen heading a tour of the musical *Kissing Time*. My last sighting of him on stage is as Norman Figgis in *The Love Race* in 1931.

Hooper married, in 1904, Ethel Marie Octavia Brookes (b. Stockwell Park Road, 16 July 1877; d. Cheltenham, 1961), by whom he had four children: Leslie William, Edward James, Doris Ethel, and Christina. I spy Ethel and Christina in Seaford in the 1939 census, and James? I imagine he is the "retired actor," James W. Hooper, "married" but living alone, in Mitcham. I'll keep chasing James; I like James.

Utopia (Limited)'s Legacy

Utopia (Limited) is, as are the other lesser works of famous writers and composers, still seen, on occasion, today. Its bitterness and bile have become watered down by time, and by present-day incomprehension of Victorian conservative politics and preoccupations, and its jollier moments—from Scaphio to Phantis and back—still appeal. But, personally, I rather feel that if the meddlers of the twenty-first century see fit to alter the words to Ko-Ko's little list, and quail at the Fairy Queen's mention of Captain Shaw, then the libretto to *Utopia (Limited)* is, today, more than a little in need of a wash and brush up.

14

The Grand Duke, or The Statutory Duel

Comic opera in two acts
Savoy Theatre, 7 March 1896

The Grand Duke was to be the last of the "Savoy operas" of Gilbert and Sullivan, and it was very far from the their most successful. It was not that the piece lacked wit or melody—in places—but it seems to have tried, too hard, to be all things to all men—and one woman. To start with, where *Utopia (Limited)* had suffered from having very little plot, *The Grand Duke* suffered, rather, from having too much, or too many. It was stuck together cleverly, of course, but . . . And, then, were they plots, or merely conceits?

Preproduction buzz said that the new show would include bits of *Thespis*. *Thespis* the text, or *Thespis* the music? Well, it certainly had one thing in common with the authors' first collaboration. The central characters were a group of actors, pretending to be something that they weren't. "Things are seldom what they seem," again. And then, somehow, the ancient Greek bit, à propos of nothing at all, got pasted in, too. But a rather more obvious inspiration for the piece was an anonymous forty-plus-year-old *Blackwood's Magazine* story titled *The Duke's Dilemma: A Chronicle of Niesenstein* (published in September 1853), in which an impecunious Duke is seen, anxious to put on a good reception for a wealthy prince whose sister he is hoping to marry. Unfortunately, his court has chosen this moment to go on strike, an event that delights nasty Baron Pippinstir, who is pressing the claims of his wealthy ward, the Margravaine of Adelburg, to the position of grand duchess. Duke Leopold is saved by the appearance of a troupe of actors, ordered for the entertainment, who agree to help by masquerading as courtiers. When the prince and his sister arrive, complications ensue. Those complications duly propose all sorts of abusive pairings before a timely death and lots of rank and wealth set everything right and the prima donna of the troupe and her original lover disappear off into the sunset.

Of course, one doesn't imagine that Mr. Gilbert had been thumbing old magazines. He didn't need to. *The Duke's Dilemma* (which was a full fifty-two pages long) had been reprinted and reprinted and even, recently, made into a comic opera, which had been playing at the Avenue Theatre while *The Gondoliers* was at the Savoy. It had originally been titled *The Grand Duke*, but it had been hurriedly retitled *La Prima Donna* when previous claims to that title had been mooted. I notice, however, that the mooter, provincial manager H. D. Burton, didn't squawk when the Savoy used "his" title. He'd had his publicity. *La Prima Donna* was a modest affair. The libretto was credited to the well-known Henry Brougham Farnie and Alfred Murray, but it ended up being largely the work of the latter, as Farnie was into his last illness. The workmanlike music was by songwriter Tito Mattei. The most successful numbers in the piece, however, were the additional ones written and performed by the actor playing the company's stage manager. Albert Chevalier would go on to fame in less old-fashioned purlieus. *La Prima Donna* played its modest sixty performances, was published and was put away. And onto its bones Gilbert grafted the other plots and fancies that would make up his libretto.

First was the concept of the statutory duel, where, instead of pistols, a pack of cards is used, and he who draws low is considered "dead," his emoluments and duties being transferred to the victor. Second was the clever use of the old theatrical tradition of "a line of parts," by which an actor/actress is contracted to play whichever role is deemed "lead," "lover," "soubrette," or "old woman," regardless of suitability. All this results in one man owning, at one stage, four—depending on which rules you go by—wives. This was all promising "Gilbertian" material. But, then, there was one particularly unfortunate and tasteless episode that it was hard to believe came from the hand of the Savoy librettist.

If there were, actually, a coherent play in there—and there very well might have been—it got further confused by other considerations. And this time, at least some of the blame has to be laid in an area that had always been (give or take a soprano or three) one of the company's great strengths: the players. It was not that they were not good performers; far from it. Newcomers such as Charles Kenningham, Robert Fishe, Florence Perry, Scott Russell, C. H. Workman, and Emmie Owen (replacing Jessie Bond) were as good, very often, as their predecessors.

But they were not their predecessors. And personalities and traditions intervened. Roles and numbers were written not because they suited the show but because they suited an actor . . . oh! how often have we seen that sad situation! . . . and so, *The Grand Duke* became lopsided. There was, in particular, far too much of Barrington, who was featured in a role of which just about the only salient point was its length. And, as cuts and alterations set in, the lopsidedness became more and more pronounced.

Last time I tried to describe the plot(s) of *The Grand Duke* it took me twenty-two lines. So, I'll stick to the characters. Walter Passmore was the titular Grand Duke, a nice and fun character in the novelette: here, he was a not very enjoyable fellow equipped with a couple of wordy songs ("When You Find You're a Broken-Down Critter") that sounded as if they might have been Barrington or Grossmith rejects. He spent half the opera being "dead"—a worse fate than that of King Gama! The manager of the theater troupe, tenor Ernest Dummkopf (Kenningham), also spent time in the virtual coffin, leaving the limelight to Ludwig, his chief comedian, played by Barrington. Barrington's first song, describing the actors' conspiracy (why?) against their employer, the duke, under the sign of a sausage roll (why? are sausage rolls funny? or are they meant to be saucy?), was a peculiar, awkward piece, which set a sad tone for the rest of the evening. If things got a little better once the ladies came on, they slumped again as soon as Ludwig unrolled another too-same-ish sausage of patter.

The Leading Lady, as remade by Gilbert (and Sullivan), definitely had possibilities. Julia Jellicoe is characterized as an English prima donna in what seems to have been a nebulously mid-European troupe. As such, she, of course, holds dear to such theatrical traditions as "lines" of roles. The role of Julia Jellicoe was constructed for and around the Hungarian megastar Ilka Pálmay, with her pretty Hungarian accent. She was to be the Englishwoman in the affair, while all those Halbpfenning actors would speak perfect Queen's English. It was a delightful conceit, even if one that was pretty much a "one-off-joke" and didn't really add to the total effect.

Ilka Pálmay (Julia Jellicoe)

Ilka Pálmay (née Ilona Pálmay Petráss; b. Ungvár, Hungary, 21 September 1859; d. Budapest, 17 February 1945) was an established megastar in central Europe. The eighteen-year-old (or thirteen-year-old, if you believe the dates given in some biographies), who had first trod the boards at Kaschau, shot to the theatrical forefront when she appeared at the Népszínház, Budapest's principal musical theater, as Serpolette, in the Hungarian première of A Kornevilli harangok (Les Cloches de Corneville, 1878). Over the next decade, during which she shed her first husband, József Szigligeti (1851–1889), and his name, she shared with Aranka Hegyi the major operatic roles—prima donna, soubrette, and travesty—at the Népszínház, as well as taking leads in many of the straight plays that made up the theater's programs.

Among the forty-eight (we are told) different musical pieces and roles she played were A Királykisasszony babui (Les Poupées de l'infante); Manola in Nap és hold (Le Jour et la nuit); Sora in Gasparone; Lisbeth (i.e., Gretchen) in Rip; Offenbach's Eurydice, his Belle Hélène and Gabrielle in Párizsi élet (La Vie parisienne); Micaëla in A Kertészleány (Le Coeur et la Main); Bronislawa in Koldusdiák (Der Bettelstudent); a

75. Ilka Pálmay: International Megastar.

travesty Barinkay in A Cigánybáró (Der Zigeunerbaron); the title-role of A Béárni leány (La Béarnaise); the Queen in A Királynő csipkekendője (Das Spitzentuch der Königin); the title-roles of the local versions of Les Noces d'Olivette, La Grande-Duchesse de Gérolstein, Donna Juanita, Marjolaine, Le Petit Duc, Niniche, and Boccaccio; Clairette in La Fille de Madame Angot; both Yum-Yum and Nanki-Poo in different productions of The Mikado; Denise de Flavigny in Nebántsvirág (Mam'zelle Nitouche); Benjamine in Jozéfa Egyiptomban (Joséphine vendue par ses soeurs); Tilly in Simplicius; Nell Gwynne in A Komédiás hercegnő (Planquette's Nell Gwynne); Phryne (apparently Phoebe) in A Gárdista (The Yeomen of the Guard); and Borka (presumably Patience) in Fejő leány (Patience). The gamut.

Frau Pálmay created starring roles in several early Hungarian operettas—including the remake of L'Étoile as Uff király (1887, Lazuli) and Béla Hegyi and Szidor Bátor's A Titkos csók (1888, Lolotte)—and the musical plays A Piros bugyelláris (1878, Török Zsófi) and Csókon szerzett võlegeny (1883, Irén Abrai), and also played such nonsinging roles as that of Zola's Nana (1882). In 1883, she appeared with the Budapest company as Micaëla, Manola, and Serpolette in a season in Vienna; and she returned there, in 1891, to spend more than two years as leading lady at the Theater an der Wien. During that time, she created the role of the little postmistress Christel in Zeller's Der Vogelhändler (1891, "Ich bin die Christel von der Post"); Ilona in the farcical Heisses Blut (1892, "written especially for her by Krenn and Lindau"); Lady Sylvia Rockhill in Millöcker's Das Sonntagskind (1892); and the title-role in Johann Strauss's Fürstin Ninetta (1893), as well as appearing as Hélène Javotte in Fanchon's Leyer (La Fille de Fanchon la vielleuse); in German versions of Anna Judic's roles of Denise de Flavigny (Mam'zelle Nitouche) and Princess Anna Semionowna Machinstoff (Die Kosakin); and introducing the little opérette La Stupida (1893 aka Das Mädchen vom Mirano). She also played at Berlin's Thomas-Theater (1892, Heisses Blut, etc.), and at the Friedrich-Wilhelmstädtisches Theater in 1893 (Das Mädchen vom Mirano, Der Bettelstudent, Mam'zelle Nitouche, and Die schöne Helena).

After a brief retirement from the stage to become the Gräfin Eugen Kinsky, she moved on to appear at the Theater Unter der Linden in Adolphe Ferron's Sataniel (1893) and, to the annoyance of Sullivan, who tried to stop it, as Nanki-Poo. She returned to Vienna in 1895 to star in travesty as Hector in Die Karlsschülerin and appeared in London, with the Saxe-Coburg Company, in Der Vogelhändler at the Theatre Royal, Drury Lane. This visit resulted in her being offered a contract by D'Oyly Carte, and in 1896–97 she created the roles of Julia Jellicoe in *The Grand Duke* and Felice in *His Majesty* and appeared as Elsie Maynard in a revival of *The Yeomen of the Guard* at the Savoy Theatre.

In 1898–99, Frau Pálmay played again in Vienna, starring at the Theater an der Wien in a series of largely new but not very impressive Operetten: *Die Küchen-Comtesse* (Lisa Schwarzen); Eugen von Taund's *Der Dreibund* (Lydia); Adolf Müller Jr.'s *Der Blondin von Namur* (Blondin); Josef Bayer's *Fräulein Hexe* (Magdalene); and as the Principessa Santiago de Merimac in Richard Heuberger's version of *Niniche, Ihre Excellenz*.

The later part of her career was spent mostly in Budapest (where, in 1901, she played Belasco's nonmusical *Madame Butterfly*), although she visited New York in 1905 and appeared there in her protean role of Ilona in *Heisses Blut* in the German-language theater. Among her latter-day appearances in Budapest, Frau Pálmay played the old Countess Irini in the local production of *Der Zigeunerprimás* (1913) and the elder Hannerl in *Médi* (1918), the Hungarian version of *Hannerl*. She did not officially retire from the stage until 1928, after a career of fifty years in which she had compiled one of the most remarkable series of performances in the history of European musical theater, a career that held the unusual distinction of including the creation of leading roles both for Johann Strauss and Gilbert and Sullivan.

If Gilbert and Sullivan had not managed to construct a bright and original role for Barrington, what would they come up with, given the acknowledged triple-threat talents of the lady, for Mme. Pálmay? Well, they duly gave her a bit of everything. Some of it—mostly the lyrical parts, such as the lovely romantic solo "Broken Every Promise Plighted"— was decidedly successful; some—"The Grand Duke's Bride"—decidedly reminiscent; and some missed the mark. An extended scena to allow the lady to display her acting rather than her vocal skills the protean "I have a rival! Frenzy-thrilled" was a nice set piece but . . . where was Sullivan? The scena would have made a splendid operatic-burlesque showpiece. But therein lay the rub: Ilka Pálmay, outstanding performer and established star that she was, was, in spite of Julia Jellicoe's claims to prima donna-dom over Lisa, the "soubrette" in the piece, was herself a soubrette. And she had never, truly, attempted to be anything but. In the resplendent piece and score of *Der Vogelhändler*, in which Carte had first seen her, she had not played the vocally substantial role of the Princess with its beautiful (and difficult) soprano airs; she had been the little Brief-Christel with her bouncy wee hit number. Here, she had a role—and I am not intending in any way to downplay her talent—that was somewhat awkwardly tailored to her measure. Damme! Where was Helene Crosmond when you needed her? Pálmay would have been wonderful as Ludwig's sweetheart, Lisa. Sullivan thought so too: when she was subsequently cast by the theater as Elsie Maynard, he expressed the opinion (undoubtedly correctly) that she would have been altogether better suited as Phoebe.

Florence Perry (Lisa)

As it happened, Carte found a splendid artist to play Lisa, whose sweet and simple little song "Take Care of Him" proved one of the better-liked numbers in the score.

Florence Julia Perry (b. London, 13 July 1869; d. Durban, South Africa, 6 December 1949) was born in Holborn, one of the large family of Welsh builder Frederick March Perry and his wife, Elizabeth (née Quincey). The "piquante, petite" Florence began her career as a stage vocalist in 1887 with Henry Leslie, at the Prince of Wales Theatre, as the little bride in *Dorothy*, alongside her brother-in-law, tenor Ben Davies, and on Leslie's tours of *The Red Hussar* and *Doris*. She and her elder sister, Beatrice, then joined the Carte touring companies, with whom she appeared as Yum-Yum, Gianetta, Phyllis, Winifred in *The Vicar of Bray*, and Phoebe in *Billee Taylor*, between 1891 and 1893. In 1893, she was promoted to the Savoy Theatre, where she created the part of Milly in *Jane Annie*, taking over latterly from Decima Moore as Bab. She followed up in *Utopia (Limited)* and *Mirette*, and played Dolly Grigg in *The Chieftain*, before leaving Carte briefly to appear for Melnotte and Wyatt as Clementine in *Baron Golosh*.

In 1895, Florence played on tour as Josephine, Yum-Yum, and both Dolly Grigg and Rita in *The Chieftain*, but she soon returned to London, where she filled in for Marie Tempest in the star role of *An Artist's Model*. She returned once more to the Savoy in 1895 as Yum-Yum in a revival of *The Mikado*, and stayed to create the part of Lisa in *The Grand Duke*, deputizing at matinées in the *Paradrolle* of Julia Jellicoe. She appeared again as Yum-Yum, as Princess Lucilla Chloris in *His Majesty*, Phoebe in *The Yeomen of the Guard*, and, finally, Wanda in *The Grand Duchess of Gerolstein*, before, in 1898, she made a foray to Australia, appearing there as O Mimosa San in *The Geisha*, Phyllis in *Iolanthe*, Rosette in *Ma mie Rosette*, and as Yum-Yum to Beatrice's Peep-Bo in *The Mikado*. On her return to England, she appeared in *The Thirty Thieves* and *HMS Irresponsible* before succeeding to the title-role of Sidney Jones's *My Lady Molly*.

Florence married Melbourne-born Francis Ernest Greig, "gentleman", "honorary 2nd lieutenant", "transport officer of the NSW Bushmen's contingent," and later captain, in the Boer War, and settled in South Africa.

Emmie Owen (Princess of Monte Carlo)

If Barrington and even Mme. Pálmay were overserved, almost all of the rest of the players in *The Grand Duke* were underserved. Rosina Brandram's role, a perfectly good part, if no Katisha or Sangazure, was cut to ribbons as what proportions the show had were sacrificed to the gods of the sausage roll. The parts of the Prince and Princess of Monte Carlo—which in olden days would doubtless have been played by Richard Temple and Miss Bond, and were now Scott Fishe and Emmie Owen—went under the same knife as well, and they appeared in the piece almost as an afterthought. Fishe's lively Roulette Song was among the crumbs of the sausage roll, and Florence Perry's "little sister" from *Utopia (Limited)* was left with a nub of a part.

Emily Mary Owen was born in Bristol, on 28 November 1871, the daughter of Henry Owen, stage carpenter at the local Prince's Theatre, and his wife, Hester (née Morgan). I first spot her in speaking parts in *Proof* and as Little Eva in *Uncle Tom's Cabin* at the Prince's in 1885, and in 1890 she was cast as So-Shi in the theater's pantomime *Aladdin*. Emmie joined the Cartesian touring ranks the following year, and appeared in *The Nautch Girl*, *The Vicar of Bray*, and *Haddon Hall*, before being summoned to the Savoy. Over the next years, she played there in *Jane Annie*, *Utopia (Limited)*, *Mirette*, and *The Chieftain*, deputizing when required, before going on the road again, now promoted to better parts, including Gianetta and Patience. She returned to the Savoy as Peep-Bo for the 1895 revival of *The Mikado*, and then was given what was left of the role of the Princess of Monte Carlo in *The Grand Duke*.

In 1896, Emmie took time out from the Savoy, to appear in *Monte Carlo* at the Avenue Theatre, but she returned to join the Cartesian company for a tour of South Africa, now as leading lady (Patience, Phyllis, Yum-Yum, Elsie), and then, once more, at the Savoy. With one break, to play in *La Périchole* with Florence St. John at the Garrick, she

76. Rosina Brandram (Lady Sophy) with her Utopian charges: Florence Perry and Emmie Owen.

remained with Carte until 1900, now as a full-fledged light leading lady (Elsie in *The Yeomen of the Guard*; Jacqueline in *The Beauty Stone*; Constance in *The Sorcerer*; Lazuli in *The Lucky Star*; Hebe in *HMS Pinafore*; and Honey-of-Life in *The Rose of Persia*).

In 1901, Emmie visited Australia to play for George Musgrove in *The Scarlet Feather* (*La Petite Mademoiselle*) and as Dandini in *Cinderella*, but when the contract ended, she decided to adventure further. She visited New Zealand and got mixed up with a local Barnum, by the name of P. F. Dix. A few months later she wrote to the press saying she and "a friend" were stranded in Auckland. Mr. Dix had a different version. And it appears he was in the right. A fund was set up to help her homeward. After her return, she appeared but rarely, before the undefined "illness" that had caused her misfortunes caught up with her. She died of cirrhosis of the liver on 18 October 1905, at the age of thirty-three.

The Grand Duke: Over and Out

If I have mentioned Sullivan but little in my tales of *The Grand Duke*, it is simply because the story and the characters seem to have inspired him but mildly. There is a lot of tuneful chorus music; the occasional lyrical gem such as Julia's and Lisa's soulful songs; and a few fun bits that ended up on the cutting-room floor, as the secondary roles were filleted, in a display of artistic and commercial suicide and poor judgment in which it is hard to believe such experienced gentlemen could have indulged. In the end, only three songs from *The Grand Duke* were published as singles—and the third one was a surprise. It was the rather *Gondoliers*-ish announcement of the arrival of the Monte Carlo family, and it was sung—oh, shades of *Lohengrin*—by "An Herald."

The Grand Duke was kept on the stage at the Savoy for four months. On 10 July 1896, it closed. It was the end of an era, an era that had ended not with a bang but a whimper. But in the years of its flourishing, the epoch of Messrs. Carte, Gilbert, and Sullivan brought to the world's English-language musical stages a body of work the like of which had, and has, never been equaled; a body of work that, nearly a century and a half since the first night of *Trial by Jury*, and 125 years after the last night of *The Grand Duke*, still flourishes on the world's stages.

I realize that I've flourished, with it, for more than half of that time; thank you, gentlemen, for three quarters of a century of music and fun and genius.

Appendix

Recommended Reading

There have been a host of books written on Gilbert, Sullivan, Carte and some of those who sailed with them. A few have become regarded as "standards." I have a couple of these on my bookshelf. They haven't been opened since I closed them for the first time, decades ago, and are about to be given to the Rotary Book Fair. As one learned PhD sighed when asked to add a vote to my best-of-G&S survey, "There has been so much *tosh* written about G&S."

For the scripts and scores of the operas . . . get just that, the script and the score, or if you don't have a piano, get a recording. In my opinion, much of the G&S on record that is available is a little disappointing. The post–D'Oyly Carte issues haven't really produced the collection of aptly cast and sung performances one might have hoped for. However, the only way to find which you prefer is to listen to them all, as I did when writing my book on vinyl recordings. Therein you may read my musings: *The Blackwell Guide to Musical Theatre on Record* (Blackwell, 1989). On the Internet, one can refer to Marc Shepherd's G&S discography at http://gasdisc.oakapplepress.com.

I'm listening to my favorite ever G&S recording as I write. Was there ever a Mabel like Arleen Auger, a Ruth like Martha Mödl, a Frederic like Peter Bahrig . . . ? Joyous tempi, effortless singing, with (mock) operatic voices. I know there are some notes that ar'n't Sullivan, but if Sullivan had had Fräulein Auger, I'll bet he would have written them.

The scripts are gathered together in an enjoyable modern edition by Ian Bradley, *The Complete Annotated Gilbert and Sullivan* (Oxford University Press, 2016), and of course there is also the Terry Rees classic

Thespis: A Gilbert and Sullivan Enigma (Dillon's University Bookshop 1964; revised edition 2003).

For just the stories of the pieces, and a brief history, you have a wide choice. I, naturally, point you toward *Gänzl's Book of the Musical Theatre*. It gives you, also, the stories and scores of the most important among other nineteenth-century shows but it lacks *Utopia (Limited)* and *The Grand Duke* (Bodley Head/Schirmer, 1988). *[An Introduction to] The Gilbert and Sullivan Opera* by Ric Woodbridge Wilson (Eastern Press, 1989) is a delightful 112-page summary by one of the great G&S experts, which I myself use as a quick reference when my elderly brain hits a blank. And, then, of course there is my three-volume *The Encyclopedia of the Musical Theatre* (Schirmer, 2001), where you will find all the facts on the plays, lots of the people, and a whole bundle of related stuff, including exhaustive lists of all the books on the subject (up to 2001), recommendable or not.

Biographies (of the Boys)

I have not read one of these since those "standards" by Jacobs (Sullivan) and Stedman (Gilbert) came out, sometime last century. In spite of being friends with both authors, I found neither of those works wholly satisfying and, actually, a bit dreary. Not what you would expect, given such a joyous subject! However, for reference, here they are:

- Arthur Jacobs, *Arthur Sullivan: A Victorian Musician* (Oxford University Press, 1984); first or second (1992) edition only, because the 2020 reissue is faulty.

- Jane W. Stedman, *W S Gilbert: A Classic Victorian and His Theatre* (Oxford University Press, 1996).

Having, thus, no opinion of my own, on twenty-first-century books, I have turned to the young folk at the Arthur Sullivan Appreciation Group, and asked them for their (English-language) recommendations. Top of the voting list (in no particular order) came:

- Michael Ainger, *Gilbert and Sullivan: A Dual Biography* (Oxford University Press, 2009).

- Andrew Crowther, *Gilbert of Gilbert and Sullivan* (The History Press, 2011).

- David Eden, *W. S. Gilbert: Appearance and Reality* (Sir Arthur Sullivan Society, 2003).

- Paul Seeley, *Richard D'Oyly Carte* (Routledge, 2018).

They gave a big nod, also, to the older Percy M. Young's *Sir Arthur Sullivan* (J. M. Dent & Sons, 1971), and another, muted, to David Eden and Meinhard Saremba's *The Cambridge Companion to Gilbert and Sullivan* (Cambridge University Press, 2010), with the caveat "largely for academics." I think that means, maybe, not me.

Such memoirs or autobiographies of the players as exist are, largely, as credible as are most showbiz autobiographies: that is, ranging from the fairly fictional to the, at least, trying-to-be-truthful. Frankly, the only ones that I have read that I would wholeheartedly recommend are George Grossmith's *A Society Clown* (J. W. Arrowsmith, 1888) and *Piano and I* (J. W. Arrowsmith, 1910). However, in more modern times, determined research has provoked a great deal of clarification of the stories of the lives and careers of the early Cartesian performers. For the details of the various people's performances in the "Savoy Operas," I turn to David Stone's website Who Was Who in the D'Oyly Carte Opera Company (https://gsarchive.net/whowaswho/index.htm) and its (and everyone's) grandfather, Cyril Rollins and R John Witts's amazing pre-Internet volume of research, *The D'Oyly Carte Opera Company in Gilbert and Sullivan Operas* (Michael Joseph, 1961, etc.).

For tales of who was really who, and what they did with the rest of their careers and lives when they weren't Carte-ing . . . well, this is where I came in. When age and infirmity stopped me traveling, I turned my blog travel diary into the home for a (very) large series of freshly minted Cartesian (and other) showbiz biographies, winkled and weaseled from the past. I think and hope those articles (descendants of a handful of which appear here) have added another layer to our knowledge of G&S. They can be read (sandwiched between other stories) at https://kurtofgerolstein.blogspot.com. The volumes issued by the Sullivan Society, containing many in-depth articles on individual players, written by a range of scholars, can be found on the Internet at www.sullivansociety.org.uk; and Gilbert, too, has a similar society and a journal that live at www.wsgilbert.co.uk.

Index

This is an index of the more featured, and relevant-to-our-subject, players and plays included in this volume.

Sisters, cousins and aunts, missing babies, and folk who are not what they seem may appear in the text, but not here.

An asterisk alongside an index entry signifies that there is a photograph of the player included, which can be found in the list of illustrations in the front matter.

Ages Ago, 38, 197
Aladdin II, 1, 2, 9, 175–76
Allen, George B., 39

Baldwin, Alice, 228, 239
Barber, Julia*, 23, 25, 27–28
Barnett, Alice*, 70, 92, 125, 128, 129, 136–38, 160–61
Barrington, Rutland*, 39, 41, 43, 56, 57, 59, 74, 112–15, 120–21, 149, 152, 154, 176–77, 189, 198–99, 202, 205, 208–12, 243, 246, 257, 260, 262
Beebe, Mary*, 157, 162–63
Bentham, George*, 40, 44–51, 55
Beverley, Dick, 78, 106, 142
Beverley, Julia, 23, 26–27, 29
Billee Taylor, 25, 44, 64, 84, 118, 124, 182, 134, 138, 155, 167, 220, 239–40, 248, 261

Billington, Fred, 103, 189, 195
Bond, Jessie*, 58, 92, 143–46, 149, 155, 177, 198–99, 209, 251, 256, 262
Bovill, Frederick*, 180–81
Bracy, Henry*, 154, 157–60
Braham, Leonora*, 123–25, 143, 149, 154, 156, 177–79, 183–85, 193, 198, 237
Brandram, Rosina*, 56, 58, 74, 92, 138, 143, 160–62, 177, 179, 198, 243, 248, 262
Brocolini, John*, 50, 90–91, 99–100, 157, 165, 168, 173
Bromley, Nellie*, 13–16, 24
Browne, George Byron, 193–95
Brownlow, Wallace*, 218–19
Brunelli, Therese, 42–43
Buhicrosan, Mynheer Tannaker, 175–76

Burbank, Percy, 203
Burke, Aileen*, 248–50
Burton, Carrie*, 133–34
Burville. Alice, 32, 75–76, 205, 211

Cadwaladr, Llewellyn, 103, 149
Cameron, Elsie*, 193–95
Campbell, Charles J.*, 29–30, 35, 83
Carleton, William Turnham*, 126, 139–43, 168
Carlton, Mr. *See* Carleton
Carritte, Nita, 229–30
Carte, Richard D'Oyly, *passim*
Carthew, Laura, 23, 25, 27–29
Cave-Ashton, Gertrude, 53, 55
Celli, Frank, 53, 111, 117, 140, 143
Cellier, Alfred, xxi, 22, 32, 95, 101, 106, 112, 118, 159, 183, 188, 208, 219, 241
Cellier, François, 64, 107, 208
Chard, Kate, 156
Charles, Harold, 202–203
Chilpéric, 18, 34, 71, 82, 140–41, 191
Clary, Madeleine*, 2–6, 9, 139
Clay, Frederic, xxi, 45, 64, 111–12, 132
Cleary, Mina, 228–29
Clifford, Amy, 23, 25–27, 29, 35
Clifton, Frederic*, 40–43, 56, 75, 113
Cloches de Corneville, Les, 29, 61, 151, 159, 166, 183, 204, 242, 258
Cloney, Edward J.*, 171–73
Comedy Opera Company, 43, 62, 73, 107
Contrabandista, The, xix, 22, 166, 183
Corelli, Blanche, 83–85
Cox and Box*, xix, 21–22, 38, 61, 96, 106–107, 142, 191
Crosmond, Helene, 62, 94, 98–99, 155, 245, 261

Cross, Emily*, 74, 108–12

D'Orme, Aileen. *See* Burke
Denny, William Henry*, 211–13, 221, 243
Dolaro, Selina, xvi, 12, 15, 19–20, 24, 29, 76, 148, 155, 173, 225
Donald, Carrie, 228, 230
Duff, James C., 78, 82–83, 165, 182, 237
Durrant, Cissie*, 23–24, 27
Dymott, Aeneas*, 71–73

Edwardes, George, 25, 114, 116, 118, 124, 162, 178–80, 184–85, 201, 218, 227, 241, 246
Erminie, 124, 132, 143, 159, 189, 226, 239
Evans's Supper Rooms, 24, 72
Everard, Harriet*, 19, 40, 56, 58, 65–70, 109, 112, 125, 161

Farren, Nellie, 2–3, 9, 22, 35, 68, 118, 139
Federici, Fred*, 103, 187–89, 192
Fille de Madame Angot, La, 12, 20, 22, 24, 29, 32, 34–35, 42, 77, 81–82, 106, 112, 131, 158–59, 167, 191, 211, 225, 227, 242, 259
Findlay, Josephine, 184–86, 201, 237
Fishe, Robert Scott, 250–51, 256, 262
Fisher, Walter Henry*, 13, 16–20, 33, 35
Forster, Kate*, 192–93
Fortescue, George H.*, 87

Geneviève de Brabant, 22, 24–25, 32, 40, 76–77, 81, 106–107, 157
Gentleman in Black, The, xxi, 37
Gilbert, William Schwenk, *passim*
Gondoliers, The, 221–40, *et passim*

Index

Gordon, Duglas*, xviii, 32, 75–77
Grand Duke, The, 255–64, et passim
Grey, Sybil*, 177–80
Grossmith, George*, 39, 43, 56, 58–59, 103–106, et passim
Grundy, Thomas, 31, 34

Halman, Ella, xi
Hatch, Alonzo, 83
Hervey, Rose*, 213–15
HMS Pinafore, 57–88 et passim
Holland, Fanny, 75
Holland, Maud, 230
Hollingsworth, Charles, 31–32
Hood, Marion*, 64, 115–17, 122, 155, 193
Hooper, James William, 251–53
Howson, Emma*, 50, 59–61, 82, 88, 112, 155
Howson, John, 61
Husk, James Baker, 31, 33–34

Iolanthe, 135–52, et passim

James, Lithgow*, 149–52
Jolly, Elizabeth, 5–9

Kelleher, Charles J., 31–33
Kenningham, Charles, 243–44, 256–57

La Rue, Lilian*, vii, xiv–xvii, 74, 116
Lang, Charles F.*, 165–67
Laurent, Henri*, 78–86, 163, 173
Lawrence, Nellie*, 231
Leighton, Rose, 87, 168
Lely, Durward*, 125, 146–49, 177, 189–90, 198–99, 201, 211, 216, 235
Lenoir, Helen (Mrs Carte), 90, 129
Lewis, Rudolph, 200–201

Loveday, Elinor, 64, 75

Manners, Charles, 149–50
Mansfield, Richard, 86, 103, 205
Mapleson, J. H., xvii, 47–50, 97–99, 101–102, 140
Mathews, Julia, 19, 24, 39, 61, 70, 106, 142
May, Alice, 8, 32, 39, 43, 55, 59, 75–76, 196
McCaull, John, 95, 129, 134, 155
Mc Creery, Wallace, 163–65
McIntosh, Nancy, 239, 244–45
Medcalf, Antonio, 214–16
Mikado, The, 175–97, et passim
Montelli, T. J., xvii
Moore, Decima*, 226–28, 239, 261

Oates, Alice, 35, 61, 78, 82–83, 166
Offenbach, Jacques, xvii, 5, 22, 106, 128, 131, 158–59, 221, 258
Our Island Home, 38, 89
Owen, Emmie*, 256, 262–63

Palliser, Esther*, 232–33, 237
Pálmay, Ilka*, 239, 257–62
Palmer, Amy, 23, 27
Par[r]ris, George, 34
Patience, 119–34, et passim
Paul, Isabella*, 39–40, 56, 58, 70, 104, 113, 144, 161
Penley, William S., 31
Pepper, Belville R., 31–32
Périchole, La, 12, 15, 20, 22, 24–25, 27, 29, 33, 35, 142, 158, 210, 211, 224, 262
Perry, Florence*, 256, 261–63
Petrelli, Emilie, xviii, 103, 122, 154
Pirates of Penzance, The, 89–118, et passim
Planché, J. L., 18, 153, 154

Pounds, Courtice*, 189–92, 211, 249, 251
Power, George*, 51, 58, 61–65, 99, 108
Price, Sidney, 205
Princess Ida, 153–74, et passim
Princess Toto, xxi, 108, 112, 114, 124, 132

Reddick, Isabel, 245–46
Reed, Priscilla, 124
Reed, T German xix, 38, 89, 112, 124, 234
Rees, Terence 3, 10
Reeves, John Sims, 17, 47, 50, 68, 109–11, 113, 127, 141, 193
Righton, Edward*, 18–19
Rising William S*, 167–70
Rita, Pauline, 35, 62, 77
Roche, Augusta*, 126–30, 136, 149
Roebuck, Disney, 17, 157
Roosevelt, Blanche*, 75, 92–95, 101, 155
Roze, Marie, 49, 142, 148–49, 216
Ruddigore, 197–206, et passim
Russell, Lillian, 44, 85, 132, 134, 138, 155, 213, 249
Ryley, John H*, 91, 95, 100, 126, 130–33, 136, 149, 157, 199, 205, 220

Santley, Kate, 20, 27, 32–33, 69, 128, 132
Saumarez, Cissie, 235
Schauspieler-Gesellschaft in Olymp, Die, 1
Schuberth, Annie, 236–37
Scott, Mazellah Ainsley*, 170–72
Shaw, J. A., 32
Sherwin, Amy, 149, 230, 236
Shirley, W. R.*, 217–18
Sinico, Clarice, 47, 53

Snyder, Lenore*, 234, 237–38
Soldene, Emily, xvi, 12, 22, 24–25, 27–30, 32, 34–35, 55, 72, 76, 81–82, 85, 106, 125, 131, 141, 169, 195, 220, 240
Solomon, Edward ('Teddy'), 15, 64, 85, 106, 108, 117, 138, 155
Solomon, Fred, 65, 85, 220
Sorcerer, The, 37–56, et passim
Squire, Emily, 234–35
St John, Florence, xvii, 20, 25, 118, 151, 241, 262
St Maur, Geraldine*, 196
Steele, Tommy, 220
Sullivan, Arthur Seymour, passim
Sullivan, Fred*, 3, 13, 21–22, 33, 35, 37, 39, 106, 131, 142

Talbot, Hugh, xviii, 95–102
Talby, Kate*, 247–48
Tanner, Cora, 157, 163
Taylor, James Gould, 3, 78, 208
Temple, George*, 74
Temple, Richard*, 40, 56, 58–59, 103, 106–108, 112, 120–22, 126, 139, 141, 149, 154, 177, 188, 198–99, 201, 204, 209, 211, 215, 234, 251, 262
Terrott, William, 18, 141
Thespis, 1–11, 22, 37, 58, 78, 142, 177, 208, 211, 255
Thompson, Lydia, 15, 25, 29, 157, 212, 225
Thorne, George*, 186–87
Thornton, Frank*, 74
Toole, John Lawrence*, 2–3, 69, 106, 132, 175
Tremaine, Annie, 2–3, 5, 8–9, 64, 75, 142
Trevor, Harris, 203
Trial by Jury, 11–36, et passim
Tuer, Arthur, 203

Ulmar, Geraldine*, 182–84, 192, 211, 228–29, 233, 237
Utopia (Limited), 241–54, *et passim*

Venne, Lottie, 15, 18, 179
Verner, Linda*, 15, 23–25, 27, 29

Walton, Lisa, 55–56
Ware, Irene, 53, 55
Warwick, Giulia*, 40, 51–55, 72, 148

West, Joseph S., 31, 34
Wilbraham, James, 204–205, 215
Wilde, Oscar, 81, 119–20, 126, 134
Wyatt, Frank*, 224–26, 251
Wyndham, Charles, 20, 32, 43, 224

Yeomen of the Guard, The, 207–20, *et passim*

Zoo, The, xxi, 106

www.ingramcontent.com/pod-product-compliance
Lightning Source LLC
Chambersburg PA
CBHW030821230426
43667CB00008B/1316